The Maker Cookbook

The Maker Cookbook

Recipes for Children's and 'Tween Library Programs

Cindy R. Wall and Lynn M. Pawloski

Foreword by Bill Derry

AN IMPRINT OF ABC-CLIO, LLC
Santa Barbara, California • Denver, Colorado • Oxford, England

Library of Congress Cataloging-in-Publication Data

Wall, Cindy R.
　The maker cookbook : recipes for children's and 'tween library programs / Cindy R. Wall and Lynn M. Pawloski ; foreword by Bill Derry.
　　pages cm
　Includes bibliographical references and index.
　ISBN 978-1-61069-661-6 (pbk : alk. paper) — ISBN 978-1-61069-662-3 (ebook)
1. Children's libraries—Activity programs.   2. Makerspaces.   3. Do-it-yourself work.   4. Workshops.   I. Pawloski, Lynn M.   II. Title.
　Z718.3.W35   2014
　027.62'5—dc23　　　2014015730

ISBN: 978-1-61069-661-6
EISBN: 978-1-61069-662-3

18 17 16 15 14　　1 2 3 4 5

This book is also available on the World Wide Web as an eBook.
Visit www.abc-clio.com for details.

Libraries Unlimited
An Imprint of ABC-CLIO, LLC

ABC-CLIO, LLC
130 Cremona Drive, P.O. Box 1911
Santa Barbara, California 93116–1911

This book is printed on acid-free paper ∞
Manufactured in the United States of America

Photographs appearing throughout book by Cindy R. Wall.

For Kelly, without your love, help, support, and nifty editing skills, this book would not have been possible. For Joe and Emily, whose love sustained me.

—CW

For James Schafer, fellow lover of libraries, letters, laughter, and infinite possibilities.

—LP

Contents

Foreword

I first encountered the "Maker Movement" and its potential for library programming at an Internet Librarians conference in 2011 where John Seely Brown stated that many librarians are still living in "the Information Age" not realizing our culture has moved into "the Imagination Age." He said that since information is now easily accessible, librarians need to help people imagine how to process it and what to do with it. He proceeded to suggest that libraries should contemplate hosting or working with Maker Faires and consider engaging patrons in activities that foster playing, tinkering, and making.

Fortunately Maxine Bleiweis, the Director of the Westport Library in Connecticut where I work, is forward thinking, and the staff is willing and able to respond quickly to implementing new ideas. Within six months we had coproduced a Mini Maker Faire and two months later opened our own MakerSpace.

As the MakerSpace has evolved, we have learned that our patrons want more and more Maker programs. Parents looking for STEAM (Science, Technology, Engineering, Arts and Math) learning activities for their children have created one of the largest demands for Maker programming. It is clear that the Maker Movement is a trend rather than a fad, and has broad appeal to members of our community.

Children's librarians have always included Maker activities in traditional library programming, typically in the areas of arts and crafts. The Maker Movement does include arts and crafts activities but also embraces and includes activities dealing with industrial arts, invention, and technology. How does a library move from traditional arts and crafts programming to more activities that are open-ended, involve creative and critical thinking skills, and deal with invention and technology? It can be overwhelming to consider where to start and how to proceed. That is where this book can be an extremely helpful resource!

Cindy and Lynn have created *The Maker Cookbook: Recipes for Children's and 'Tween Library Programs* to provide multiple starting points for any person involved in programming for kids. Each community is unique as is the staff of the organization providing the Maker programming. With this book youth programming coordinators and instructors can "play" with selecting and implementing activities to determine their community's interests and needs as related to Maker programming.

The book not only appeals to a broad level of patron interests and skill levels, but also, more importantly, meets the experience and skill levels of staff members who are grappling with the confidence to present and work with science and/or technology-related topics. With the 30+ Maker "recipes" and the description of strategies to vary the activities, there is an entry point for everyone. Through their cooking analogy, Cindy and Lynn have used common terms such as "variations" and "recipe substitutions" to help the user think of alternate ways of implementing the recipes. They even provide a "Fusion Box" for some recipes to add an optional helping of technology!

Cindy and Lynn have created an accessible, informative and easy-to-follow *Maker Cookbook* for public and school libraries (and any other organization serving youth) that includes activities focused on arts and crafts, 3D printers, cooking, sewing, animation, building, how to use a Raspberry Pi, and much more! This book may be the first in your Maker Resource Toolbox or a useful addition to your current holdings!

Merry Making!

Bill Derry
Assistant Director for Innovation & User Experience
The Westport Library
Westport, CT 06880

Introduction

The Maker Cookbook: Recipes for Children's and 'Tween Library Programs is a step-by-step guide for public librarians wishing to embrace Maker programming in their libraries but who are hesitant due to budget, staffing, space, skill limitations, or technology comfort levels. Media specialists and educators may adapt these programs on their own for use in an academic setting or use the suggestions provided in the Recipe Substitutions section. Maker, today's DIY, encourages collaboration among participants and does not require a designated MakerSpace, for every library is a MakerPlace.

The Maker philosophy empowers people with the knowledge that they can create the things that they want and need. In the ideal Maker world, when people have a need, they do not wait for a corporation to acknowledge that need and create a product; instead they make the new product themselves. Therefore, library Maker programming should empower participants to believe in their ability to create something through experimentation and trial and error. The Maker Movement allows individuals to free and shift their thinking; it allows everyone to think in terms of unlimited possibilities.

It is easy to be intimidated by the Maker Movement and its perceived reliance on high-tech gadgets and electronics. But the Maker Movement is so much more. It includes art, music, cooking, sewing, crafting, and any of the do-it-yourself skills you can think of. It is best to offer a variety of as many of the different disciplines of the Maker Movement as possible to determine what your community desires. While one community may be heavy on high-tech gadgets (3D printing, iPads, Arduino boards), another community may gravitate toward crafting (crocheting, knitting, weaving) and yet another community may focus on the arts (painting, sculpting, photography). All of these communities will have embraced the Maker Movement in their own unique way. In addition to providing the community the Maker programs they already love, be sure to offer a variety of new activities that they don't know that they love yet.

Most children's librarians entered the field of library science hoping to pass the love of reading onto others, never anticipating entering a world of unfamiliar territory. Without minimizing this original mission, the library world recognizes that we need to move forward and build upon the traditional offerings of story times and book groups. Maker programs will attract nontraditional patrons who have yet to discover the variety and depth of programming at the contemporary library. Once the newly attracted patrons are in the library, librarians may then foster the love of reading with this new audience.

What stands between many children's librarians and successful Maker programming is a dash of inexperience and a heaping helping of fear. We have learned that experience counts less than you might think in Maker programming. Don't be afraid to try a program with a subject matter you feel as though you have yet to master. Together, you and the program participants may experiment with different ideas and learn from each other. If your program does not turn out as you originally anticipated, embrace the program that was. No program is a failure if you challenged yourself and you offered the children a fun, positive learning experience in a safe, respectful environment. Ultimately, it's all about the process not the product.

So how do you start? It all comes back to that perennial musical story time favorite, the "Hokey Pokey." You have to put your right foot into the Maker Movement and not be afraid to shake it all about. Start small. You may wish to add a Maker element to a program the library already offers, such as a book discussion. As you become more comfortable, build upon your successes. In addition to offering Maker elements as an added component, you will soon serve up Maker programming as a main dish. Before you know it, you won't think twice about tackling a new Maker project. And that's what it's all about.

The program recipes in this book will include offerings in science and technology, arts and crafts, and home skills. The recipes are divided into traditional cookbook entries: "Appetizers," "Side Dishes," "Main Entrees," and "Desserts." "Variations" are included to offer additional ways to present the program recipe ideas either to another audience and/or with other related activities. Media specialists and educators may adapt the programs for classroom use by following the "Recipe Substitutions." Some recipes include a "Fusion Box" that adds an optional helping of technology, "Leftover" suggestions, and a "Garnish of Books to Be Displayed during the Program." Be sure to read through *all* of the recipe steps before beginning a program. If you do not have all of the ingredients on hand, you may wish to switch out the ingredients with those readily available, or simply let the projects in this book inspire you to create your own recipes.

To someone who is not a librarian, library programming may seem deceptively simple. As children's librarians, we know how much hard work and preparation is involved in presenting each library program. Therefore, in addition to the user-friendly directions and instructions, the appendices of this book will provide a treasure-trove of the time-consuming minutia that is often left to the last minute. The appendices are meant to be reproducible. You may photocopy, fill in the blank, and check it off your list. Appendices include a "Recipe Planning Checklist," letters to parents and caregivers, book discussion questions, a list of the apps used in the recipes, and program handouts.

You won't want to skip the index of this book. In it, you will find money- and time-saving entries. We know how expensive art and craft supplies can be. Most recipe ingredients have been indexed individually, so you may find a program to present that will utilize the supplies you already have on hand. Clear out your pantry with the programs in the "Craft Closet Cleanout" index entry. "Fruitcake" recipes, programs that can be repackaged for use with multiple age groups or ideas, have also been indexed.

The Well-Stocked Pantry (Craft Closet)

Just as you can't make a recipe without the ingredients, you can't hold a program without the necessary supplies. Therefore, a well-stocked pantry or craft closet is essential. The following is a list of the ingredients or items you will likely use most. You may already have many of these items on hand. Purchase any items you don't currently own when making the recipe that requires them. Don't invest your whole programming budget into purchasing every supply on this list or your craft closet will runneth over and your pockets will be empty. Simply buy the necessary supplies as you go.

Crayons in a variety of colors
Washable markers in a variety of colors
Colored pencils in a variety of colors
Cray-Pas in a variety of colors
Drawing paper
Construction paper in a variety of colors
Poster board in a variety of colors
Pencils
Erasers
Washable tempera paint in a variety of colors
Watercolor paints in a variety of colors
Watercolor paper
Paintbrushes
White school glue
Craft glue
Glitter glue in a variety of colors
Glue sticks
Cellophane tape
Book tape
Masking tape
Duct tape
Sequins in a variety of colors

Feathers in a variety of colors
Pom-poms in a variety of colors
Ribbon in a variety of colors
Tissue paper in a variety of colors
Craft jewels
Glitter
Pipe cleaners
Assorted stickers
Stamps
Ink pads
Craft sticks
Bamboo skewers
Scissors
Plastic tablecloths
Baby wipes
Paper towels
Foam, paper or plastic disposable bowls
Foam, paper or plastic disposable plates
Foam, paper or plastic disposable drinking cups
Heavy-duty aluminum foil
Plastic zippered bags, large and small
Disposable aluminum lasagna pans

Menu and Meal Planning

Now that your pantry is well stocked, it's time to open up the cookbook. The sections in *The Maker Cookbook: Recipes for Children's and 'Tween Library Programs* are divided into traditional cookbook categories. Each of the categories includes programs from three different areas: science and technology, arts and crafts, and home skills. Science and technology programs utilize iPads, computers, and 3D printers. Crafts, photography, and music are included in arts and crafts programs. Home skills programs feature cooking, gardening, and interior design.

Appetizers: Maker elements are suggested for those wishing to add a taste of the Maker Movement into their existing book discussion groups. Each appetizer comes complete with recommended book titles for different age ranges and a list of book discussion questions. As in a restaurant, sometimes an appetizer hits the spot, so feel free to use the activities without the recommended book. Other recipes with book discussions are also sprinkled throughout the book.

Side Dishes: The entries in this category are suited for those with limited staff, budget, space, or any combination of the three.

Main Entrees: Though these programs require a longer time commitment, they allow attendees to delve deeper into the subject matter. They are suitable for one lengthy event or a series of events over multiple days. More preparation time is required for these recipes.

Desserts: These recipes are fun, feel good, lower tech programs for young children.

Program Recipes

Each recipe begins with a brief introduction outlining what the attendees will make, why the recipe is appealing, or the benefits to the participants and/or the library.

Cost: The next component in each recipe is the cost. This is an estimate of the anticipated costs associated with the program. Keep in mind that the dollar amounts provided are approximate and depend on a multitude of factors, including the region in which your library is located and whether or not items may be purchased on sale, at a discount, or in bulk.

However, some programs may have little or no cost, as many of the ingredients are already in most libraries' craft closets. Some recipes include suggestions on how to lower the cost of the program by using alternate ingredients.

Time: Time encompasses both the time spent in the preparation of the program and the actual length of the program. These are merely estimates; you may find in creating a sample that you may need more or less time. Your library may already have an established program length that works for you. Feel free to adapt the time allotment to meet your library's and/or patron's needs.

Early Bird Special(s): These entries are the tags that reveal the recipe's "nutritional value." "Craft Closet Cleanout" lists programs that necessitate a variety of common art and craft supplies. "Fruitcake" recipes are programs that can be repackaged for use with multiple age groups. "Smorgasbord" recipes allow each participant the chance to partake in any or all of the activities. "Low Cost Programs" and "Time Saving Programs" are just that—low cost and time saving. You will also find entries for these tags in the index.

Serving Size: Serving Size encompasses the most basic program information, including the suggested targeted age ranges for your program and the number of participants. You may wish to alter the age and/or number of the attendees to suit your library's needs. Some program recipes will appeal to a wide range of ages. You may find that older participants shy away from programs that are open to children several years younger. If interest is high in all age groups, it may be best to hold more than one session, grouping the children by age.

Recommendations are made where registration may be helpful in order to ensure that you have the necessary supplies to accommodate all of the participants. Some programs include food among their ingredients. For medical reasons, registration prior to the program may be necessary to obtain allergy information to avoid serious food allergies or reactions. Other recipes may include images of the child participants that are displayed either at the library or on social media site(s). Each library should have its own process for obtaining permission to use the images of children. In this book, it is referred to as the photo permission form. Carefully examine your own library's policies and follow them precisely.

Staff Size: The recipes suggest the minimum staffing requirements. If the opportunity presents itself, collaborative work adds to a program exponentially. It helps to have another staff member to bounce ideas off of, to add to your knowledge base, to present a different point of view, and to provide support.

Ingredients: Just like a recipe in a traditional cookbook, the ingredients are the specific items and quantities necessary to present each program. In the creation of the sample, you may find that alternate ingredients work equally as well or that you need to modify the quantity to suit your taste, budget, or the supplies you have on hand.

Preheat: Preheat encompasses all of the activities that take place prior to the program, from the weeks or days before the program to minutes before the children arrive. This may include the purchasing of ingredients, the preparation of an inspirational slideshow, the creation of a program sample, the setup of the program room, and the layout of the supplies.

Bake: Bake is a list of the step-by-step instructions of the specific activities that take place during the program. It may also contain tips and hints for the staff member(s) to increase participation.

Food Styling: Some programs suggest an additional component to highlight the work of the program participants. Food styling offers ways to showcase the children's work and provides family members and library patrons the opportunity to view not only the specific projects created but also offers an avenue to advertise other library programs they may not have known existed.

Variation(s): Variations provide suggestions for ways the recipes may be altered for different ages, to add additional concepts and/or components, or different ingredient combinations.

Fusion Box: iPad apps offered in this section add another dimension to a program. They expand the program's appeal to a wider audience. The greatest selection of apps is currently available in iPad format. Therefore, the apps recommended in the program recipes are created for use with an Apple device. They may also be available for Android devices. If the specific apps are not available in your device's format, perform an online search to find equivalent apps.

Occasionally an app that meets the specific needs of the program you are presenting is available only in iPhone format. Do not automatically discount this app. You should be able to enlarge most iPhone apps to fit an iPad screen. Be sure to check that the enlargement does not pixelate or distort the graphics of the app.

Recipe Substitution(s): Recipe Substitutions suggest the ways media specialists and educators may adapt the program recipes for either library or classroom use.

Leftovers: Ingredients are expensive and difficult to store. To save money and storage space, at the end of many recipes, the Leftovers component identifies other programs using the same ingredients.

Garnish of Books to Be Displayed during the Program: This section contains a bibliography of recommended materials to promote in conjunction with the program recipe. These materials are not meant to be a comprehensive listing of resources. Feel free to substitute other quality books from your collection. Recommended titles for book discussions have also been included.

Now You're Cooking!

So, you've chosen a recipe. What's next? Read the entire recipe in order to make sure it is suitable for your library's needs, the intended audience, and your budget. Some of the recipes in this book include food and/or edible ingredients. The ingredients included are suggestions based on a group of participants who have no known food allergies. It is your responsibility to adjust the ingredients list or the program itself, based on the medical needs of the participants in your program.

Although it is tempting to forego the creation of a sample due to time and staff limitations, this step is essential. It will familiarize you with the process used to create the projects and aid in the presentation of your program. You will also be better able to answer questions and assist the program attendees. In order to avoid any additional complications, it is necessary to create the sample with the exact ingredients that will be given to the participants. Once the sample is created, feel free to adjust, add, or take away any ingredients or steps to modify the project for you and/or your participants' needs.

If you are using a recommended app, eBook, or book title in a program, you should try out the app and/or read the book prior to planning the program. You need to make sure the app or book is suitable for your patrons and that you think that it would complement the program. Remember, there are new apps and books published daily. Check online to be sure that you are using the best materials and resources for your program.

Although one of the tenets of the Maker philosophy is the individuals' exploration and/or creation of new ideas or materials or tools, some attendees may find themselves stuck on where to start. Due to program time restrictions, realistically you may wish to prepare a few program prompts to jump-start the creative process.

It makes everyone's life easier if the program participants are asked to *Dress for a Mess*. Put this request on all flyers, advertisements, and publicity, and reiterate this to parents and caregivers upon registration. Some libraries have strict dress codes for their employees. If your library does not have a strict code, the staff member(s) conducting the program should *Dress for a Mess* as well. If your library does have a strict dress code, consider purchasing a smock or apron, or asking your supervisor for a program day exemption.

Program Publicity

If a tree falls in a forest and no one is around to hear it, does it make a sound? If a library offers a program and no one is aware of it, is it a success? To maximize the number of attendees at a program you have invested so much of yourself in, publicity is a crucial step for the success of any program and should not be skipped.

Social Media

Social media web sites are a great place to let your community know what the library is doing and allow the children to share their library program creations with friends and family near and far. Social media web sites are some of the most popular sources of direct information dissemination today and have fervent groups of followers. In order to best promote the hard work you and the children have put into library programs, you should familiarize yourself with popular social media web sites. These include YouTube, Pinterest, Facebook, Twitter, Instagram, Tumblr, Vine, and others. New social media sites are always cropping up, so keep an eye on the latest trends. Your library is most likely already using several of these social media sites in some capacity. Providing yourself with a deeper knowledge of these sites and all their complexity will allow you to better use the many different capabilities of the sites. If your library belongs to a consortium or association, they may offer free classes on using social media web sites. Take advantage of as many of these free opportunities as possible.

Other Marketing Sources

The following is a checklist to be used in the creation of successful library program flyers or signs:

- The name of the program
- The date and time of the program
- The age requirements
- Any items the participants may be asked to bring with them on the day of the program (e.g., an empty shoebox)
- Whether or not registration is required
- A brief visual and/or written description of the program
- A clean, clear layout or design
- An inviting or attention-grabbing hook to make participants and/or parents or caregivers want to learn more about the program

Flyers and signs may be used to promote library programs in many different ways. They may be physically posted inside and outside of the library and throughout the community. Places you frequent are likely to be popular with other members of your community. Consider asking businesses, doctors (especially pediatricians), and the local community center you patronize to post library programming flyers. Local elementary and middle schools may also be willing to display your flyer or sign with their own publicity. Image-based forms of publicity, like a sign or a flyer, lend themselves to be posted on your library's social media site(s) as well. You may need to convert your sign into a graphic format before posting on sites such as Facebook and Instagram.

Other opportunities exist for visual library promotion. Many libraries have a continuous slideshow on display on large screen monitors at different points of service. Take advantage of this and create a presence in this slideshow to promote all of your programming. For an ongoing program, consider asking your program regulars to produce a commercial to distribute on social media and public access outlets.

In order to reach the widest audience possible, programs need written publicity in addition to the more graphic flyer or sign. The written publicity should include the same elements as the flyer or sign with the exception of the visual. You must create the inviting or attention-grabbing hook through verbal means rather than visually. Disseminate the written publicity in any library written and/or electronic newsletters, local school written and/or electronic newsletters, local newspapers, community calendars, local blogs or discussion boards, and on community access television.

You're Connected

You aren't just connected to others via printed publicity or virtually through social media and the like. Whether or not you realize it, you have other connections. Think about your coworkers, friends, and family members. It is likely that most of them have an interest or talent that other people would like to learn about. These connections could add to the variety in your library's program offerings. Grandma might be thrilled to teach either you or your program attendees the skill of crochet. Uncle Joe's bottle cap collection could provide you with an idea for an upcycled art program.

You may also want to reach out to your "extended" family, the members of your community. A local hardware store may want to provide instruction on assistance with the use of power tools. The library would receive a free program while the business owner may attract new customers to his or her establishment.

Local residents may wish to share their hobbies with future generations. They may also wish to donate outgrown plastic interlocking building blocks, craft, or art supplies. Reach out to your Friends of the Library group. They may have talents or supplies that they wish to share. An enthusiastic Friends group might also be willing to help fund some of your expenses. You never know what valuable resources the people in your community are until you ask.

Temporary MakerSpace

To promote programming, to gauge the community interest, and to find out what the people of your community have to offer, consider setting up a temporary Maker-Space. Create different sections in your program room where children and families can experience the wonders of the Maker Movement. You may either purchase supplies or use what you have on hand to design your stations. For example, you may have a crafting station where you provide yarn and knitting needles. You may have a Break-It station with old electronics and tools for families to disassemble. You may provide a technology station that offers whatever technology or devices your library owns for program participants to explore at their own interest level or pace. The program may take place for as little as one hour or as long as a weekend. Add as many stations as your program room and/or your budget can accommodate. To save money, don't purchase, but consider borrowing or renting tools and safety equipment for the event. You may wish to use events such as this to generate interest and support for the creation of a permanent MakerSpace. In the meantime . . .

Make Your Library a MakerPlace!

Your library is already a place where people gather together to learn new skills and exchange ideas. The addition of Maker programming simply highlights and expands this mission. Keep calm and you can do it! Start by adding a Maker component to an existing library program. As you grow more comfortable, you may add Maker-centered programming to your library's offerings. Before you know it, your library will be a MakerPlace.

And, that's what it's all about . . .

I

Appetizers

Maker elements are suggested for those wishing to add a taste of the Maker Movement into their existing book discussion groups. Each appetizer comes complete with recommended book titles for different age ranges and a list of book discussion questions. As in a restaurant, sometimes an appetizer hits the spot, so feel free to use the activities without the recommended book. Other recipes with book discussions are also sprinkled throughout the book.

Alternate Reality

At one time or another, everyone has wondered what would happen if he or she could go back and alter one event in his or her life. Would his or her life change? On a grander scale, the *Alternate Reality* program proposes a change to the history of flight. (For other *Alternate Reality* ideas, see the Alternate, Alternate Reality Ideas, Projects and Discussion Questions in Appendix D on page 225.) Over 500 years ago, Leonardo da Vinci drew sketches of a flying machine. What if his design had been successful?

Leonardo da Vinci was one of the most famous and prolific of all Makers. He explored all facets of scientific experimentation. More importantly, he documented his entire thought process in his notebooks, some of which survive to this day. The *Alternate Reality* program opens with a discussion on how the world would have been different if Leonardo da Vinci had lifted us into the aviation era by inventing the world's first helicopter. The program begins with a book discussion of the child inventors in the book *The Templeton Twins Have an Idea* by Ellis Weiner for 9- to 12-year-olds or the time travelers in *Da Wild, Da Crazy, Da Vinci* by Jon Scieszka for 7- to 10-year-olds. In the final activity, the children will create their own flying vehicle, either modeled after Leonardo da Vinci's sketch or based on a design of their own creation. If the children are agreeable, you may post their preliminary sketches and photos of their flying machines on the library's social media site(s).

Cost: The cost of this program is minimal. Most of the necessary ingredients should already be in your craft closet.

Time: Most of the preparation time will be split among reading *The Templeton Twins Have an Idea* or *Da Wild, Da Crazy, Da Vinci*, creating an inspirational slideshow, and gathering the ingredients. If you must Interlibrary Loan copies of the book yourself or choose not to use *The Templeton Twins Have an Idea* book discussion questions in Appendix A on page 178 or the *Da Wild, Da Crazy, Da Vinci* in Appendix A on page 177, but instead create your own set of book discussion questions, you will need to allow additional preparation time. This program should last approximately one hour.

Early Bird Specials: Craft Closet Cleanout, Fruitcake, Low Cost Program

Serving Size: Twelve to fifteen 7- to 12-year-olds, with a separate program for each age-appropriate group. Registration should be required in order to obtain the correct number of copies of *The Templeton Twins Have an Idea* or *Da Wild, Da Crazy, Da Vinci* and to estimate the necessary ingredients.

Staff Size: One staff member.

Ingredients

One copy of the book *The Templeton Twins Have an Idea* or *Da Wild, Da Crazy, Da Vinci* for each registered child plus an additional copy for the staff member

Paper plates of different sizes and strengths

Craft sticks

Pencils to be used in the construction of the flying vehicle

Paper and writing utensils with which to sketch the designs

A selection of muslin and canvas

Wax paper

Twine

Scissors

Bamboo skewers

An assortment of tape that should include cellophane, book, masking, duct, etc.

(Optional) Pieces of heavy cardboard

(Optional) Utility knife or box cutter (to be used by the staff member before the program)

Inspirational slideshow of Leonardo da Vinci's inventions

Preheat

1. Interlibrary Loan enough copies of *The Templeton Twins Have an Idea* or *Da Wild, Da Crazy, Da Vinci* for each registered child to be available at the time of registration plus an additional copy for the staff member.
2. Purchase and/or gather the necessary ingredients.
3. Photocopy the list of *The Templeton Twins Have an Idea* book discussion questions provided in Appendix A on page 178 or the *Da Wild, Da Crazy, Da Vinci* book discussion questions provided in Appendix A on page 177 or create your own list of questions.
4. Perform an online search for images of Leonardo da Vinci's ideas and/or inventions with which to create an inspirational slideshow for the program participants. Be sure to end the slideshow with an image of Leonardo da Vinci's helicopter and leave this image up while the children create their helicopters.
5. If you wish to offer the children cardboard circles to use in the creation of their flying machines, use the utility knife or box cutter to pre-cut cardboard circles in a variety of sizes.
6. As the children will each be creating their own unique flying machine and not using step-by-step instructions, it is not absolutely necessary to create a sample helicopter. However, if you choose to make one, it may allow you to better assist the participants with their designs. It will also provide more inspiration for them to draw from.
7. On the day of the program, arrange the ingredients on the supply table.

Bake

1. Gather the children in your favorite book discussion formation.
2. Explain the concept of alternate realities and hold a discussion on what would have been different today if Leonardo da Vinci had successfully invented the helicopter in the 1500s.
3. Hold the book discussion on either *The Templeton Twins Have an* Idea or *Da Wild, Da Crazy, Da Vinci*.
4. Present the inspirational slideshow on Leonardo da Vinci's ideas and/or inventions.
5. If you made a sample flying machine, share it with the program participants.
6. Explain to the children that they will each be creating their own flying machine using ingredients from the supply table. Suggest that the children sketch out an idea on paper, as Leonardo da Vinci did, before building their own flying machine.
7. Ask the program participants if they would like to have their sketches and photos of their flying machines posted on the library's social media site(s).
8. Allot the remainder of the program time to the children's helicopter design and creation.

In addition to a program that encourages creativity and explores science and history, the *Alternate Reality* program promotes a discussion of causality, one of the basic components of philosophy since the time of Aristotle. The program may bring about a difference in the participants' way of thinking regarding the events in their own lives and the world around them. Who knows what change could come from that?

Variation: For a list of other *Alternate Reality* themes and activities, see the Alternate, Alternate Reality Ideas, Projects, and Discussion Questions in Appendix D.

Fusion Box: Use the Monster Physics app, a physics-inspired contraption-building game, in addition to or as a substitute for either the book discussion or the helicopter design project. If you chose to add the Monster Physics app to the recipe as is, add an additional 15 minutes to the length of the program.

Recipe Substitutions: Pair with a science teacher and hold this program in conjunction with a unit on the Scientific Method, the science of flight, or early scientific pioneers.

Leftovers: A variety of recipes use the bamboo skewers and paper plates. You will find these items listed individually in the index.

Garnish of Books to Be Displayed during the Program

Brezenoff, Steve. *Time Voyage*. Mankato, MN: Stone Arch Books, 2012.
Enz, Tammy. *Build Your Own Car, Rocket and Other Things That Go*. Mankato, MN: Capstone Press, 2011.
Krull, Kathleen. *Leonardo da Vinci*. New York: Viking Children's, 2005.
Osbourne, Mary Pope and Natalie Pope Boyce. *Leonardo da Vinci: A Nonfiction Companion to Magic Tree House #38*. New York: Random House Books for Young Readers, 2009.
Strasser, Todd. *Fallout*. Somerville, MA: Candlewick Press, 2013.
Wurge, B. B. *The Last Notebook of Leonardo*. Teaticket, MA: Leapfrog Press, 2010.

Balloon Zip Line

Who hasn't dreamed of flying like a superhero? Add a little zip to a book discussion of *Powerless* by Matthew Cody with the *Balloon Zip Line* recipe. To present this program to a group of children ages 7 to 10, substitute the book *The Curse of the Bologna Sandwich* by Greg Trine. Children will create their own superhero out of art supplies and grant it the super power of flight by attaching it to a balloon and sending it flying across a zip line made from yarn.

Cost: Depending on the ingredients you have on hand, the cost of this program should be less than $25.

Time: Most of the preparation time will be split between reading *Powerless* or *The Curse of the Bologna Sandwich*, creating a sample to familiarize yourself with the process, and setting up the zip lines in the program room. If you must Interlibrary Loan copies of the book yourself and/or choose not to use the *Powerless* book discussion questions in Appendix A on page 181 or *The Curse of the Bologna Sandwich* book discussion questions in Appendix A on page 180, but instead create your own set of book discussion questions, you will need to allow additional preparation time. The program should last 45 minutes to one hour.

Early Bird Specials: Fruitcake, Low Cost Program

Serving Size: Twelve to fifteen 7- to 12-year-olds, with a separate program for each age-appropriate group. Registration is required in order to obtain the correct number of copies of *Powerless* or *The Curse of the Bologna Sandwich*, to estimate the necessary ingredients and to determine the number of zip lines.

Staff Size: One staff member.

Ingredients

One copy of the book *Powerless* or *The Curse of the Bologna Sandwich* for each registered child to be available at the time of registration plus an additional copy for the staff member

One piece of 8½ inch by 11 inch white drawing, printer, or copy paper per registered child plus two extra pieces to create the sample, for demonstration, and for the inevitable mishaps

A selection of crayons, markers, colored pencils, and/or pastels in a variety of colors

Scissors

One skein of medium-weight yarn of any color

One 12 inch balloon per registered child plus several more to create the sample, for demonstration, and for the inevitable mistakes and breakage

One plastic drinking straw per registered child plus two additional straws to create the sample and for demonstration, and for the inevitable mistakes and misfires. Straws that do not bend are preferable.

One roll of masking tape or painter's tape

One roll of duct tape

(Optional) One roll of double-sided tape

(Optional) Bamboo skewers, plastic knitting needles or other thin, pointed threading implements with which to thread the yarn through the straws

Preheat

1. Interlibrary Loan enough copies of *Powerless* or *The Curse of the Bologna Sandwich* to accommodate the Serving Size, plus an additional copy for the staff member.
2. Photocopy the list of *Powerless* book discussion questions provided in Appendix A on page 181 or *The Curse of the Bologna Sandwich* book discussion questions provided in Appendix A on page 180 or create your own list of questions.
3. Purchase and/or gather the necessary ingredients.
4. Find an area in which to test your balloon zip line. The area does not have to be in the room where the program will take place. All you need is two flat vertical surfaces (e.g., two walls, a wall and cabinet, two cabinets) on which to attach your yarn, resembling a clothesline.
5. Create a sample to familiarize yourself with the process:
   a. Draw the rough outline of a superhero on one piece of the drawing, printer, or copy paper. You do not have to create a fancy outline or color it in, as it is simply to be used as a test to make sure the process works for you.
   b. Cut out the rough outline of the superhero.
   c. If you are using a bendable straw, cut off the bendable portion, leaving the largest part of the straw intact.
   d. Thread the piece at the free end of the skein of yarn through the drinking straw using one bamboo skewer or other threading implement.
   e. Once threaded, take the free end of the yarn and tape it to one of the flat vertical surfaces at approximately eye level with a piece of masking or painter's tape. Painter's tape may be preferable if your flat surface is a painted wall.
   f. Pull the skein end of the yarn, releasing yarn as you go, to the opposite flat surface. Pull the yarn as taut as possible. The tighter the yarn tension, the easier it is to propel the balloon from one side of the zip line to the other.
   g. Tape the skein end of the yarn to the opposing flat surface with a piece of masking or painter's tape.

    h. Cut the yarn from the skein.

    i.   If necessary, pull the straw to one end of the zip line.

    j.   Stretch out one balloon, inflating and deflating it two or three times.

    k. At this point, you will need another set of hands with which to attach the balloon and superhero drawing. During the program, you may ask one of the children to assist you. For now, ask another staff member for assistance.

    l.   Blow up the balloon and pinch it closed to ensure that air does not escape.

    m. Hold the balloon parallel to and touching the bottom of the straw with the mouth or opening of the balloon pointed toward the closest flat surface to which the yarn is taped.

    n. Cut a 4–6 inch piece of duct tape.

    o. Place the tape perpendicularly atop the straw and balloon, securing the balloon to the straw.

    p. With the balloon still pinched, one staff member should cut a 3–4 inch piece of masking or painter's tape and roll it into a loop, sticky side out. (You may prefer to use a 2 inch piece of double-sided tape instead.)

    q. Place the loop of masking or painter's tape or piece of double-sided tape in the center of the back of the superhero drawing.

    r.   Secure the superhero to the bottom of the balloon, opposite the straw. To achieve the best visual result, attach the superhero parallel to the balloon with its head facing its destination or opposing flat surface.

    s.   Stand back and let go of the balloon. Your superhero should "fly" to the other side of the room.

6. Create one more superhero to be used as a demonstration in front of the children. This superhero should be colored in to provide inspiration for the program participants.

7. Decide how many zip lines the program will offer. (Leave half of the program room without zip lines to provide an area for the participants to create their superheroes.) It is preferable for each child to have his or her own zip line, but if the program space is limited, participants may take turns. Be sure to reserve one zip line spot to send your sample superhero flying. While attaching your zip lines, you may wish to thread two straws onto the yarn, one at each end, and have two children share the same zip line. The straws will most likely be unable to be used for more than one balloon due to the strength of the adhesive used in the duct tape. Secure the chosen number of zip lines to the flat vertical surfaces of the program room. Remember to consider the age and average height of the participants so that they will not have difficulty reaching the balloon and straw to tape them together.

8. Arrange the art supplies on the supply table. To avoid distractions, place the balloons, straws, and the duct tape on the supply table while the children are creating their superheroes.

Bake

1. Gather the children in your favorite book discussion formation.
2. Explain the components of the program to the participants.
3. Hold the *Powerless* or *The Curse of the Bologna Sandwich* book discussion.

4. Introduce the concept of the zip line and explain the steps the participants will use to make their superheroes fly.
5. With the assistance of one your participants, attach your demonstration superhero to one zip line and make it fly according to the steps outlined in Preheat 5i–s.
6. Instruct the children to create their own superheroes using the art supplies on the supply table.
7. While the children are drawing, place the straws (if you have not chosen to thread the straws onto the yarn as in Preheat 7), balloons, and duct tape on the supply table. Cut one 4–6 inch piece of duct tape for each child and stick one end of the strip of tape to the supply table. This step saves the staff member time and trouble while attaching the balloons to the zip line straws, as the participants will not need to stop and cut the tape.
8. Fifteen minutes before the end of the program or activity, ask the children to complete the instructions outlined in Preheat 5i–s. To speed up this process, ask the children to help one another attach their balloons to their straws and their superheroes to their balloons.

SHAZAAM!!! Take your participants up, up and away, with this laughter-inducing, fun-filled program.

Recipe Substitution: In cooperation with a science teacher use the media center or classroom in this nontraditional way to present a riotous participatory science lesson on aerodynamics.

Leftovers: Use the leftover yarn from this program in the *Look Ma, No Needles!* program on page 48.

Garnish of Books to Be Displayed during the Program

Anderson, John David. *Sidekicked*. New York: Walden Pond Press, 2013.
Brown, Jeff. *Flat Stanley*. New York: HarperTrophy, 2003.
Cody, Matthew. *Powerless*. New York: Alfred A. Knopf, 2009.
DiCamillo, Kate. *Flora & Ulysses: The Illuminated Adventures*. Somerville, MA: Candlewick Press, 2013.
Kirby, Stan. *Captain Awesome to the Rescue!* New York: Little Simon, 2012.
Trine, Greg. *The Curse of the Bologna Sandwich*. New York: Henry Holt, 2006.

3

Off to the Races!

Toy cars are one of the most popular children's toys. Racing invokes a competitive spirit. Put the two together and you have an exciting addition to a book discussion of *A Whole Nother Story* by Dr. Cuthbert Soup for 9- to 12-year-olds or *Barfing in the Backseat: How I Survived My Family Road Trip* by Henry Winkler and Lin Oliver for 7- to 10-year-olds. In this program, children will take part in a book discussion and create cars powered by the air inside of a balloon and race them against one another in friendly competition.

Cost: The largest cost for this program is the plastic interlocking building block car wheels. You can purchase these online—look for a box containing ONLY car wheels. To avoid this cost, experiment with wine corks or other small discs or circular materials to be used as substitutes or request donations of building block car wheels from patrons and/or staff well in advance of the program. If you choose to use small disc or circular materials as wheel substitutes, be sure to triple check that your substitute wheels work before providing this option to the children. The remaining materials may be purchased inexpensively at a dollar or discount store. Including the cost of the plastic interlocking building block car wheels, the cost of the program should total less than $100.

Time: Most of the preparation time will be split between reading *A Whole Nother Story* or *Barfing in the Backseat: How I Survived My Family Road Trip* and purchasing and gathering the necessary ingredients. If you must Interlibrary Loan copies of the book yourself and/or choose not to use the *A Whole Nother Story* book discussion questions in Appendix A on page 185 or the *Barfing in the Backseat: How I Survived My Family Road Trip* book discussion questions in Appendix A on page 184, but instead create your own set of book discussion questions, you will need to allow additional preparation time. An additional 30 minutes or so will be necessary to assemble your demonstration model. The program itself may run 45 minutes or more depending on the amount of time allotted for racing.

Early Bird Special: Fruitcake

Serving Size: Twelve to sixteen 7- to 12-year-olds, with a separate program for each age-appropriate group. Registration is required in order to obtain the correct number of copies of *A Whole Nother Story* or *Barfing in the Backseat: How I Survived My Family Road Trip* and to determine the necessary ingredients.

Staff Size: One staff member.

Ingredients

One copy of the book *A Whole Nother Story* or *Barfing in the Backseat: How I Survived My Family Road Trip for* each registered child to be available at the time of registration plus an additional copy for the staff member

One empty plastic 16.9 ounce water bottle per registered child, plus one for the demonstration model (ridged water bottles work best)

One 12 inch balloon per registered child, plus extra for the demonstration model and any balloon mishaps

Six plastic drinking straws per registered child, plus six for the demonstration model

One roll of duct tape per table

One roll of electrical tape per table

Scissors

Four plastic interlocking building block car wheels per registered child, plus one additional set for the demonstration model

(Optional) Four wine corks or other small discs or circular materials to be used as wheels per registered child plus one additional set for the demonstration model

One bamboo skewer per child, plus one for the demonstration model

Utility or craft knife (to be used by the staff member before the program)

One zippered plastic bag, paper plate, or disposable foil lasagna pan per registered child

Tape measure

Preheat

1. Interlibrary Loan enough copies of *A Whole Nother Story* or *Barfing in the Backseat: How I Survived My Family Road Trip* to accommodate the Serving Size, plus an additional copy for the staff member.
2. Photocopy the list of *A Whole Nother Story* book discussion questions provided in Appendix A on page 185 or *Barfing in the Backseat: How I Survived My Family Road Trip* book discussion questions provided in Appendix A on page 184 or create your own list of questions.
3. Save twenty 16.9 ounce empty plastic water bottles and/or ask staff members to donate bottles.
4. Purchase and/or gather the remaining ingredients.
5. Create a sample car for demonstration and to familiarize yourself with the process.
   a. Remove and discard the water bottle cap from one 16.9 ounce empty plastic water bottle.
   b. Use the utility or craft knife to cut an X in the empty plastic water bottle approximately 3½ inches from the open mouth of the bottle.

c. Place one plastic drinking straw horizontally on a table.

d. Lay the water bottle vertically on top of the plastic drinking straw.

e. Cut the straw so that it is slightly longer than the widest part of the bottle. This will be used to make one part of an axle for one pair of wheels.

f. Remove the drinking bottle and cut another piece of straw the same length as the first.

g. Bamboo skewers are difficult to cut with scissors. For this step, you should snap the bamboo skewer with your hands and trim the excess strands with scissors. Snap one bamboo skewer into two pieces, each piece 1 inch longer than the measured drinking straw segments. If you are using large wheels, you may need to snap your bamboo skewer pieces 2 inches longer or more to accommodate the width of the larger wheels.

h. Lay the water bottle on the table, with the cut X side down. Place one plastic drinking straw segment perpendicular to the water bottle approximately 3 inches down from the open mouth. This will comprise the axle for the front wheels. If you are using ridged water bottles, the ridges of the bottle will hold the straw in place. If you are using a smooth water bottle, the straws will need to be secured individually.

i. Place the remaining plastic drinking straw segment perpendicular to the water bottle approximately 1 inch from the bottom. This will comprise the axle for the back wheels.

j. Secure the two plastic drinking straw segments with one piece of duct tape running the length of the bottle.

k. Turn the bottle over and make sure the plastic drinking straw segment closest to the mouth of the bottle is above the cut X.

l. Insert one bamboo skewer piece into each drinking straw segment. There should be at least ½ inch of bamboo skewer hanging out of each side of the plastic drinking straw segment.

m. Attach one building block car wheel or wine cork or other small disc or circular material to each one of the four bamboo skewers sticking out of the plastic drinking straw segments.

n. Cut a small piece of electrical tape and wrap it around the tip of the bamboo skewer to firmly secure each wheel.

o. Turn the water bottle wheel side down onto the table to make sure all four wheels touch the table. You may need to adjust the wheel position by applying gentle pressure to the bottle. If this does not change your wheel position, adjust the duct tape accordingly.

p. Stretch out one balloon, inflating and deflating it three times.

q. In one hand, gather five plastic drinking straws like a bouquet of flowers. Tape the five straws together with the duct tape, being careful not to collapse or otherwise damage the straws.

r. Insert the straws into the balloon opening. Secure the balloons to the straws by wrapping the duct tape around the opening of the balloon to make an airtight seal.

s. Insert the straws into the cut X and push the straws out the open bottle neck until a sufficient length of the straws is sticking out of the bottle to comfortably blow up the balloon.

t. Blow into the straws to inflate the balloon.

u. Pinch the base of the balloon to prevent the balloon from deflating.

v. Now that your sample is done, it is time to try it out. Set the car on a hard, flat surface. Lower the flag, let go of the balloon, and you are off to the races!

6. Remove and discard all the remaining empty plastic water bottle caps.

7. Use the utility or craft knife to cut an X into each of the remaining empty plastic water bottles.

8. Count out the correct number of straws, bamboo skewers, and wheels or wine corks or small discs or other circular materials for each child and place them into the zippered plastic bags or onto the paper plates or disposable foil lasagna pans. This will ensure that each child has the correct number of pieces with which to construct his or her car.

9. Arrange the tables along the perimeter of the program room, leaving space for car races in the middle of the room.

10. Place one complete set of ingredients at each work space. Children may share the scissors, electrical tape, and duct tape.

Bake

1. Gather the children in your favorite book discussion formation.
2. Explain the components of the program to the participants.
3. Hold the *A Whole Nother Story* or *Barfing in the Backseat: How I Survived My Family Road Trip* book discussion.
4. Show the participants your demonstration model and explain the steps used to create it.
5. Blow up the balloon and let the car race across the open space.
6. Instruct the children to create their own car using the steps in Preheat 5a–u. Walk around the perimeter of the room, answering any questions that may arise.

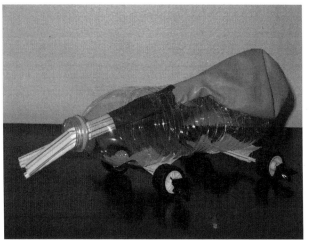

7. Once all the cars are completed, it is race time. Depending on the size of your room you can race individually, measuring the result with the tape measure, race in heats, or all at once.

The *Off to the Races* program provides opportunities not only for fun but also for discussing the importance of family and friendship.

Variation: Have the children embellish their cars with stickers and/or decorate their uninflated balloons with markers.

Recipe Substitutions: Add this project to a science unit studying Sir Isaac Newton's Laws of Motion or use it as a lively way to teach measurement and/or the metric system.

Leftovers: Use the leftover bamboo skewers or plastic drinking straws to help create your Cardboard aMAZEment on page 25.

Garnish of Books to Be Displayed during the Program

Ballard, Carol. *Exploring Forces and Movement*. New York: Rosen Publishing Group, Inc., 2008.
Barber, Phil. *From Finish to Start: A Week in the Life of NASCAR Race Team*. Excelsior, MN: Tradition Books, 2003.
Gorman, Carol. *Dork in Disguise*. New York: HarperCollins Publishers, 1999.
Krull, Kathleen. *Isaac Newton*. New York: Puffin Books, 2008.
Oxlade, Chris. *Forces and Motion: An Investigation*. New York: Rosen Publishing Group, Inc., 2008.
Soup, Cuthbert. *A Whole Nother Story*. New York: Bloomsbury, 2010.
Winkler, Henry and Lin Oliver. *Barfing in the Backseat: How I Survived My Family Road Trip*. New York: Grosset & Dunlap, 2007.

4

Cardboard aMAZEment

Throughout history, children have used their imagination to create their own games to entertain themselves. In this high-tech world of apps and video games, this program provides an old-fashioned but creative and fun alternative. After a book discussion of *The Gollywhopper Games* by Jody Feldman for 9- to 12-year-olds or *Judy Moody & Stink: The Mad, Mad, Mad, Mad Treasure Hunt* by Megan McDonald for 7- to 10-year-olds, the children will design and construct a unique maze. This simple-to-construct maze will be created using a cardboard box and some craft supplies likely already in your craft closet. It is sure to provide hours of screen-free amusement.

Cost: Ask the cataloging or acquisitions department to save empty cardboard shipping boxes from book orders. Purchase or collect from your craft supply cabinet the remaining ingredients. As long as your cupboard isn't bare, this program has little or no cost.

Time: Most of the preparation time will be split between reading *The Gollywhopper Games* or *Judy Moody & Stink: The Mad, Mad, Mad, Mad Treasure Hunt*, cutting the cardboard boxes to the specified height, purchasing and/or gathering the ingredients and creating your sample maze. If you must Interlibrary Loan copies of the book yourself and/or choose not to use *The Gollywhopper Games* book discussion questions in Appendix A on page 189 or the *Judy Moody & Stink: The Mad, Mad, Mad, Mad Treasure Hunt* book discussion questions in Appendix A on page 188, but instead create your own set of book discussion questions, you will need to allow additional preparation time. The program should last 45 minutes to one hour.

Early Bird Specials: Craft Closet Cleanout, Fruitcake, Low Cost Program

Serving Size: Twelve to sixteen 7- to 12-year-olds, with a separate program for each age-appropriate group. Registration is required in order to obtain the correct number of copies of *The Gollywhopper Games* or *Judy Moody & Stink: The Mad, Mad, Mad, Mad Treasure Hunt* and to estimate the necessary ingredients.

Staff Size: One staff member.

Ingredients

One copy of the book *The Gollywhopper Games* or *Judy Moody & Stink: The Mad, Mad, Mad, Mad Treasure Hunt* for each registered child to be available at the time of registration plus an additional copy for the staff member

One empty cardboard shipping box per registered child plus one box to create the sample

One box cutter (to be used by the staff member before the program)

Masking tape or book tape

A large quantity of 3-mm bamboo skewers and/or plastic drinking straws

One bottle of white glue per registered child

Scissors

Pencils, crayons, and markers

One ruler per registered child

Pom-poms, self-adhesive note paper, and any other items or materials that may be used as bumpers or barriers

One small-to-medium-sized marble per child

Newspapers

Baby wipes and paper towels (to be used in cleanup)

Inspirational maze design slideshow

Preheat

1. Interlibrary Loan enough copies of *The Gollywhopper Games* or *Judy Moody & Stink: The Mad, Mad, Mad, Mad Treasure Hunt* to accommodate the Serving Size, plus an additional copy for the staff member.

2. Photocopy the list of *The Gollywhopper Games* book discussion questions provided in Appendix A on page 189 or *Judy Moody & Stink: The Mad, Mad, Mad, Mad Treasure Hunt* book discussion questions provided in Appendix A on page 188 or create your own list of questions.

3. Research maze designs either online or in books to provide the children with examples of successful maze line placement.

4. Create an inspirational slideshow showcasing a variety of simple maze design images.

5. Purchase and/or gather the necessary ingredients.

6. Create a sample *Cardboard aMAZEment* game to familiarize yourself with the process and to show to the children. If you are using this recipe with the book *Judy Moody & Stink: The Mad, Mad, Mad, Mad Treasure Hunt*, you may wish to create a pirate-themed maze that showcases the clues used in the book's treasure hunt.

   a. Using the box cutter, cut down one empty cardboard shipping box to a 3½ inch to 4 inch height.

   b. If the box is taped or glued on the bottom, reinforce the closure with masking or book tape to prevent the marble from falling out of the maze box.

   c. Use a pencil and ruler, if desired, to draw the track lines of your maze. Make sure your lines are spaced far enough apart to accommodate your marble. Note this measurement to instruct the children how far apart their track lines should be.

   d. Using crayons or markers, decorate your game with a background design or themed elements. If you are not using a pirate theme, consider basing your design on a fairy tale, having the marble pass by the different settings. For example, the marble may visit the houses of the three little pigs. Be sure to make the background design around the pencil maze lines.

e. Use bamboo skewers and/or plastic drinking straws to mark the boundaries of your maze. Bamboo skewers are difficult to cut with scissors. For this step you should snap the skewer with your hands and trim the excess strands with scissors. Snap bamboo skewers or cut plastic drinking straws into pieces, with each piece measuring the length of one of the pencil-drawn maze lines.

f. Glue the bamboo skewer pieces or plastic drinking straw segments onto the pencil-drawn maze lines on the empty cardboard shipping box.

g. Glue pom-poms and/or stick self-adhesive note paper folded into accordion pleats, or any other bumper items or materials onto the empty cardboard shipping box throughout the course of the maze to provide obstacles to the marble's path.

h. Allow the glue to dry completely before using your maze.

7. Use the box cutter to cut down the remaining empty cardboard shipping boxes.

8. Cover the tables with newspaper.

9. Place one pre-cut empty cardboard shipping box at each work space.

10. Arrange the remaining ingredients on the supply table in like groups (e.g., pencils with rulers, skewers with straws, crayons with markers). Do not put the marbles on the supply table.

Bake

1. Gather the children in your favorite book discussion formation.

2. Explain the components of the program to the participants.

3. Hold *The Gollywhopper Games* or *Judy Moody & Stink: The Mad, Mad, Mad, Mad Treasure Hunt* book discussion.

4. After the book discussion has ended, show the participants your sample maze.

5. Present an inspirational slideshow containing examples of successful maze line placement designs.

6. Discuss the steps used to create the maze.

7. Instruct the children to select ingredients from the supply table and begin creating their mazes using the steps in Preheat 5c–h.

8. Walk around the room answering any questions that may arise.

9. At the end of the program, hand out one marble to each child. As you are handing out the marbles, explain to each child that they should wait to try their maze until the glue is completely dry and that they must keep the marbles in a safe place out of the reach of small children, as the marbles may be a choking hazard.

The mazes may be made as simple or elaborate as time permits. Allow the children to let their imaginations soar and think OUTSIDE of the box!

Variations: *Cardboard aMAZEment* may be used as a starting point for a series of programs on recycled crafts. You might also use this program for a different take on Family Game Night and have families create a maze together. If you can find a number of large appliance boxes, consider breaking the participants into groups to

create a number of giant mazes and displaying them at the library for the community to enjoy.

Fusion Box: Provide examples of successful maze line placement using maze apps on your library's iPad(s). Mouse Maze, Fairytale 123 Maze, and Magic Maze are examples of interesting maze designs from which the children may take inspiration.

Leftovers: Use the leftover bamboo skewers or plastic drinking straws to help create your *Off to the Races* car on page 20. You might also use the Mouse Maze, Fairytale 123 Maze, and Magic Maze apps from this program's "Fusion Box" in the *Fondant Game* program on page 130. Consider pairing the book discussion of *Judy Moody & Stink: The Mad, Mad, Mad, Mad Treasure Hunt* with one or more of the components of the "Pirate Loot Bag" project in the *Maker Marketplace* program on page 106.

Garnish of Books to Be Displayed during the Program

Baccalario, Pierdomenico. *The Door to Time.* New York: Scholastic, 2006.

Berlin, Eric. *The Puzzling World of Winston Breen.* New York: G.P. Putnam's Sons, 2007.

Feldman, Jody. *The Gollywhopper Games.* New York: Greenwillow Books, 2008.

McDonald, Megan. *Judy Moody & Stink: The Mad, Mad, Mad, Mad Treasure Hunt.* Somerville, MA: Candlewick Press, 2010.

Munro, Roxie. *Amazement Park.* San Francisco: Chronicle Books, 2005.

Munro, Roxie. *Ecomazes: Twelve Earth Adventures.* New York: Sterling Publishing Company, Inc., 2010.

Nilsen, Anna. *Mousemazia: An Amazing Dream House Maze.* Cambridge, MA: Candlewick Press, 2000.

Riordan, Rick. *The Maze of Bones.* New York: Scholastic, 2008.

The Fake Spill

Who said Maker programs can't be funny? This project was inspired by sculptor Jacci Den Hartog's work, *Pink Accident*, and it appeals to kids' natural affinity for practical jokes. After a book discussion of *Pickle: The (Formerly) Anonymous Prank Club of Fountain Point Middle School* by Kim Baker for 9- to 12-year-olds or *The Get Rich Quick Club* by Dan Gutman for 7- to 10-year-olds, the children will create a simple, artistic rendering of a fake spill using materials you likely already have on hand.

Cost: Your library may have many of the listed ingredients on hand. However, if you had to buy all of the materials, the cost should still be under $50. Remember, the dollar store is your friend.

Time: Most of the preparation time will be split between reading *Pickle: The (Formerly) Anonymous Prank Club of Fountain Point Middle School* or *The Get Rich Quick Club* and creating the sample. If you must Interlibrary Loan copies of the book yourself and/or choose not to use the *Pickle: The (Formerly) Anonymous Prank Club of Fountain Point Middle School* book discussion questions in Appendix A on page 192 or *The Get Rich Quick Club* book discussion questions in Appendix A on page 191, but instead create your own set of book discussion questions, you will need to allow additional preparation time. The project can be made in 10–15 minutes but, BE WARNED, it takes four or more days to dry. This program should last approximately 45 minutes to one hour.

Early Bird Specials: Fruitcake, Low Cost Program

Serving Size: Twelve 7- to 12-year-olds, with a separate program for each age-appropriate group. You may accommodate up to 20 participants, but this will increase the cost. Registration is required in order to obtain the correct number of copies of *Pickle: The (Formerly) Anonymous Prank Club of Fountain Point Middle School* or *The Get Rich Quick Club* and to estimate the necessary ingredients.

Staff Size: One staff member.

Ingredients

One copy of the book *Pickle: The (Formerly) Anonymous Prank Club of Fountain Point Middle School* or *The Get Rich Quick Club* for each registered child to be available at the time of registration, plus an additional copy for the staff member

One 4 ounce bottle of white glue per registered child plus one additional bottle to create the sample

One disposable foam or plastic bowl per registered child plus one additional bowl to create the sample

Washable tempera paint in a variety of colors

Craft sticks or coffee stirrers

One plastic cup per registered child plus one additional cup to create the sample

One foil disposable lasagna pan per registered child plus one additional pan to create the sample

One roll of wax paper

Masking tape

Straws, plastic spoons, life-sized toy bugs, or anything you have on hand that may be used to make the spill appear more realistic

Plastic tablecloths

Baby wipes and paper towels (to be used in cleanup)

Inspirational slideshow of fake spills

Preheat

1. Interlibrary loan enough copies of *Pickle: The (Formerly) Anonymous Prank Club of Fountain Point Middle School* or *The Get Rich Quick Club* to accommodate the Serving Size, plus an additional copy for the staff member.

2. Photocopy the list of *Pickle: The (Formerly) Anonymous Prank Club of Fountain Point Middle School* book discussion questions provided in Appendix A on page 192 or *The Get Rich Quick Club* book discussion questions in Appendix A on page 191 or create your own list of questions.

3. Perform an online search for an image of Jacci Den Hartog's sculpture *Pink Accident* and any other fake spills (an online image search should produce many other examples). Use the images to create an inspirational slideshow for the program participants.

4. Purchase and/or gather the necessary ingredients.

5. At least four days in advance of the program, decide what type of fake spill you'd like to create and make your sample fake spill:

   a. Line the lasagna pans with wax paper. To prevent the wax paper from shifting, secure the wax paper to the bottom of the pan with masking tape.

   b. Pour the entire contents of the 4 ounce glue bottle into a bowl.

   c. Choose a paint color appropriate for the spill. (NOTE: To make a milk spill you must add white paint to the glue as glue becomes transparent as it dries.)

   d. Squeeze three drops of paint into the glue.

   e. Stir the paint into the glue with a craft stick or coffee stirrer.

   f. If you haven't achieved the proper color, add one paint drop at a time until it looks right. Be careful not to add too much paint or the paint may make the glue too watery to set.

   g. Pour the glue/paint mixture into a plastic cup.

   h. Have the lasagna pan at the ready.

   i. Starting at one end of the pan, slowly tip the cup toward the wax paper liner.

j. Gently set the cup down, as if it had fallen.

k. Place the straws, spoons, or other materials on top of the glue/paint mixture and press lightly.

6. Line the remaining foil lasagna pans with wax paper, securing the wax paper to the bottom of the pans with masking tape.

7. On the day of the program, cover all of the tables with plastic tablecloths.

8. Arrange the supplies on the supply table.

Bake

1. Gather the children in your favorite book discussion formation.

2. Explain the components of the program to the participants.

3. Hold the *Pickle: The (Formerly) Anonymous Prank Club of Fountain Point Middle School* or *The Get Rich Quick Club* book discussion.

4. Show the participants the inspirational slideshow.

5. Have the children decide what type of fake spill they would like to make.

6. Inform the children that the spills take four days or more to dry. In order not to ruin their project, strongly suggest that they leave their spills at the library to set.

7. Whether the project remains at the library or goes home with the child, once the project is COMPLETELY dry, the wax paper must be carefully peeled off the spill and the cup before placing it realistically on a countertop or tile or wood floor.

At some point during the program, be sure to emphasize that practical jokes are not meant to be mean. Though the children should have fun with their fake spills, they need to be responsible. The execution of any prank should be enjoyed by EVERYONE.

Recipe Substitutions: Pair with an art teacher in conjunction with a unit on contemporary American artists, women artists, or humorous art.

Garnish of Books to Be Displayed during the Program

Baker, Kim. *Pickle: The (Formerly) Anonymous Prank Club of Fountain Point Middle School.* New York: Roaring Brook Press, 2012.

Bell-Rehwoldt, Sheri. *The Kids' Guide to Pranks, Tricks and Practical Jokes.* Mankato, MN: Capstone Press, 2009.

Gutman, Dan. *The Get Rich Quick Club.* New York: HarperCollins, 2004.

Hargrave, John. *Mischief Maker's Manual.* New York: Grosset & Dunlap, 2009.

Holm, Jennifer L. and Matthew Holm. *The Power of the Parasite.* New York: Random House, 2012.

Jocelyn, Marthe. *Sneaky Art: Craft Surprises to Hide in Plain Sight.* Somerville, MA: Candlewick Press, 2013.

YES Mag. *Hoaxed! Fakes & Mistakes in the World of Science.* Toronto: Kids Can Press, 2009.

6

Meteorite Strike!

Wonderstruck by Brian Selznick is a story that has widespread appeal for children ages 9 to 12. Through text and illustrations, this book incorporates adventure with an exploration of the universal themes of friendship, family, and a sense of belonging. Though the two main characters are separated by time, Selznick connects them through a meteorite exhibit at the American Museum of Natural History in New York. The *Meteorite Strike!* program is a delicious way to allow the participants to bond with the characters, learn about meteorites, and make colorful meteorite cookies to eat.

For younger children, ages 7 to 10, rename this program *Cookie Tales*, omit the inspirational slideshow, and pair it with the book *How to Save Your Tail: If You Are a Rat Nabbed by Cats Who Really Like Stories about Magic Spoons, Wolves with Snout-warts, Big, Hairy Chimney Trolls . . . and Cookies, too* by Mary Hanson. This fairy tale –inspired book takes a humorous look at the classic stories children know and love and provides an opportunity for participants to create a delicious no-bake cookie.

Cost: The purchase of the listed food ingredients is the most expensive part of the cost of this program. Since food prices vary by region and retail establishment, expect this program to cost between $75 and $100. For less-expensive *Meteorite Strike!* program ideas, see the "Variations" section at the conclusion of this recipe.

Time: Most of the preparation time for this program will be split between reading *Wonderstruck* or *How to Save Your Tail: If You Are a Rat Nabbed by Cats Who Really Like Stories about Magic Spoons, Wolves with Snout-warts, Big, Hairy Chimney Trolls . . . and Cookies, too*, creating the slideshow if applicable, shopping for the ingredients, and preparing the cookie sample. If you must Interlibrary Loan copies of the books yourself and/or choose not to use the *Wonderstruck* book discussion questions in Appendix A on page 195 or the *How to Save Your Tail: If You Are a Rat Nabbed by Cats Who Really Like Stories about Magic Spoons, Wolves with Snout-warts, Big, Hairy Chimney Trolls . . . and Cookies, too* book discussion questions in Appendix A on page 194, but instead create your own set of book discussion questions, you will need to allow additional preparation time. This program should last approximately one hour.

Early Bird Special: Fruitcake

Serving Size: Twelve 7- to 12-year-olds, with a separate program for each age-appropriate group. Registration should be required in order to obtain allergy information to avoid serious food allergies or reactions, to obtain the correct number of copies of *Wonderstruck* or *How to Save Your Tail: If You Are a Rat Nabbed by Cats Who Really Like Stories about Magic Spoons, Wolves with Snout-warts, Big, Hairy Chimney Trolls . . . and Cookies, too*, and to estimate the necessary ingredients.

Staff Size: One staff member.

Ingredients

As indicated by the list of suggested ingredients, this program involves the use of food and edible ingredients. The ingredients included are suggestions based on a group of participants who have no known food allergies. It is your responsibility to adjust the ingredients list based on the medical needs of the participants in your program.

One copy of the book *Wonderstruck* or *How to Save Your Tail: If You Are a Rat Nabbed by Cats Who Really Like Stories about Magic Spoons, Wolves with Snout-warts, Big, Hairy Chimney Trolls . . . and Cookies, too* for each registered child to be available at the time of registration plus an additional copy for the staff member

Two cups or four sticks of butter or margarine (prior to the creation of the meteorite cookie recipe, leave the butter or margarine out at room temperature to soften)

Four 12 ounce packages of semisweet, milk, or dark chocolate chips

One tablespoon plus one teaspoon of vanilla extract

Eight cups of chocolate-covered malted milk balls

Four 10.5 ounce bags of multicolored miniature marshmallows

Five packages of chocolate sandwich cookies with a chocolate or vanilla filling or an equivalent of packaged, pre-crushed cookie crumbs (one of the five bags of sandwich cookies is for the inevitable culinary mishap)

Stove, hot plate, or microwave oven

One large saucepan or large microwavable bowl

One metal or wooden spoon

One rubber spatula per registered child

One plastic medium size bowl per registered child

Two ½ cup measuring cups

One ¼ teaspoon measuring spoon

One roll of wax paper

Three zippered plastic bags per registered child, plus two to create the sample

One kitchen knife (to be used by the staff member)

One foam, paper or plastic plate per registered child, plus one to create the sample

One 12 inch ruler per registered child (if you do not own enough rulers, paper rulers may be found online and printed)

Paper napkins

One book (preferably weeded and/or discarded) or other blunt instrument with which to crush the chocolate sandwich cookies into crumbs

Plastic tablecloths

Baby wipes and paper towels (to be used in cleanup)

Inspirational meteorite slideshow

Preheat

1. Interlibrary Loan enough copies of *Wonderstruck* or *How to Save Your Tail: If You Are a Rat Nabbed by Cats Who Really Like Stories about Magic Spoons, Wolves with Snout-warts, Big, Hairy Chimney Trolls . . . and Cookies, too* to accommodate the Serving Size, plus an additional copy for the staff member.

2. Photocopy the list of *Wonderstruck* book discussion questions provided in Appendix A on page 195 or the *How to Save Your Tail: If You Are a Rat Nabbed by Cats Who Really Like Stories about Magic Spoons, Wolves with Snout-warts, Big, Hairy Chimney Trolls . . . and Cookies, too* book discussion questions provided in Appendix A on page 194, or create your own list of questions.

3. Purchase and/or gather the necessary ingredients.

4. Perform an online search for cross-section or interior images of meteorites with which to create an inspirational slideshow for the program participants. Be sure to include a selection of colorful images, at least one image of an intact meteorite and any other factual information about meteorites you would like to highlight.

5. If you do not already own enough rulers, perform an online search for a 12 inch paper ruler. Print out one 12 inch ruler for each registered child.

6. Create a sample batch of meteorite cookies to familiarize yourself with the recipe and to serve during the book discussion. To aid in shopping for this program, the list above contains the ingredients needed to make enough cookies for the entire program. Use ¼ of the ingredients to make the sample.

   a. If you are using a stove top or a hot plate:
      1. Place ½ cup of butter or margarine and one 12 ounce package of chocolate chips into the large saucepan.
      2. Heat the saucepan on low, stirring constantly until the chocolate chips are completely melted.

   b. If you are using a microwave oven:
      1. Place ½ cup of butter or margarine and one 12 ounce package of chocolate chips into the microwavable bowl.
      2. Microwave the butter or margarine and the chocolate chips for 30 seconds. Remove them from the microwave and stir. Continue in 20-second increments, stirring between each until the chocolate chips are almost melted. Reduce the time to 10-second increments, stirring between each, until the chocolate chips are completely melted.

   c. Add one teaspoon of vanilla extract and stir.

   d. Let the chocolate mixture cool, but not harden. This should take approximately 5–15 minutes.

   e. While the mixture is cooling, measure and cut two 18 inch pieces of wax paper.

   f. Place one half of one package of chocolate creme-filled sandwich cookies in a zippered plastic bag and crush the cookies with the book or other blunt instrument. Pour the crumbs onto the foam, paper or plastic plate. Repeat the process with the remaining cookies. Leave the second batch of crushed ookie crumbs in the zippered plastic bag until all the cookie crumbs on the plate have been used.

    g. Place two cups of the chocolate-covered malted milk balls in a second zippered plastic bag and crush them with the book or other blunt instrument.

    h. Once the chocolate mixture has cooled, use a rubber spatula to fold in the colored miniature marshmallows and the crushed chocolate-covered malted milk balls.

    i. Spoon half of the mixture lengthwise onto the edge of one of the pre-cut pieces of wax paper and shape the mixture into a 12 inch by 2 inch log.

    j. Sprinkle the chocolate creme-filled sandwich cookie crumbs from the plate on the remaining area of the wax paper.

    k. Roll the log over the cookie crumbs, evenly coating the outside of the entire log.

    l. Wrap the log tightly in the wax paper, folding the ends snugly and tucking them underneath the log.

    m. Repeat Preheat 6i–l using the other half of the cooled cookie mixture and the remaining cookie crumbs in the zippered plastic bag.

    n. Chill the meteorite cookie logs in the refrigerator until firm, at least two hours or overnight. This recipe should yield 24 one quarter inch meteorite cookies.

6. Cut one 18 inch piece of wax paper per registered child.

7. Place ½ cup of chocolate-covered malted milk balls into one zippered plastic bag for each registered child and set aside.

8. Place 7–8 chocolate creme-filled sandwich cookies into an additional zippered plastic bag for each registered child and set aside.

9. Cover all of the tables in the program room with plastic tablecloths.

10. If your library does not have kitchen facilities available for program use, designate one table in the program room as the cook station and place the hot plate or microwave oven, chocolate chips, colored miniature marshmallows, vanilla extract, and the spoon on the cook station table.

11. Place the weeded and/or discarded books or other blunt instruments, rubber spatulas, plastic bowls, plastic zippered bags of the creme-filled sandwich cookies and chocolate-covered malted milk balls and pre-cut wax paper pieces on a table separate from the cook station.

12. Take the remaining butter or margarine out of the refrigerator to soften for approximately one hour before use.

13. Minutes before the start of the program, remove the sample cookie logs from the refrigerator and place them on the cook table. The staff member will be slicing the cookie logs in front of the children. Be sure that the knife is secure and kept away from the children during the entirety of the program.

Bake

1. Gather the children in your favorite book discussion formation.

2. Explain the components of the program to the participants.

3. Present the inspirational meteorite slideshow, if applicable.

4. Compare the cookie log sample to an intact meteorite, if applicable, and then slice the meteorite cookie log into ¼ inch slices in front of the children to reveal the colorful interior.

5. Serve the cookies on napkins to the children.

6. Hold the *Wonderstruck* or *How to Save Your Tail: If You Are a Rat Nabbed by Cats Who Really Like Stories about Magic Spoons, Wolves with Snout-warts, Big, Hairy Chimney Trolls . . . and Cookies, too* book discussion while the children eat their cookies.

7. After the book discussion has concluded, gather the children around the designated cook station table and complete the steps in Preheat 6a–c. Let the mixture cool as directed in Preheat 6d.

8. While the meteorite cookie mixture is cooling, instruct the children to retrieve one book or other blunt instrument, one rubber spatula, one zippered plastic bag filled with chocolate-covered malted milk balls and a second zippered plastic bag filled with chocolate creme-filled sandwich cookies from the supply table and place them at their work space.

9. Instruct the children to use the book or other blunt instrument to crush the chocolate-covered malted milk balls and the chocolate creme-filled sandwich cookies zippered in their respective bags.

10. Once the 5–15 minutes cooling time has elapsed and the cookie mixture is cooled, ask the program participants to line up at the cook station with their bowls. Scoop ½ cup of the cooled chocolate mixture and ½ cup of the colored miniature marshmallows into each child's bowl. Take care to use one ½ cup measuring cup for the chocolate mixture and a separate ½ cup measuring cup for the marshmallows.

11. Take an empty bowl, the saucepan or whatever is at hand, and a rubber spatula and demonstrate to the participants the technique of folding ingredients into batter. Instruct the children to add the crushed chocolate-covered malted milk balls and the colored miniature marshmallows to the bowl and use their rubber spatulas to fold them into the batter.

12. Have the children follow the remaining steps in Preheat 6i–l to finish their meteorite cookies.

13. Let the program participants know they should take home and chill their meteorite cookie logs for at least two hours, but preferably overnight, before asking an adult to slice the cookies into ¼ inch individual cookies.

Don't feel guilty about plying the children with cookies when you are feeding their brains with quality literature. Brian Selznick excels in seamlessly combining illustrations and storytelling. Any opportunity to expose children to this high standard of authorship should not be missed. The minds of younger children benefit from the exposure to fairy tales, and Mary Hanson offers a fresh take on the genre.

Variations: The meteorite cookie recipe is only one program idea that can be added to a *Wonderstruck*-themed program. The illustrations included in *Wonderstruck* also lend themselves to an instructional drawing

or illustration program. Another art-themed idea is to have the children create their own colorful meteorite cross sections through scratch art. You may purchase scratch art paper or boards or instruct the children on how to make their own with common items such as card stock, crayons, and black paint. Because the two main characters are deaf, sign language is discussed in the text and illustrations. Give the participants a copy of the American Sign Language alphabet and practice the letters as a group. Create your own sign language quiz using alphabetic illustrations and test the children's knowledge.

Fusion Box: For a technological variation on the *Meteorite Strike!* or *Cookie Tales* programs, allow participants to explore the Silent Film Studio app and create a short silent film, much like a film the mother of the main character in *Wonderstruck* would have appeared in. Or, consider creating a rendition of one of Bob's fairy tales from *How to Save Your Tail: If You Are a Rat Nabbed by Cats Who Really Like Stories about Magic Spoons, Wolves with Snout-warts, Big, Hairy Chimney Trolls . . . and Cookies, too*. For tips and techniques, refer to the *Silent Film* program on page 81.

Recipe Substitutions: The *Meteorite Strike!* program could be used in conjunction with a history unit on the Roaring Twenties or the 1970s. An earth science teacher could add more in-depth information on meteorites and present this program in conjunction with a unit on astronomy. In *Wonderstruck*, the North Star leads the two main characters home. The North Star is part of the Little Dipper constellation. In a language arts unit on myths, students may design their own constellation and write a myth describing its creation.

Leftovers: Use the Silent Film Studio app from the "Variations" section above to present the *Silent Film* program on page 81.

Garnish of Books to Be Displayed during the Program

Bucholz, Dinah. *The Unofficial Harry Potter Cookbook: From Cauldron Cakes to Knickerbocker Glory—More Than 150 Magical Recipes for Wizards and Non-wizards Alike*. Avon, MA: Adams Media, 2010.

Goodman, Susan E. *How Do You Burp in Space?: And Other Tips Every Space Tourist Needs to Know*. New York: Bloomsbury Publishing Plc, 2013.

Hanson, Mary. *How to Save Your Tail: If You Are a Rat Nabbed by Cats Who Really Like Stories about Magic Spoons, Wolves with Snout-warts, Big, Hairy Chimney Trolls . . . and Cookies, too*. New York: Schwartz & Wade Books, 2007.

Hobbs, Will. *Go Big or Go Home*. New York: HarperCollins Publishers, 2008.

Poynter, Margaret. *Doomsday Rocks from Space*. Berkeley Heights, NJ: Enslow Publishers, 2011.

Selznick, Brian. *The Invention of Hugo Cabret: A Novel in Words and Pictures*. New York: Scholastic Press, 2007.

Selznick, Brian. *Wonderstruck: A Story in Words and Pictures*. New York: Scholastic Press, 2011.

II

Side Dishes

The entries in this category are suited for those with limited staff, budget, space, or any combination of the three.

7

Scratch That Technology Itch

The *Scratch* computer program, invented by the Lifelong Kindergarten Group at the MIT Media Lab, presents the perfect introduction to computer programming for 'tweens and teens. Scratch allows children to build computer code by dragging and dropping colored blocks inscribed with computer commands that snap together like plastic interlocking building blocks. The program offers the opportunity to utilize your library's computer lab or create your own ad hoc computer lab with monitors and the purchase of $35 Raspberry Pi computers. For a list of the components required to create a Raspberry Pi workstation, see the Raspberry Pi Workstation Essentials in Appendix D on page 228.

Currently, there is a Scratch iPhone app available entitled Start Scratch. Although it works on the iPad, it is not a fully functional version of the Scratch program. Start Scratch provides theoretical tutorials and quizzes that may be useful, but do not allow users to create Scratch projects. If your library already owns multiple iPads, but you do not have access to a computer lab or desire to create an ad hoc Raspberry Pi computer lab, you may wish to investigate whether the Start Scratch app is a viable beginning teaching tool as is or has been updated or improved enough to satisfy your programming goals. You may also wish to consider using the Hopscotch app. This app provides an experience similar to the Scratch computer program. For more information on using Hopscotch with this program, see the "Fusion Box" section at the end of this recipe.

Cost: Since downloading Scratch is free, if your library has a computer lab that may be reserved for programming, there is no cost for this program. If your library does not have a computer lab, does not allow the computer lab to be reserved for program use, or you want a simple way to introduce Raspberry Pi, create an ad hoc computer lab using computer monitors and Raspberry Pi computers. Without any donations, a new Raspberry Pi workstation may be assembled for approximately $200. The cost can be greatly reduced if you can secure donations or use existing cables, monitors, or HDTVs (which can be used as monitors).

Time: The bulk of the preparation time for this program will be spent teaching yourself how to use the basic components of the Scratch program. Remember, you do not have to become an expert. The children will learn and then teach you as you all progress. If you are creating Raspberry Pi workstations, you will need to spend a significant amount of time ordering the components. Consider adding additional time to the length of this program and allowing the children to assemble the Raspberry Pi workstations themselves.

Serving Size: The number of 'tweens and/or teens you register to participate in this program depends exclusively on the number of workstations available. To encourage peer teaching, ask the children to work in pairs. Registration is recommended in order to seat no more than two participants at each workstation and obtain permission from their parents or caregivers for the children to open a Scratch account.

Staff Size: One staff member.

Ingredients

One computer workstation for every two registered participants

Scratch program

A selection of online websites and print materials with which to teach yourself and the participants the basics of Scratch (see the "Garnish of Books to Be Displayed during the Program" section at the end of this recipe.)

Preheat

1. Decide whether you wish to use the library's existing computer lab or create an ad hoc Raspberry Pi computer lab.
   a. If you are using the library's computer lab, reserve the lab or the specified number of workstations.
   b. If you choose to create your own ad hoc Raspberry Pi computer lab with the purchase of Raspberry Pi computers, see the Raspberry Pi Workstation Essentials in Appendix D on page 228 for a list of supplies.
2. Gather a collection of current print and online materials about the Scratch program that include tutorials. Because Scratch is a work in progress, new updates may be released at any time. Keep this in mind while researching or purchasing print materials that are likely to be released in revised editions. Be sure to select the newest edition whether already published or scheduled to be published. Also, check the version of Scratch used in each online tutorial you consider using. Tutorials may or may not be altered to reflect a Scratch update. If your library does not already own printed material on the Scratch program, you may wish to make use of Interlibrary Loan.
3. Download the newest version of the Scratch program onto a computer that you will be able to use undisturbed for an extended amount of time. (WARNING: do not attempt this at a public service desk.) This is the best way to provide an environment conducive to concentration and one that will allow you to more easily teach yourself the basics of Scratch.
4. Create a free online Scratch account and re-create the steps from a variety of current tutorials to learn the fundamentals of Scratch.

5. If you choose to create your own Raspberry Pi workstations:
   a. Gather a selection of print and online materials about Raspberry Pi. If your library does not already own printed material on Raspberry Pi, you may wish to make use of Interlibrary Loan.
   b. Order the supplies needed to create your Raspberry Pi Workstation.
   c. Use the documentation that accompanies the Raspberry Pi computer, online sources, and printed material to assemble and test your Raspberry Pi workstation.
   d. If your SD card is not already preloaded with the Scratch program, download and install Scratch onto your SD card and the SD cards the program participants will use.
   e. Open and test the Scratch program to ensure that it runs properly on the Raspberry Pi computer.
   f. If you are not going to allow the participants to assemble their own Raspberry Pi workstations, then you must assemble all but one of the remaining Raspberry Pi workstations. Arrange the components of one full Raspberry Pi workstation to be assembled in front of the children on the supply table.
   g. If you are allowing the children to assemble their own Raspberry Pi workstations, place the components for one full Raspberry Pi workstation in a disposable bag large enough to accommodate them. Repeat this process for each full Raspberry Pi workstation remaining to ensure that each pair of participants has the correct components.
6. If you are using the library computer lab, or a collection of computers and/or laptops in the program room, download and install Scratch on each reserved workstation.
7. Create your own or choose a tutorial that you are familiar with to use to teach the fundamentals of Scratch to the program participants.
8. Search the Scratch website for cool and interesting examples of completed Scratch projects. Choose at least one example each of the Scratch project categories: animation, game, interactive art, music and dance, and story, to give the children a range of ideas of what they can eventually create using the Scratch program. Bookmark the URLs so that you may easily access the examples. If you desire, you may also put them into a slideshow presentation.

Bake

1. If you are using Raspberry Pi computers to create an ad hoc computer lab:
   a. Gather the children around the supply table.
   b. Explain what Raspberry Pi is, the things that may be done with Raspberry Pi computers and provide the program participants with a very brief history of Raspberry Pi.
   c. Show the attendees the different parts of the computer.
   d. Assemble a Raspberry Pi workstation in front of the children.
   e. If the participants will assemble their own Raspberry Pi workstations, hand out one prepared kit in a disposable bag to each pair and allow sufficient time for the children to assemble their Raspberry Pi workstations.

     f. Instruct the program participants to test their Raspberry Pi workstations to be sure they can access and use the Scratch program.

2. Whether you are using an ad hoc Raspberry Pi computer lab, your library's computer lab or a collection of computers and laptops in the program room:

     a. Give a brief explanation and history of the Scratch computer program.

     b. Show the participants the Scratch samples you have bookmarked or placed in a slideshow.

     c. Instruct the children on how to create their own Scratch accounts and then allot time for the children to open them.

     d. As a group, have the participants re-create the steps of the tutorial you created or chose. While you verbally walk the children though the tutorial, look around the room to make sure that they understand and are able to follow the directions. Check their screens as you go.

     e. After the tutorial is complete, allot the remaining program time for the creation of their new and exciting Scratch projects.

Computer programming is fast becoming a necessary life skill. In the near future, children will need, at minimum, a basic knowledge of the workings of computer programming and coding. Scratch provides a fun way to expose children to the world of computer programming and encourages children to gain this necessary skill.

Fusion Box: If your library is fortunate enough to have multiple iPads and you wish to teach computer coding exclusively with apps, substitute iPads for the computers and install the free Hopscotch app (which was inspired by Scratch) onto each iPad. In addition to coding by dragging and dropping colored blocks like Scratch, this app allows users to control their projects by shouting at, shaking, or tilting their iPads. Perform your online search for Hopscotch tutorials to practice and to show to the program participants. Be sure to check out the official Hopscotch blog for recommendations for interesting Hopscotch projects to display.

Garnish of Books to Be Displayed during the Program

Ford, Jerry Lee, Jr. *Scratch 2.0 Programming for Teens*. Stamford, CT: Cengage Learning PTR, 2014.

Majed, Marji. *Learn to Program with Scratch: A Visual Introduction to Programming with Art, Science, Math and Games*. San Francisco: No Starch Press, 2014.

McManus, Sean. *Scratch Programming in Easy Steps: Covers Versions 1.4 and 2.0*. Warwickshire, UK: In Easy Steps Limited, 2013.

The Lead Project. *Super Scratch Programming Adventure! (Covers Version 2.0): Learn to Program by Making Cool Games*. San Francisco: No Starch Press, 2013.

Whitemore, Craig. *Computer Programming for Kids with Scratch*. lulu.com, 2012. (NOTE: This title is a 54-page teaching guide.)

8

All the World's a Puppet Stage

Open up the world of puppetry to children with this program's simple puppet theater and stick puppets. Puppetry allows children to work through the trials and tribulations of childhood, re-enacting the highlights of their day while controlling the outcome. Children also enjoy the creativity of becoming different characters, experimenting with alternate voices, and testing a variety of emotions.

Cost: The cost of this program can be drastically reduced if you can find the foam or cardboard tri-fold display boards at your local dollar store. Otherwise, the boards range in cost from $3 to $10 each. The rest of the supplies will most likely be found in your craft closet.

Time: The largest amount of preparation time will be spent cutting "windows" in your puppet stage. You will also need time to perform an online search for a variety of coloring sheets with simple images of animals or people, and to cut the poster board into 5 inch square stick puppet backs. This program should last approximately 45 minutes to one hour.

Early Bird Special: Craft Closet Cleanout

Serving Size: Twelve 5- to 8-year-olds each creating their own puppet stage and four stick puppets.

Staff Size: One staff member.

Ingredients

One foam or cardboard tri-fold display board per registered child plus one additional board to embellish in front of the children

One ruler

Box cutter or utility knife (to be used by the staff member before the program)

Crayons

Markers

Design elements (ribbon, pom-poms, streamers, tissue paper, etc.)

One bottle of white glue per child

A selection of poster board of any color (enough to cut four 5 inch squares per registered child plus 11 additional squares)

A variety of coloring sheets with simple images of animals or people sized to fit on the 5 inch squares of poster board. Provide enough coloring sheets for each child to select four and one additional coloring sheet image for demonstration

Scissors

One pair of child safety scissors per registered child

Four craft sticks per registered child

One glue stick per registered child

Newspapers

Baby wipes and paper towels (to be used in cleanup)

Preheat

1. Purchase and/or gather the foam or cardboard tri-fold display boards and any other necessary ingredients.
2. Using the box cutter or utility knife, cut a window in the center portion of the foam or cardboard tri-fold display boards. The windows should be located 3 inches from the top and 3 inches from each side fold to create a window frame. The size of the window or opening depends on the dimensions of the display board. The bottom of the window should not extend past the halfway point of the height of the display board.
3. Cut the poster board into 5 inch squares. Provide 4 poster board squares per registered child plus an additional 11 squares for the demonstration and the inevitable mishaps.
4. Perform an online search for a variety of coloring sheets with simple images of animals or people. If necessary, resize the images to fit on the poster board squares. Print out the images. You should be able to fit four images on one standard sheet of letter-sized printer paper. Cut the letter-sized paper into the individual images.
5. Arrange the supplies on the tables according to like groups (e.g., crayons with markers, pom-poms with ribbon, craft sticks with poster board and coloring sheet images, etc.)

Bake

1. Gather the children in front of you.
2. Take one foam or cardboard tri-fold display board and discuss how they will use it to create a puppet stage.
3. Quickly adhere a few design elements to the display board to demonstrate how the children will add elements to their puppet stage. Explain to the children that they will want to use the art supplies and add many more design elements than you have used and that they are free to use whatever supplies they wish.
4. In front of the children, make one stick puppet:
   a. Color a small area of one coloring sheet image, but explain to the children that while you don't have time to color in the entire image now, they will.

    b. Glue the image to one 5 inch poster board square.

    c. Cut out the character image following the outline of the image.

    d. Glue the craft stick to the poster board on the reverse side of the image. Be sure to glue the image half-way down the stick so the image remains upright.

5. Have the children choose an area on the floor as their work space and cover it with newspaper.

6. Instruct the children to take one foam or cardboard tri-fold display board to their work space. They may then return to the supply table and choose art supplies and design elements.

7. Walk around the room and offer assistance to those in need, but give the children the opportunity to succeed in their project themselves.

8. Once the children feel their puppet stages are complete, instruct them to begin working on their stick puppets.

9. At the end of the program, invite parents and caregivers into the program room to help carry their child's puppet stage home.

10. When the parents and caregivers arrive, encourage any willing children to perform impromptu puppet shows.

Not only does this program provide an activity at the library, it also creates an opportunity for endless hours of entertainment at home. Parents and caregivers will be pleased to take home this free educational toy that provides an outlet for creativity and increases verbal skills.

Variation: With this alternate idea, parents and caregivers will actually want their children to watch television, also known as Kellyvision or Carlosvision. Use the child's first name and the suffix "vision" to create the name of this project variant. By cutting a larger opening or window, your display board becomes a television. Now that their child is the star, they will never again complain that there is nothing good to watch on television.

Recipe Substitution: Educators can encourage children to improve their writing and storytelling skills by creating a script for a puppet show either individually or as a group. The children will then perform their script using their newly created stick puppets and puppet stage.

Garnish of Books to Be Displayed during the Program

Carreiro, Carolyn. *Make Your Own Puppets & Puppet Theaters*. Nashville, TN: Williamson Books, 2005.

Kennedy, John. *Puppet Mania!* Cincinnati, OH: North Light Books, 2004.

Kennedy, John. *Puppet Planet: The Most Amazing Puppet-Making Book in the Universe*. Cincinnati, OH: North Light Books, 2006.

MacNeal, Noel. *10-Minute Puppets*. New York: Workman Publishing Company, 2010.

Sadler, Wendy. *Puppets*. Chicago: Heinemann Library, 2005.

Schoenbrun, Diana. *Puppet Play: 20 Puppet Projects Made with Recycled Mittens, Towels, Socks and More*. Kansas City, MO: Andrews McMeel Publishing, 2011.

Toraya, Norma V. *Paper Puppet Palooza: Techniques for Making Moveable Art Figures and Paper Dolls*. Beverly, MA: Quarry Books, 2009.

9

Look Ma, No Needles!

This knitting recipe is a handy little finger food to serve when your cupboards are bare. Finger knitting is the only librarian-approved five-finger discount, as all you need for this program is one large skein of yarn and opposable thumbs. Finger knitting is exactly what it sounds like. Participants will learn to use their fingers as knitting needles. They can then go on to create a variety of projects from this basic skill.

Cost: This program has little to no cost. Yarn may be purchased at discount stores or donated by staff members and/or patrons. To save even more money, purchase economy-size skeins of yarn and divide them into individual portions for each program participant.

Time: Most of the preparation time for this program will be spent teaching yourself to finger knit and performing an online search to create a slideshow of visual step-by-step finger knitting directions. If you have chosen to purchase economy-size skeins of yarn, you must also allow yourself time to divide the yarn into individual portions. This program should last 45 minutes to one hour.

Early Bird Specials: Fruitcake, Low Cost Program

Serving Size: The number of children in this program depends upon the ages of the participants. The younger the participants are, the smaller the size of the group should be. Registration should be required for this program in order to ensure that each child is able to receive assistance from the staff member if and when he or she needs it.

Staff Size: One staff member.

Ingredients

> One large, economy-size skein of yarn to be divided into individual portions, or multiple skeins of yarn in a variety of colors
> Scissors
> Slideshow of visual step-by-step finger knitting directions

---

Preheat

1. Purchase and/or gather the necessary ingredients.
2. Perform an online search for visual step-by-step finger knitting direction images to be used to create a slideshow.

3. Perform an online search for objects to create with the basic finger knitting chain.
4. Create a slideshow of the step-by-step directions and project ideas.
5. Before you create your sample:
   a. Do not cut a length of yarn for your sample, but create the sample directly off the skein. This way, when you have reached the desired length of finger knitting, you may then cut it from the skein, unravel the knitting, and measure the length of yarn needed for an individual portion.
   b. If you do not wish to measure the length of yarn, simply roll the yarn into a ball and duplicate that size yarn ball for each individual portion.
   c. Regardless of which method you choose, you may wish to create a few larger-sized individual portions for children who already know how to finger knit. Consider creating a few extra yarn balls for children who catch on quickly.
6. Create the sample to familiarize yourself with the process and to show to the program participants. Remove all your rings and any other hand or wrist jewelry to prevent the yarn from snagging.
   a. Lay the yarn in between your thumb and your pointer finger, leaving a 3 to 4 inch tail.
   b. Hold the tail by pressing your thumb flat against your hand and wrap the yarn around the front of your pointer finger and pull it behind your middle finger. Then, pull the yarn up and over your ring finger and finally behind your pinky.
   c. Pull the yarn up and over your pinky, behind your ring finger, up and over your middle finger and behind your pointer finger.
   d. Once again, wrap the yarn around the front of your pointer finger and pull it behind your middle finger. Then, pull the yarn up and over your ring finger and finally behind your pinky.
   e. Pull the yarn up and over your pinky, behind your ring finger, up and over your middle finger and behind your pointer finger. Next, pull up the skein end of the yarn and lay it diagonally across your palm. Each finger should now have two loops of yarn. Widen the space between your fingers to loosen the yarn.
   f. Starting with your pinky finger, take the bottom loop of yarn and pull it up and over the top loop of yarn and your finger. Continue on pulling the loops up and over the ring and middle fingers.
   g. Take the tail and drop it over the back of the "v" between your pointer and middle fingers.
   h. Pick up the skein end of the yarn from your palm and wrap the yarn around the front of your pointer finger and pull it behind your middle finger. Then, pull the yarn up and over your ring finger and finally behind your pinky.
   i. Pull the yarn up and over your pinky, behind your ring finger, up and over your middle finger and behind your pointer finger. Next, pull up the skein end of the yarn and lay it diagonally across your palm. Each finger should now have two loops of yarn. Starting with your pinky finger, take the bottom loop of yarn and pull it up and over the top loop of yarn and your finger. Repeat this process in order with your remaining three fingers.

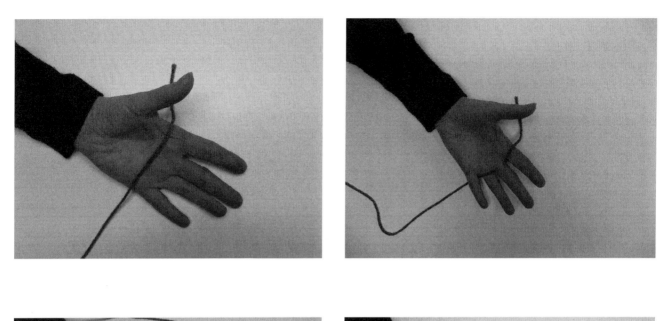

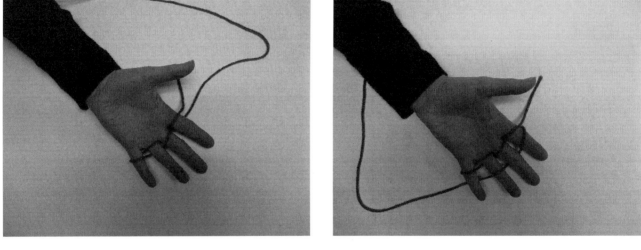

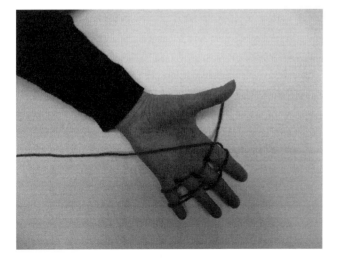
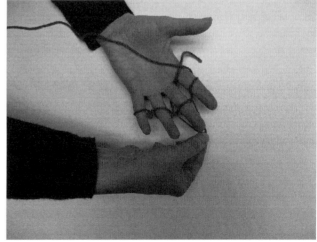

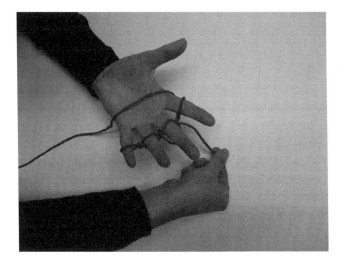 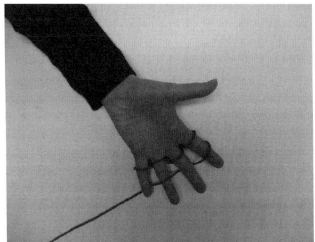

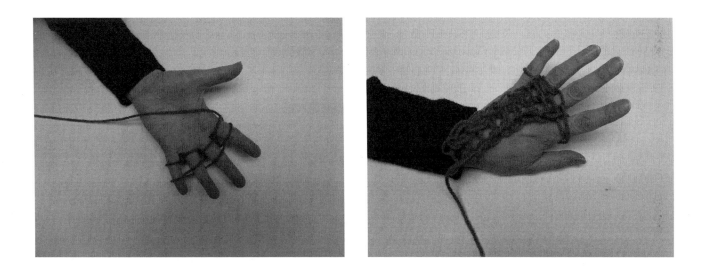

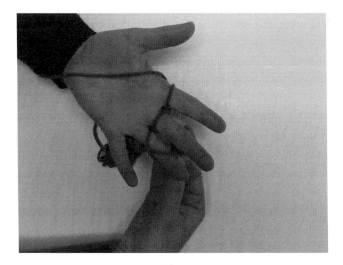 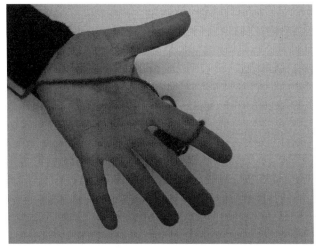

j.   Repeat the steps in Preheat 6h—j until your finger knitting is the desired length for your project.

k.   You will now begin the casting off process to remove your project from your hand and finish the edges. Each finger should have only one loop on it. Let the skein end of the yarn hang down off the back of your hand in between your pointer and middle fingers. Take the loop on your pinky finger off and place it on your ring finger. Now you have two loops on your ring finger. Pull the bottom loop of your ring finger over the top.

l.   Repeat the process in Preheat 6k one finger at a time until you have only one loop left on your pointer finger. Cut the yarn off of the skein leaving a 4 inch tail. Remove the last loop from your pointer finger and insert the newly cut end through the loop. Pull it tight. The original tail at the starting end of your project should also be pulled tight.

7.   Arrange the yarn balls on the supply table.

Bake

1.   Explain the technique of finger knitting to the program participants.
2.   Present the visual step-by-step finger knitting directions and project ideas slideshow in its entirety.
3.   Return the slideshow to the first directional slide.
4.   If you are using one color of yarn, pass out the individual portions to each child. If you are offering a variety of colors, allow the children to choose their own portion of yarn.
5.   Allot the rest of the time for teaching the finger knitting technique and finger knitting itself.
6.   Walk around the room noting the children's progress and answering any questions that may arise. Advance the slideshow to follow the majority of the participants.
7.   Five minutes before the conclusion of the program time, remind the children of the options for further project ideas to create from their newly acquired finger knitting skills.

Old Mother Hubbard's got nothing on you when you present this fun, frugal program that may be tailored to a variety of ages. This new skill opens up a world of opportunities for children to create an unlimited range of further projects at home. For the attendees, the introduction of finger knitting may also become a gateway skill for other yarn crafts.

Variation: If you wish to make a project larger than the skinny scarf, increase your allotted program time and create bracelets, headbands, twisted and knotted scarves, hair clips, or barrettes. To increase the number of participants, add one staff member for every six additional attendees.

Leftovers: Use the leftover yarn in the *Balloon Zip Line* program on page 16.

Garnish of Books to Be Displayed during the Program

Chorba, April. *Pom-Pom Puppies: Make Your Own Adorable Dogs.* Palo Alto, CA: Klutz, 2013.

Darsie, Richard. *String Games.* New York: Sterling Publishing Co., Inc., 2005.

Ferrer, J. J. *The Art of Stone Skipping and Other Fun Old-Time Games: Stoopball, Jacks, String Games, Coin Flipping, Line Baseball, Jump Rope, and More.* Watertown, MA: Imagine! Publishing, 2012.

Jones, Jen. *Knitting for Fun!* Minneapolis, MN: Compass Point Books, 2005.

Kay, Adel. *Knitting.* London: QED Publishing, 2013.

10

Zen Garden

Life today is hectic and overscheduled. Children need to learn constructive ways to stop, calm, and relax just as adults do. They need to develop their own inner sense of tranquility. Traditionally, the Japanese have used the Zen Garden as a place to get away from it all. A Japanese Zen Garden is a minimalistic place of contemplation that may include sand, gravel, moss, rocks, or trees representing the elements of nature. In most Zen Gardens, the patterns raked in the sand and/or gravel mimic rippled water. The Zen Garden promotes a peaceful harmony within.

Most libraries don't have the acreage to create a full-size Zen Garden. However, children can easily make and benefit from the creation of their own tabletop versions.

Cost: You control the budget for this project. You can spend more money by purchasing ceramic dishes as a base for each child's garden or simply use shoeboxes. You can buy polished rocks or go outside and collect them. Sand may be purchased from a garden or craft store; however, if you're heading to the beach, bring an extra pail and it's free! (Note: more expensive fine white craft sand is cleaner and produces a more distinct pattern when raked).

Time: Beyond purchasing or collecting the supplies and creating a sample of colored sand, there is little preparation for this program. However, we do recommend creating a slideshow of Zen Garden images for inspiration that should be shown at the beginning of the program and kept running on a loop throughout the program. The program should last 30–45 minutes.

Early Bird Special: Fruitcake

Serving Size: Twelve to 20 school-aged children working individually, with a separate program for each age-appropriate group. Registration is required in order to estimate the necessary ingredients.

Staff Size: One staff member.

Ingredients

Shoeboxes, which may be donated by staff members or requested from the children upon registration (save the lids to use as covers for a spill-free ride home), ceramic dishes, or inexpensive plastic containers

Plastic cups, scoops, or beach shovels

Sand (approximately 12 cups of sand per child, depending on the size of the container)

Rocks (three to six per child)

Decorative features (e.g., craft jewels, shells, aquarium stones, marbles)

Design tools (e.g., plastic forks, bamboo skewers, pencils or pens)*

Colored sidewalk chalk in a variety of vivid colors

(Optional) Glitter

One disposable foam or plastic bowl per registered child plus an additional two bowls for the creation of the sample and for the demonstration

Fan blender paintbrush (a paintbrush with the bristles in the shape of a fan)

Newspapers

Inspirational Zen Garden slideshow

Preheat

1. Purchase and/or gather the necessary ingredients.
2. Perform an online search for images of both full-size and tabletop Zen Gardens.
3. Prepare an inspirational slideshow of the Zen Garden images to present to the participants.
4. Create a sample to familiarize yourself with the process and to show to the participants:
   a. If you wish to use colored sand in your Zen Garden:
      1. Scoop ¼ cup of sand or salt into a foam or plastic disposable bowl.
      2. Choose a piece of colored chalk, insert it into the sand, and alternate between a stirring motion and a grinding technique similar to using a mortar and pestle. Be sure to scrape the bottom of the bowl with each stir. The longer you mix the chalk and sand, the greater the color saturation.
      3. Periodically shake the bowl to evenly distribute the pigment.
      4. If you are using glitter, sprinkle the glitter into the bowl and stir and/or shake to distribute the glitter as evenly as possible.
   b. Fill your sample container with colored sand, uncolored sand, or a mixture of both.
   c. Shake the container gently to evenly distribute the sand in preparation for the addition of the design elements.
   d. Choose the decorative elements (e.g., rocks, jewels) that you wish to include.
   e. Arrange all of the decorative elements before using the design tools.
   f. Using the design tools or your fingertips, either allow a design to flow freely or create a distinct pattern in the sand. If you wish to change your entire design, gently shake the container and begin again. If you wish to redesign only a portion of the sand pattern, lightly brush the affected area with the fan blender paintbrush. After the area is flattened, blow very gently until enough sand covers the slight ridges made by the fan blender paintbrush.
5. Cover the tables with newspaper.

---

*If your budget allows, consider purchasing miniature rakes, combs, or small cacti from a garden and/or craft supply store.

6. Fill each of the remaining disposable foam or plastic bowls with ¼ cup of sand.
7. Arrange the supplies on a table buffet style, by item, in the order in which they will be used.

Bake

1. Explain the concept of Zen Gardens to the group. Let the children know that elements are not usually placed in straight lines but are often grouped in threes or multiples of three. Rocks are traditionally used to symbolize mountains, valleys, cascading water or even boats, with the patterns in the sand representing the surrounding water. While it is important to provide a framework of the practice of Zen Gardens by discussing traditional elements, allow the children to create a Zen Garden of their own choice.
2. Present the inspirational slideshow to the program participants.
3. Have the children plan the arrangement of their garden's elements. Give the children a few minutes to think about the decorative features they will choose. Will the placement of their garden's elements represent an animal or person? What sorts of patterns will they try? Will they use straight lines, circles, checkerboards, names, or even doodle? Does their garden represent an existing place or an imaginary landscape?
4. Have each child choose a container, a piece of colored chalk, a disposable foam, or plastic bowl pre-filled with sand and take them to their work area.
5. Instruct the children on how to create their own Zen Gardens using the directions used to create the sample in Preheat 4a–f.
6. Before the end of the program, reiterate that the fun and relaxation of the Zen Garden lies in its constant re-creation and redesign.

The *Zen Garden* program is meant to be a harmonious activity. Each garden should be as unique as the person creating it. There is no right or wrong way to compose a Zen Garden. Since the children will be bringing their Zen Gardens home, encourage them to continue to add to and manipulate the elements.

Recipe Substitutions: Media specialists and educators may wish to include the tabletop Zen Garden in a social studies unit on Japan. Health classes may incorporate this project into a section on stress management. Language arts teachers may modify the project for a poetry unit by having students paint the rocks a dark color; and once dry, write one word on each rock with a white or silver paint pen or permanent marker. Rocks can then be arranged and rearranged into poems, similar to magnetic poetry. This may be done individually, in groups or with an entire class.

Fusion Box: Use the iZen Garden app to visually explain the concept of the Zen Garden. The children can practice creating gardens to see what design elements and features they would like to include in their own projects.

Leftovers: Use up the leftover sand, rocks, and colored sidewalk chalk in the *Project Planet* program on page 160 and use the colored sidewalk chalk in the *Chalktography* program on page 89.

Garnish of Books to Be Displayed during the Program

Buckley, A. M. *Japan*. Edina, MN: ABDO Publishing Company, 2012.
Callery, Sean. *100 Things You Should Know about Rocks and Minerals*. Broomall, PA: Mason Crest Publishers, 2011.
Dyer, Hadley. *Potatoes on Rooftops: Farming in the City*. Toronto: Annick Press, 2012.
Hoffman, Steven M. *Gems, Crystals, and Precious Rocks*. New York: Power Kids Press, 2011.
Meredith, Susan. *Rocks, Minerals, and Soil*. Vero Beach, FL: Rourke Publishing, 2010.
Scheunemann, Pam. *Cool Stuff for Your Garden: Creative Handmade Projects for Your Kids*. Edina, MN: ABDO Publishing Company, 2012.

III

Main Entrees

Though these programs require a longer time commitment, they allow attendees to delve deeper into the subject matter. They are suitable for one lengthy event or a series of events over multiple days. More preparation time is required for these recipes.

11

Maker Open House

This program allows the entire library to present a *Maker Open House* to patrons and future patrons showcasing the theory and practice of the Maker Movement. Visitors to the library will take part in a hands-on experience at five different Maker stations (you may customize the number of stations offered to suit your library), each located in a different area of your library. Both children and adults should be encouraged to enjoy this experience together.

The artist Marcel Duchamp believed that the idea of any artist was the actual art. The medium chosen by the artist (e.g., paints, clay, found objects) was a secondary consideration. Duchamp felt that it was more important to formalize an idea first and then determine the media that would best convey its meaning. His inclusive philosophy frees people who think they are not capable of creating art to explore different avenues of artistic expression. For example, people who think they do not paint well may find they have a talent for graphic design.

Cost: This program can cost as little or as much as you wish to invest. Depending on the anticipated turnout, you may use existing materials, solicit donations, or purchase additional supplies.

Time: Most of the preparation time will be spent arranging the logistics of the stations and the staff. You will also need additional time to purchase and/or gather the necessary ingredients and set up the individual stations. The program should last approximately two hours. In this recipe, we suggest five stations, allowing 20 minutes at each station and an extra 20 minutes for travel between the stations and any fluctuation in program presentation lengths in individual stations. For suggestions on how to hold this program as an all-day event, see the "Variations" section at the end of this recipe.

Early Bird Special: Craft Closet Cleanout, Smorgasbord

Serving Size: This program is designed to serve an unlimited number of people. Adults should be required to attend with younger children in order to encourage their Maker experience. Registration is suggested in order to create groups to ensure that no one station becomes overcrowded and attendees have the opportunity to explore all of the stations.

Staff Size: At least one staff member per station plus an additional staff member to direct program participants to the individual stations and to answer general questions.

Ingredients (listed by station)

For this program you will create stations representing different facets of the Maker Movement, such as art, craft, iPad, computer, 3D printer, and so forth. Use whatever resources your library has and/or whatever offerings your library would like to highlight. Art and craft supplies may need to be purchased, but more often than not will already be in your craft closet. A staff member may need to download computer software and/or apps prior to the program. Make sure the staff member at the Computer and/or iPad Station has had the chance to become familiar with the software and/or apps. The 3D Printer Station should be demonstrated by the staff member most familiar with its use.

In addition to the individual ingredients listed by Maker Station, you will need:

Plain labels or solid colored stickers to denote group affiliation and help route the flow of patrons from station to station

Multiple copies of the *Maker Open House* Survey (see Appendix C on page 210)

Maker Art Station

Clay (It is preferable to purchase air drying, art clay sold by school supply stores online or in craft stores, in large economical slabs usually weighing 25 pounds. More expensive clay sold in individual packets is available, but this will add to the cost of your program.)

Fishing line

Scissors

Foam, paper or plastic plates

A large quantity of drawing, printer, or copy paper

Colored pencils, markers, crayons, Cray-pas, paint pens, etc.

Pencils

Erasers

Washable tempera paint in a variety of colors

Watercolor paint in a variety of colors

Paintbrushes

Watercolor paper

(Optional) Art canvases

Foam, paper or plastic disposable cups or bowls filled with water

A large quantity of foam, paper or plastic plates (to be used as paint palettes)

Plastic tablecloths

Newspapers upon which to transport wet art projects home

Baby wipes and paper towels (to be used in cleanup)

Maker Craft Station

An assortment of yarn in a variety of colors, textures, and weights to be used for crocheting and knitting

Crochet hooks in a variety of sizes

Paired knitting needles in a variety of sizes

Potholder loom kit(s) and additional cotton loops

Latch hook canvas cut into 6 inch squares

Masking tape (to finish the edges of the cut squares of canvas)

Latch hooks

Yarn in a variety of colors (of a suitable weight to easily maneuver into and out of your latch hook canvas) cut to into 3 inch lengths

How to Knit handout

How to Crochet handout

How to Create a Loop Potholder handout

How to Create a Latch Hook handout

Maker iPad Station

iPads or other tablet devices
A selection of apps that may include:
123D Sculpt
Painting with Time
Soundbrush
The Chihuly App
PlayArt
MoMA Art Lab
Design Museum Collection

Maker Computer Station

Computer workstations
3D printer software design choices to consider downloading:
3dtin
Tinkercad
Sketchup
OpenSCAD
Wings3D
Scupltris
Autodesk 123D
Blender
(Optional) Inexpensive thumb drives

Maker 3D Printer Station

3D printer
Assortment of colored filaments
Handout with a list of instructional videos specific to the library's make and model of 3D printer

At each station, the staff member(s) will be expected to perform a different function:

> At the Maker Art Station, the staff member(s) should encourage the program attendees either to find the media that best expresses an idea that they may have or to freely explore the art supplies.
>
> The role of the staff member(s) at the Maker Craft Station will be to answer questions and assist participants learning basic techniques of their chosen craft.
>
> At the Maker iPad Station, the staff member(s) should answer questions involving the use of the specific apps. If there is more than one staff member at this station, one person may be dedicated to posting app creations on the library's social media site(s).
>
> The staff member(s) at the Maker Computer Station will guide patrons in the use of 3D printer design software. Patrons who are unable to complete a design within the allotted 20-minute time period may be given an inexpensive thumb drive on which to store their design or should be encouraged to email a copy of the design file to themselves. This will allow the participants to complete their designs at a later date and time.
>
> The staff member(s) at the Maker 3D Printer Station will provide a demonstration on how to load a design file, insert filament, adjust any hardware settings, and print a 3D design. At the conclusion of the demonstration, the staff member(s) should reserve future 3D printer usage time for any interested program participants.

Preheat

1. Decide what stations your library will offer. Plan your *Maker Open House* according to the number of ready and willing staff members and the available space.
2. Purchase and/or gather the necessary ingredients, including art supplies, craft supplies, apps, computer software, and 3D printer supplies.
3. Research online or in print sources the basic techniques for knitting, crocheting, loop pot holder creation, and latch hooking. Create one handout for each. Instructions should be clear and concise. Be sure to include photos or illustrations. Print enough copies for each registered participant.
4. Install the 3D printer design computer software onto the computers designated for this program.
5. Install the apps onto the iPads or other tablet devices.
6. Research online and create the list of instructional videos specific to the library's type and model of 3D printer. Print enough copies for each registered participant.
7. The staff members in charge of the computer, iPad, and 3D printer stations should familiarize themselves with the offerings at their stations. They should be able to explain, instruct, and troubleshoot.
8. Each station should provide ample seating and work space.
9. Clearly designate each station with a sign that explains the station and represents the activities available at that station.

10. If directions are required, they should be displayed prominently.
11. Cover the tables in the Maker Art Station with the plastic tablecloths.
    a. At the Maker Art Station, arrange the art supplies on the supply table(s) in like groups (e.g., the paintbrushes with the paint, the drawing implements with the drawing paper).
    b. Designate one table(s) in the Maker Art Station as a drying table. Participants should be able to leave their wet art projects there as they rotate among the stations.
12. In order to prevent everyone from patronizing the same station at the same time, you will need to divide the attendees into groups that will rotate among the stations. So as not to divide family members or friends attending together, give one labeled sticker to each group. Write the word MAKER on one large adhesive label or each letter on many small adhesive labels or stickers. If you are using one large adhesive label, cut out the individual letters. Repeat the process until all the registered groups are assigned a letter.
13. Decide which letter starts at each station. For example, each group with the letter M will begin at the Maker Art Station, each group with the letter A will begin at the Maker Craft Station, and so on.

Bake

1. Gather the program attendees in one central location and welcome them to the *Maker Open House* program. Outline the activities that are available at each station. Explain the lettered sticker rotation system and the 20-minute time limit allotment for each station. Encourage the program participants to think about an idea they may wish to artistically explore, but also present them with the choice of simply utilizing the materials offered at each station.
2. Announce the location of the first station designated in Preheat 13 for each lettered group.
3. Using the public address system, announce the start and the conclusion of each 20-minute time allotment. Remember to include time in between 20-minute allotments for the program participants to travel between the stations.

The *Maker Open House* program offers a unique opportunity for patrons to see the library as a space for nontraditional materials and activities. The role of the library and its staff is adapting and innovating to meet the community's needs, and this program is a great example with which to highlight this change. Additionally, it allows participants to visit areas of the library which they may not have recently patronized.

Variations: This program may also be held as an all-day open house with stations beginning and ending on the half-hour or hour. Instead of the lettered sticker station rotation system outlined in the recipe, a staff member stationed at the library's main entrance with a smartphone to gather traffic information will direct the flow of incoming patrons to begin their rotation at the less-populated stations. You may or may not need to purchase additional supplies.

The library may wish to take advantage of this nontraditional program to ask participants what types of future programs they would like the library to offer. Have an informal survey and pencils available at each station for participants to complete. A sample *Maker Open House* Survey for you to use is available in Appendix C on page 210. You may also wish to post the survey online for participants who were unable to fill it out at the library or any other interested patrons. Consider using a free product like SurveyMonkey to post this informal survey on the library's social media site(s).

Leftovers: The leftover clay from the Maker Art Station may also be used in the programs *My, What Big Claws You Have* on page 117 or *It's All about Me* on page 103.

Garnish of Books to Be Displayed during the Program

Anderson, Chris. *Makers: The New Industrial Revolution*. New York: Crown Business, 2012.
Diana, Carla. *Leo the Maker Prince: Journeys in 3D Printing*. Sebastopol, CA: Maker Media Inc., 2013.
Evans, Brian. *Practical 3D Printers*. New York: Apress, 2012.
Kemp, Adam. *The Makerspace Workbench: Tools, Technologies, and Techniques for Making*. Sebastopol, CA: Maker Media, Inc., 2013.
Lang, David. *Zero to Maker: Learn (Just Enough) to Make (Just about) Anything*. Sebastopol, CA: Maker Media, Inc., 2013.

12

Animation Exploration

Many of the first characters children relate to are animated cartoon characters. What better way to teach storytelling than to allow children to create their own animated cartoon? In the *Animation Exploration* program, children can place themselves in the middle of the action alongside historical figures, stock characters, and even their friends.

Cost: With the exception of the iPads, the $4.99 Puppet Pals 2 app is the only expense for this program.

Time: The bulk of the preparation time will be spent installing the Puppet Pals 2 app on the iPads and familiarizing yourself with the use of the app. Additional time is recommended to research a brief history of animation to present to the program participants. The program should last approximately 45 minutes to one hour and may conclude with an optional premiere for family and friends.

Early Special: Fruitcake, Low Cost Program, Time Saver

Serving Size: Twenty 9- to 12-year-olds, with a separate program for each age-appropriate group, working individually or in pairs, with each individual or pair receiving one iPad to create an animated, interactive cartoon puppet show. Upon registration, obtain written photo permission to post the children's photographs on your library's web site and other social media sites. If applicable, inform the parents of the time and date of the film premieres.

Staff Size: One staff member.

Ingredients

One iPad per registered individual or pair
Puppet Pals 2 app
One photo permission form per registered child
(Optional) Writing utensils
(Optional) Scrap paper
(Optional) Projector to screen the films

Preheat

1. Purchase the Puppet Pals 2 app and install the app on the iPads.
2. Page through the tutorial on the app's home screen.

3. Tap *Options* on the home screen and then *Teacher's Guide* to access tips and tricks for using the Puppet Pals 2 app.
4. Create a short animated interactive cartoon puppet show sample to familiarize yourself with the process and to show to the program participants.
   a. Tap *Play* and choose a background or location where the puppet animation will take place.
   b. The icons in the upper left-hand corner of the screen allow you to add or change location, rides (vehicles or animals) or actors. You may also add a photograph of yourself or others or add photos saved on the iPad's camera roll. The last icon permits you to add or change music.
   c. Choose a location, ride, actor, and music. To create a short sample, simply have the chosen actor/puppet move and speak one or two lines of dialogue.
   d. Practice the movement and dialogue before tapping the red circular record button in the upper right-hand corner of the screen.
   e. View the animation and decide whether you would like to save it or delete it. If you choose to save the animation, you may save it in a choice of two sizes, normal or best. "Normal" is designated as the size for sharing on a social media web site(s), while "best" indicates the creation of a large file. You may show either size at your premiere.
      1. Perform an online search or read printed material on animation to provide the children with a brief history and explanation of the animation process.
      2. Make one copy of the photo permission form for each registrant.

Bake

1. Provide the program participants with an overview of the history and techniques of animation and show the short sample animated interactive cartoon puppet show you created to the program participants.
2. Provide the children with an overview of character development and effective storytelling.
3. If your library is fortunate enough to be able to provide one iPad for each participant, ask the children to decide whether they wish to work on their own or with a partner. Allow the children a moment to choose a partner, if they desire.
4. Using an iPad, show the group the location, ride, actor, and music icons and explain what each icon does.
5. Hand out one iPad to each individual or pair.
6. Ask the children to choose an actor, location, and ride (they will choose the music at a later time).
7. Instruct the children to develop a story they wish to portray using their chosen location, actor, and ride. They should also think of the dialogue and lines they

will record for their characters. This will aid in creating a smoother recording process and produce a better-developed story, which is the key to an animation the audience will understand and enjoy.

8. Walk around the program room answering questions and facilitating the animation creation process.

9. In the event you will be holding a premiere, instruct the children to prepare a short verbal introduction to their animated interactive cartoon puppet shows. Provide the children with pieces of scrap paper and writing utensils with which to write down their introduction ideas.

Food Styling

1. Once the animations are complete, use the Puppet Pals 2 app to email them to a library email address. From there, you may post them on one of the library's social media site(s) or account(s) to show at the premiere. In addition, post the animations on a variety of additional social media sites to afford friends and family unable to attend the premiere the opportunity to view the animated interactive cartoon puppet shows.

2. Arrange the chairs in your program room in theater-style seating. Invite participants, friends, and family into the screening.

3. Welcome your audience and explain the concept of animation.

4. Have the individuals or pairs present their short introductions to the animations.

5. Serve their animated dishes and cue the applause.

The world of animation is a universally happy place for children and adults alike. If at all possible, try to provide a screening of the children's animated interactive cartoon puppet shows for family and friends. Adults may derive special pleasure from this screening, as it allows them to recapture moments from their childhood and share them with their own children.

Recipe Substitution: Many of the stock characters included in the Puppet Pals 2 app are famous historical figures (e.g., William Shakespeare, Albert Einstein, Mark Twain, Benjamin Franklin, George Washington, Martin Luther King Jr.). The *Animation Exploration* program provides a fun, nontraditional activity for use across the curriculum. Educators may reinforce subjects studied in the classroom by having students reenact historical events, explain scientific concepts, or explore the process of creative writing through animation.

Leftovers: The Puppet Pals 2 app may be used with two of the program concepts listed in the Alternate, Alternate Reality List of Ideas, Projects and Discussion Questions located in Appendix D on page 225.

Garnish of Books to Be Displayed during the Program

Bliss, John. *Art That Moves: Animation around the World*. Chicago: Raintree, 2011.

Hamernik, Harry. *Cartoon 360: Secrets to Drawing Cartoon People and Poses in 3-D*. Cincinnati, Ohio: Impact, 2010.

LaBaff, Stephanie. *Draw Cartoon People in 4 Easy Steps: Then Write a Story*. Berkeley Heights, NJ: Enslow Publishers, Inc. 2012.

Levete, Sarah. *Make an Animation!* London: Arcturus Publishing, 2012.

Tashjian, Janet. My *Life as a Cartoonist*. New York: Henry Holt and Company, 2013.

13

Necessity Is the Mother Nature of Invention Convention

In today's workplace, one of the most prized skills is the ability to think outside of the box. Future workers need to understand how to adapt and change to create, solve problems, and participate in a global society. One of the best ways to help build these skills is to look to the most diverse and valuable example of adaptation and change—Mother Nature. In this program, participants will choose an adaptive behavior of an animal and apply it to a real-world problem to come up with a nature-inspired solution. For example, Velcro, invented by George de Mestral, was inspired by the cockleburs that would stick to his trousers.

The examination of natural processes and the attempt to adapt and reproduce them to solve human problems is called biomimicry. *The Necessity Is the Mother Nature of Invention Convention* program introduces the participants to the concept of biomimicry and challenges them to use the process to create a new way(s) to solve a problem or fill a need in everyday life. Children will create an artistic representation and brief written description of their idea to be entered into a contest. The winner and their invention should be publicized through the library's social media site(s). An appropriate prize may be awarded.

Cost: The prize(s), should you choose to award them and are unable to secure a donation(s), is the only cost for this program. The materials used to create the artistic representations will most likely already be in your craft closet.

Time: The majority of the preparation time for this program will be spent researching animal adaptive behavior. To save time, use the suggestions listed in the Adaptive Animal Behavior Sheet located in Appendix D on page 229. The length of the program during which children create their projects should last 45 minutes to one hour. The projects may be displayed in the library for as long as necessary to obtain an appropriate number of voting submissions from your community.

Early Bird Specials: Low Cost Program, Time Saver

Serving Size: This program allows the opportunity for as many children who are interested to attend. The recommended age for this program is 8 and up. Registration is not required, but may be helpful in determining the number of art supplies required and the program room setup.

Staff Size: One staff member.

Ingredients

One biomimicry list either researched and created by the staff member or one photocopy of the Adaptive Animal Behavior Sheet located in Appendix D on page 229

Scissors

One fish tank or fish bowl (Think Tank) or hat (Thinking Cap)

One piece of drawing, printing, or copy paper per child plus several extra sheets for mistakes or preliminary sketching

Crayons, markers, and colored pencils in a variety of colors

Pencils with sizable erasers

One piece of lined paper per child plus several extra pieces for the inevitable mistakes

Voting ballots or small strips of scrap paper

Golf pencils

(Optional) Prize(s)

Inspirational biomimicry slideshow

Preheat

1. Familiarize yourself with the concept of biomimicry by exploring online and/or print resources.
2. Decide whether or not you will use the Adaptive Animal Behavior Handout located in Appendix D on page 229. If you are not using the Adaptive Animal Behavior Handout, perform an online search and create a list of at least 15 adaptive animal behaviors. If you list any adaptive animal behaviors that have been used to inspire an invention, do not include any information regarding the invention. Print out a copy of the list you created or the pre-prepared Adaptive Animal Behavior Sheet.
3. In your research, select images that depict examples of biomimicry (e.g., cockleburs and Velcro) and images that represent the adaptive animal behaviors from the Adaptive Animal Behavior Sheet or from the list you created. Use both the biomimicry images and the adaptive animal behavior images to create an inspirational slideshow to present to the program participants.
4. Decide upon the specific details of the contest:
   a. Where and how long will the artistic representations be displayed?
   b. Will patrons, local dignitaries, and/or the participants' peers choose the winner(s)?
   c. Will you develop criteria for the winning entry or entries, or will it be up to each judge's personal discretion?
   d. Will you award a prize to the winning entry or entries?
   e. Do you want to hold an award ceremony and/or publicize the announcement of the winning entry or entries?
3. Purchase and/or gather the necessary ingredients.
4. Cut each individual example of adaptive animal behavior into a paper strip.

5. Fold the strips of paper in half and place them into your Think Tank or Thinking Cap.
6. Using the voting ballots provided in Appendix C on page 231, create your own voting ballots or simply cut strips of scrap paper to be used as ballots.
7. Arrange the art supplies on the supply tables.

Bake

1. Introduce and discuss the concept of biomimicry with the program participants.
2. Disclose the specific details of the contest.
3. Explain the creation of the artistic representations and the brief written descriptions required to enter the contest. Note the fact that the brief written description will be on display alongside the artistic representation.
4. Show the inspirational slideshow.
5. Allow the children to decide whether they would prefer to work alone or in pairs.
6. Each child or duo should approach the Think Tank or Thinking Cap and choose one folded strip of paper containing their adaptive animal behavior. If both parties are agreeable, children may swap slips of paper to exchange their adaptive animal behaviors.
7. Allow time for the children to brainstorm ideas. The amount of time allotted will vary from one individual to another and among pairs.
8. Invite the children to the supply table to choose their art supplies.
9. Allot the remainder of the time for the creation of their artistic representations and brief written descriptions. Instruct the children not to write their names on any portion of their projects, but instead to include the name of their project on both the artistic representation and the brief written description.
10. As you walk around the room answering any questions the children may have, make a list of each creation and the name of each inventor(s). This list is necessary in order to display the items without the names of the children to remove the possibility of any voting bias.
11. Toward the end of the program, reiterate the details of the contest, emphasizing that the projects will remain on display until the end of the contest and/or the award ceremony.

Food Styling

1. Arrange the artistic representations and brief written descriptions within the children's department or throughout the library.
2. Place a sign at the children's desk inviting judges to obtain voting ballots and a golf pencil before touring the entries.
3. After viewing all of the entries, judges may then turn in their voting ballots at the children's desk.
4. On the specified date of the end of the contest, either hold your award ceremony or contact the inventor(s) of the winning entry or entries.

5. If there is no award ceremony, invite the winner(s) to the library. Whether at the award ceremony or at a later date, obtain a signed photo permission form from their caregiver(s) and photograph the winner(s) and their winning entry.

6. Upload the photograph to the library's social media site(s).

Children should be reminded that humans are not the source of all ideas. The *Necessity Is the Mother Nature of Invention Convention* program demonstrates that nature has been efficiently adapting and inventing for billions of years. Before our society retreats further into a completely telecommunicating virtual world, people need to be mindful that some of the world's greatest inspirations come not from looking down at the newest device but from stepping outdoors and noticing what is around you. Occasionally, you should allow the earth to be your tablet and scroll through nature's bounty.

Variation: Present the *Necessity Is the Mother Nature of Invention Convention* as a passive program with the children creating their projects at home. Create a brochure detailing adaptive animal behavior and biomimicry to be given to the children upon registration. Allow children to enter, alone or in pairs, and hold the program as a contest in which the artistic representation and brief written description are created at their leisure and submitted at the library by a specific date. Since the projects are made at home, allow the children to use any materials they wish in their artistic representations. The only staff involvement in this program is the creation of the brochure and the details of the judging process.

Recipe Substitution: Recruit enthusiastic teachers from across the curriculum to help establish a school-wide challenge. A winner from each grade should be chosen.

Garnish of Books to Be Displayed during the Program

Burnie, David. *How Animals Work*. New York: DK Publishing, 2010.

Jenkins, Steve. *How to Clean a Hippopotamus: A Look at Unusual Animal Partnerships*. Boston: Houghton Mifflin Books for Children, 2010.

Lee, Dora. *Biomimicry: Inventions Inspired by Nature*. Toronto: Kids Can Press, 2011.

Ripley Entertainment, Inc. *Ripley's Believe It or Not! Curious Creatures*. Broomall, PA: Mason Crest, 2013.

Winston, Robert M. L. *Life as We Know It*. New York: DK Publishing, 2012.

14

Plastic vs. Plastic

Take the plastic challenge and determine whether you're old school or high tech. This multisession program allows participants to compare a homemade plastic object made from milk and vinegar to a plastic object created on a 3D printer. (NOTE: If you don't have a 3D printer, don't turn the page; skip ahead to the "Variation" section at the end of this recipe. In the first session of this program, participants will choose an object to build on the 3D printer from the Thingiverse web site. Then, they will cook up a batch of milk plastic and mold it into a comparable shape. The second session should be held after all the objects chosen from Thingiverse have been printed. This session will include a book discussion of *Schooled* by Gordon Korman, a personality quiz and the side-by-side reveal of all the objects.

If your library is fortunate enough to own a 3D scanner, consider using it in this program. If you chose to use the 3D scanner, you must create the milk plastic object first. Then, use the 3D scanner to scan in the object to create a design for the 3D printer to build. If you are NOT using a 3D scanner, then choose the item to be printed with the 3D printer first so that you may then create a close facsimile from the milk plastic.

Cost: Assuming you already own a 3D printer or are using the directions in the "Variation" section of this recipe, the only cost for this program will be that of the milk and vinegar.

Time: The bulk of the time for this program will be spent building the 3D printed objects. If you build the 3D printed objects yourself, while you are waiting, time may also be spent creating a list of book discussion questions or you may photocopy and use the *Schooled* book discussion questions in Appendix A on page 197. You may also create your own personality quiz while you wait or photocopy and use the Old School vs. High Tech Quiz in Appendix C on page 212. If you must Interlibrary Loan copies of the book yourself, you will need to allow additional preparation time to do so. Each of the two sessions should run 45 minutes to one hour.

Early Bird Special: Low Cost Program

Serving Size: Twelve to fifteen 9- to 12-year-olds working individually. If you have a teen group interested in 3D printing, recruit a number of them to volunteer to build the 3D printed objects. Registration should be required in order to obtain allergy information to avoid serious food allergies or reaction, to obtain the correct number of copies of *Schooled*, and to estimate the necessary ingredients.

Staff Size: One staff member.

Ingredients

As indicated by the list of suggested ingredients, this program involves the use of food and/ or edible ingredients. The ingredients included are suggestions based on a group of participants who have no known food allergies. It is your responsibility to adjust the ingredients list based on the medical needs of the participants in your program.

One copy of *Schooled* by Gordon Korman per registered child plus an additional copy for the staff member

Stove or hot plate(s)

One large saucepan, if you are cooking one large batch, or one small saucepan per registered child, if each child is making his or her own milk plastic mixture

One large metal or wooden spoon, if you are cooking one large batch, or one metal or wooden spoon per registered child if each child is making his or her own milk plastic mixture

One large fine weave strainer, if you are cooking one large batch, or one small fine weave strainer per registered child, if each child is making his or her own milk plastic mixture

One 1- or 2-cup liquid measuring cup, if you are cooking one large batch, or one 1-cup liquid measuring cup per registered child, if each child is making his or her own milk plastic mixture

One 1 tablespoon measuring spoon, if you are cooking one large batch, or one 1 tablespoon measuring spoon per registered child, if each child is making his or her own milk plastic mixture

One large slotted spoon, if you are cooking one large batch, or one

large or medium slotted spoon per registered child, if each child is making his or her own milk plastic mixture

Two gallons of whole milk

One bottle of distilled white vinegar

Four coffee filters per registered child plus an additional four to create a sample

One roll of wax paper

An assortment of cookie cutters

One foam or plastic plate per registered child plus one to create the sample

One roll of plastic wrap

Plastic tablecloths

Baby wipes and paper towels (to be used in cleanup)

(Optional) One large bowl or bucket

(Optional) One 3-mm bamboo skewer per registered child

(Optional) Food coloring, in a variety of colors

(Optional) Glitter, in a variety of colors

One piece of scrap paper per registered child

One pencil per registered child

One copy of the Old School vs. High Tech Quiz in Appendix C on page 212 or the personality quiz you created per registered child

Preheat

1. Interlibrary Loan enough copies of *Schooled* by Gordon Korman to accommodate the Serving Size plus an additional copy for the staff member.
2. Purchase and/or gather the necessary supplies.
3. Create a sample object using the 3D printer to familiarize yourself with the process and to show to the program participants.
   a. Perform an online search on Thingiverse to find an object that you can create on the 3D printer and also re-create with a cookie cutter or shape by hand. When you are searching Thingiverse, be sure to choose an object that has a photograph of the finished item, not just a picture of the design in the 3D design software, and/or positive reviews from users who have downloaded the design and successfully printed the object.
   b. If you are planning to add food coloring to your milk plastic, choose a corresponding color of filament with which to create your 3D printed item. If you are not planning to add food coloring, choose white-colored filament to match the color of the milk plastic.
   c. Allot ample time to build your object on the 3D printer.
4. Libraries are notorious for having older appliances in their staff kitchens. Consider testing your hot plate or stove to ensure that it heats properly.
5. Create a sample of milk plastic to familiarize yourself with the process and to show to the program participants.
   a. Place your saucepan onto your heat source and pour two cups of whole milk into the saucepan.
   b. Heat the milk until it is very hot, but DO NOT LET THE MILK BOIL.
   c. Add two tablespoons of vinegar and remove the saucepan from the heat source.
   d. Stir the mixture gently, allowing it to separate into clumps.
   e. Stir again gently.
   f. Place the strainer in the sink or, if no sink is available, over a large bowl or bucket.
   g. Pour the contents of the saucepan into the strainer so that all of the excess water drains into the sink, bowl, or bucket.

   h. Place one coffee filter inside of another. Gather together the clumps left in the strainer and place them in the two coffee filters.
   i. Hold your hands over the sink, bowl, or bucket and squeeze the coffee filters

in your hands to get the remaining water out of the milk plastic. If the coffee filters get too wet, transfer the milk plastic mixture to two dry coffee filters placed inside of each other and squeeze again.

j. Remove the milk plastic from the coffee filters. It should be a solid or paste, not a liquid. Place the milk plastic on a piece of wax paper to dry for five minutes.

k. If you desire, you may add food coloring or glitter to the milk plastic while it is still wet.

l. After the initial five-minute drying time is over, gently shape the plastic into a ball.

m. Place the ball back onto the wax paper and flatten it partially with your hand. Turn the milk plastic over and finish flattening it to the desired thickness. The plastic will not be completely smooth.

n. Using a cookie cutter, your hand, or any other small tools with which you wish to experiment, create a shape that closely resembles the object chosen to be printed on the 3D printer.

o. If you would like to make a piece of jewelry, use the optional bamboo skewer to poke a hole into the milk plastic shape to create a place through which to thread a cord, necklace, or bale for a pendant.

p. Place the milk plastic shape onto the foam or plastic plate.

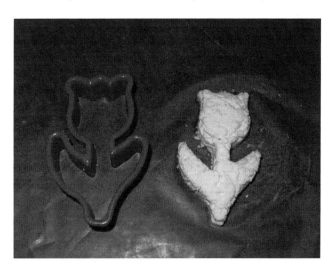

q. Allow the milk plastic shape to dry for two hours in an area free from pets and small children.

r. Turn the plastic over and allow the milk plastic shape to dry for an additional two hours.

s. The drying time will vary depending on the thickness of the milk plastic shape you have created. However, the plastic will not be fully hardened for at least two days. As it dries, the milk plastic object will become smoother, but may not lose all of its original texture.

6. If your library has a computer lab, reserve it for the first 15 to 20 minutes of the first *Plastic vs. Plastic* session so that the program participants may individually search Thingiverse for an object to print. If you don't have access to a computer lab and your program room doesn't already have a computer in it, bring a computer, laptop, or iPad to the program room. If you have multiple computers, laptops, iPads, or any combination of the three, it is best to bring enough so that each registered child may search Thingiverse individually. If you do not have access to multiple devices, then everyone may search as a group. You may wish to add 10 to 15 additional minutes to the program time in order to accommodate all the searches.

7. Arrange the supplies on the supply table.

Bake Session 1

1. Tell the participants about the *Plastic vs. Plastic* program and the different components that will take place in each session.
2. Explain to the children the steps required to make milk plastic.
3. Show the program participants your milk plastic sample.
4. Show the participants your selection of cookie cutters to provide an inspiration for objects to choose on Thingiverse.
5. Allot time for the children to choose their objects to be printed on the 3D printer from Thingiverse.
6. As each child decides upon his or her Thingiverse object, ask them to use the blank piece of scrap paper to note their Thingiverse object choice, the title of the object, the name of the creator, and the color of filament they wish to be used to print their object. Be sure to collect all of the pieces of scrap paper before starting the process of making the milk plastic.
7. Leave the computer lab and assemble in the program room (or kitchen facilities) or put away all the computers, laptops, and/or iPads to prepare to create the milk plastic mixture.
8. If you are making one large batch of milk plastic:
   a. Gather the children around the heat source and prepare the milk plastic according to the steps in Preheat 5a–g.
   b. Ask the children to take two coffee filters from the supply table and place one coffee filter inside of the other.
   c. Using the large slotted spoon, drain one to two spoonfuls of the clumped milk plastic mixture into each of the children's coffee filters.
   d. Instruct the children to complete the steps in Preheat 5i–p.
   e. Explain the drying process in Preheat 5q–s to the participants.
9. If each child will have their own heat source, ingredients, and utensils to cook up an individual batch of milk plastic:
   a. Instruct the children to complete the steps in Preheat 5a–p.
   b. Explain the drying process in Preheat 5q–s to the participants.
10. Collect the milk plastic objects and place them in a safe place in the library to complete the drying process.
11. Reiterate to the children that in the next session they will take part in a book discussion of *Schooled*, take the Old School vs. High Tech Quiz or other personality quiz, and compare their milk plastic and 3D printed objects.

In between the first and second sessions, you or a group of teen volunteers will need to use the children's 3D printer choices written on the scraps of paper to build the program participants' 3D printed objects.

Bake Session 2

1. Gather the participants in your favorite book discussion formation.
2. Hold the book discussion for *Schooled* with your own book discussion questions or those provided in Appendix A on page 197.

3. Hand out one copy of the personality quiz you created or the Old School vs. High Tech Quiz in Appendix C on page 212 to each child. Allot time for the children to take the quiz. Discuss the results.

4. Now it is time for the big reveal! To build suspense, hand out all the milk plastic objects to their creators. Deliver the corresponding 3D printed objects to the correct children. Ask the participants to examine their items and compare and contrast them.

5. Encourage a group discussion of the advantages and disadvantages of the two methods of plastic creation.

6. At the conclusion of the program, invite participants to take both their plastic objects home.

Plastic vs. Plastic offers the participants the opportunity to discuss out-of-the-box thinking and different ways to achieve the same end. You may also want to talk about the changing world we live in and whether or not the children appreciate the onslaught of technological changes taking place. The program is sure to provide a thought-provoking experience.

Variation: If your library does not own a 3D printer, present *Plastic vs. Plastic* in one 45-minute to one-hour program. Begin with a book discussion of *Schooled* by Gordon Korman, questions for which are provided in Appendix A on page 197. Next, cook up a large batch or provide the program participants with the supplies and a heat source to create their own individual batches of milk plastic. While the milk plastic cools, take the Old School vs. High Tech Quiz in Appendix C on page 212. After the quiz, allot the remaining program time for the children to sculpt their milk plastic.

Recipe Substitution: Team with a willing science teacher for a hands-on, three-dimensional, kitchen-based lesson on molecules, monomers, and polymers.

Garnish of Books to Be Displayed during the Program

Bardhan-Quallen, Sudipta. *Kitchen Science Experiments: How Does Your Mold Garden Grow?* New York: Sterling, 2010.

Coelho, Alexa. *Why Is Milk White? & 200 Other Curious Chemistry Questions*. Chicago Review Press, 2013.

Connolly, Sean. *The Book of Totally Irresponsible Science*. New York: Workman Publishing, 2008.

Field, Jon Eben. *Kitchen Chemistry*. New York: Crabtree Publishing, 2011.

Heinecke, Liz Lee. *Kitchen Science Lab for Kids: 52 Family Friendly Experiments from the Pantry*. Minneapolis, MN: Quarry Books, 2014.

Korman, Gordon. *Schooled*. New York: Hyperion Books for Children, 2008.

Scheunemann, Pam. *Cool Plastic Projects: Creative Ways to Upcycle Your Trash into Treasure*. Minneapolis, MN: ABDO Publishing, 2013.

15

Silent Film

You wouldn't think technology would bring rise to the phrase everything old is new again, but it does. Apps allow users to bring what was cutting edge in an earlier time back to the forefront. One of the best examples of this is the Silent Film Studio app, which resurrects the Silent Era of motion pictures for modern audiences.

Libraries and media centers are places where traditional media like books and periodicals are merged with new technology. What better place and subject matter for a newfangled silent film?

The silent film can be used to highlight whatever aspect or service of the library you desire. The film could be a general overview of the library and its resources, a way to showcase new materials, or illustrate library rules. But most of all, it is a creative, fun way for the participants and the viewers to learn about the library.

Cost: The .99 Silent Film Studio app and the .99 in-app purchase theme pack are the only required purchases. The app works on an iPad or iPhone. If your library doesn't own an iPad, you may consider asking a staff member to loan you his or her iPad or iPhone. You will need to purchase index cards if you do not have any. Further costs are negligible as the library is both the subject and the setting of the film. However, in order to increase the entertainment or comedic value, it is recommended to use simple costumes, perhaps featuring a period look (e.g., Chaplinesque moustaches, hats, long dresses, shawls) and simple props.

Time: To plan the time for this program, you need to decide whether or not you will write the entire script, just a framework or have the participants write the script. If you have a specific lesson with required content, you will need to plan time to write the narrative and dialogue, referred to in the Silent Film Studio app as the title cards, in addition to the time required for rehearsal and filming. To retain control over the subject, but allow the participants creative license, you will need to provide a framework or open-ended prompt understanding that additional time for the children to write the title cards is necessary. More program time will be needed if the children have free reign over the film in its entirety; however, less preparation time will be required on your part.

The exact amount of time for writing, rehearsing, and filming depends on the complexity of the subject and the final product you wish to achieve. The best results will be obtained by maintaining continuity throughout the film. All of the work should be completed in a compressed time frame (e.g., one long program or a series of shorter programs scheduled within the same week).

The program may conclude with a premiere for friends and family.

Early Bird Special: Low Cost Program

Serving Size: Ten to twelve children, ages 7 to 10, working in a group to complete one film. Registration is recommended to ensure enough, but not too many, participants. Upon registration, obtain written photo permission to post the children's images in the films on your web site, YouTube, and other social media site(s).

Staff Size: One staff member.

Ingredients

One iPad or iPhone
Silent Film Studio app with the in-app purchase theme pack
Pencils
Index cards
One photo permission form per registered child
Storyboard Worksheet(s) (see Appendix C on page 215)
(Optional) One copy of the script per child
(Optional) One copy of the framework per child
(Optional) Projector (to show the finished films to friends and family)

Preheat

1. Choose the film's topic:
   a. Understanding the Dewey Decimal System is an appropriate subject for title cards you write without the children's input. This type of program gives you complete control over the film. You will do everything but the acting.
   b. Library rules are the perfect framework to provide as a subject for participants to create their own visual explanations. You provide the rules while the children create the narrative and decide how they will visually represent the rules.
   c. For a totally open-ended program, giving the children complete creative control, suggest they create films about why they like the library.
2. If you are the sole author of the script, as in the Dewey Decimal System topic suggested in Preheat 1a, write the title cards and create a storyboard.
3. If you are sharing authorship with the children, as in the library rules topic suggested in Preheat 1b, provide a written framework for the children to add to.
4. The children will need a completed storyboard. If you have created one, as you would with the Dewey Decimal System topic, make copies to give to the participants. If you are providing a framework or leaving your film open-ended, make copies of the blank Storyboard Worksheet in Appendix C on page 215 for the children to fill in.

5. Make a copy of the photo permission form for each registrant.
6. Perform an online search to find clips of silent films to show to the participants.
7. Install the Silent Film Studio app and in-app purchase theme pack onto the iPad or iPhone.
8. Create a simple, short silent film to familiarize yourself with the use of the app and to use as an example.
9. Shoot a very short silent film in front of the children on the day of the program to show them how to use the app. Prepare a set of index cards, with each index card representing one title card, so you may expedite the process of creating your on-the-spot silent film. A few seconds of film and one or two title cards are all that is needed.
10. Gather the optional costumes and props.

Bake

1. Present an overview of the *Silent Film* program and provide an explanation of what a silent film is.
2. Display the examples of silent film clips gathered from your online search either projected on a screen or shown on a computer or iPad.
3. Show the Silent Film Studio app tutorial, which can be found in the app and on YouTube.
4. Explain the concept of a storyboard: a visual representation of the plot in comic book form. Give the children the Storyboard Worksheet you filled in or a blank Storyboard Worksheet and pencils.
5. Reinforce the concept of the title cards. Hand out index cards and explain that each index card represents one title card. Participants should immediately number the cards to keep the cards in order.
6. Gather the children around and choose two of them to be actors while you shoot a very short sample silent film to familiarize the participants with the process. Refer to the index cards you prepared in Preheat 9 to enter the text in the title cards of the app.
7. Show the participants the silent film you created on the spot.
8. Provide the children with the script, framework, or the open-ended prompt.
9. If you have total control of the film, as in the Dewey Decimal System topic, use the Storyboard Worksheet and index cards you created to direct the children.
10. If you have given the participants either the framework or an open-ended prompt, help the children through the process of filling out the Storyboard Worksheets and index cards, but allow them creative control.
11. For the best results, the staff member should act as the director/camera person. If you did not write the Storyboard Worksheet or index cards, review the Storyboard Worksheet and the index cards to familiarize yourself with the plot before beginning to film.
12. Quiet on the set and ACTION!

Food Styling

1. Once the film is completed, use the Silent Film Studio app to upload the films to YouTube.
2. Arrange the chairs in your program room in theater-style seating. Invite participants, friends, and family into the screening.
3. Welcome your audience and explain the concept of silent filmmaking.
4. Introduce each actor individually to give everyone their time in the spotlight.
5. Roll tape.
6. Post the films on a variety of social media sites to afford friends and family unable to attend the showing the opportunity to view the film.

This is a unique way to present a library tutorial. When children see other children using a complex system like the library, it gives them confidence that they can successfully navigate the library as well. Your participants also learn more about the library without even knowing it.

Variation: To present this program for older children, use an open-ended prompt. They will be more enthusiastic about a project when they have total creative control. Allow them to shoot and direct the film, but be sure to preview their Storyboard Worksheets and index cards for inappropriate material before filming begins. If your library is fortunate enough to have multiple iPads, let the participants choose their own partners or groups and create multiple films.

Recipe Substitutions: Have each grade film a tutorial for an age-appropriate library lesson. The older the children are, the more control they should have over the final product. Another option is to collaborate with a history teacher and introduce the Silent Film Studio app in a unit on any topic taking place during the Silent Era, 1894–1929.

Leftovers: Use the Silent Film Studio app in the *Meteorite Strike!* program variation on page 33.

Garnish of Books to Be Displayed during the Program

Avi. *Silent Movie*. New York: An Anne Schwartz Book/Atheneum Books for Young Readers, 2003.

Clee, Paul. *Before Hollywood: From Shadow Play to the Silver Screen*. New York: Clarion Books, 2005.

Fleishman, Sid. *Sir Charlie: Chaplin, the Funniest Man in the World*. New York: Greenwillow Books, 2005.

Friedman, Lise. *Break a Leg! The Kids' Guide to Acting and Stagecraft*. New York: Workman Publishing, 2002

Keenan, Sheila (adaptor). *The History of Movie: Animation and Live-Action, from Silent to Sound, Black-and-White to Color*. New York: Scholastic, 1995.

Kenney, Karen Latchana. *Cool Scripts & Acting: How to Stage Your Very Own Show*. Edina, MN: ABDO Publishing Company, c2010.

Platt, Richard. *Eyewitness: Film*. New York: Dorling Kindersley Education, 2000.

Selznick, Brian. *Wonderstruck: A Story in Words and Pictures*. New York: Scholastic, 2011.

16

Stop Motion Films

Can you take a photograph? Then you can make a stop motion film. Stop motion films are created by stringing together a series of photographs that, when put into motion, create a movie. This technique has been used by amateurs and professionals for more than a century. Movies like *Frankenweenie* and *Wallace & Grommit* and classics like *Gumby* are well-known examples. Stop motion filmmaking is an ideal program in that it allows children total creative freedom. They choose the characters, setting, props, storyline and shoot the films themselves.

Cost: With the exception of the iPad(s), the $1.99 Stop Motion Studio app plus an additional $3.99 for the Feature Pack (the price of one app and one feature pack covers 10 iPads or less), this program may be staged using items you and/or the children already own. These items may be the characters, props, or scenery in your film. Plastic interlocking building blocks, clay, dolls, self-adhesive notes, small toy cars, candy, or kitchen utensils make excellent choices. Children may also wish to star in their own productions.

Time: Although this program requires more time than most, children work independently for the bulk of the time. The program can be completed in one (very long) day, but is best suited for multiple sessions. The program should conclude with a premiere for friends and family.

Early Bird Specials: Low Cost Program

Serving Size: Twenty 9- to 12-year-olds working in groups, with each group receiving one iPad or the entire class using one iPad to create a single movie. If you are offering a multi-iPad program, you should require registration to ensure the proper iPad-to-child ratio. Upon registration, obtain written photo permission to post the children's photographs on your library's web site and other social media sites. If applicable, inform the parents of the time and date of the film premieres.

Staff Size: One to two staff members are required for this program.

Ingredients

As indicated by the list of suggested ingredients, this program may involve the use of food and/or edible ingredients. The ingredients included are suggestions based on a group of participants who have no known food allergies. It is your responsibility to adjust the ingredients list based on the medical needs of the participants in your program.

iPad(s)
Stop Motion Studio app
Feature Pack (in-app purchase)
(Optional) iPad tripods
Storyboard Worksheet(s) (see Appendix C on page 215)
Stop Motion Films Storytelling Sheet(s) (see Appendix C on page 214)
Props for characters and scenery
Notebooks or paper and writing utensils
One copy of the your library's photo permission form for each registered child
(Optional) Projector to screen the films

Preheat

1. Find examples of stop motion films on YouTube and other video sites to familiarize yourself and the participants with the genre. Films created by other children are most likely to make the biggest impression.
2. Photocopy at least one Storyboard Worksheet and one *Stop Motion Films* Storytelling Sheet per registered child.
3. Purchase and install the Stop Motion Studio app and the Feature Pack onto the iPad(s).
4. The best way to instruct others is to learn by doing. Create your own stop motion film with whatever you have on hand. It doesn't need to be elaborate or lengthy. Making your own stop motion film allows you to understand the process and provides the children with a standard they can easily surpass.
5. Make one copy of the photo permission form for each registered child.

Bake

1. Explain the concept of stop motion films and present examples, including your own sample stop motion film, to the program participants. If you do not have a projector, the films may be shown on a computer or iPad.
2. If you are offering a multi-iPad program, ask the children to choose a partner or group. If the children are unable to choose their own partners or groups, poll the children on what type of theme or medium they are interested in exploring and create groups accordingly.
3. Provide the children with an overview of character development, effective storytelling, and photography mechanics. Review the *Stop Motion Films* Storytelling Sheet together.
4. Have the group(s) choose props and/or a medium (e.g., clay or self-adhesive notes), to use in their stop motion film(s).
5. Explain the concept of a story-board: a visual representation of the plot in comic book form. Distribute the Storyboard Worksheets and the writing utensils.

6. Allow the children an ample amount of time to develop their story arcs. By now, the children will be itching to get their hands on an iPad, so it is important to emphasize that a well-developed story is the key to a film the audience will understand and enjoy.

7. After the groups have completed their storyboards, explain the process of creating a shot list and hand out the notebooks or paper. A shot list is a written outline of the composition of each photograph—the characters, scenery, and props. Every second of a stop motion film requires 24 individual photographs. Therefore, a 10-second film requires 240 photographs! A shot list of 50 or more photograph compositions helps the children narrow their focus and define the film's pivotal images.

8. In order to familiarize the participants with the actual mechanics of the app, while the children watch, create a three-second film. Don't concern yourself with the content; it is for demonstrative purposes only.

9. Now is the time everyone has been waiting for. Distribute the iPad(s) and tripod(s), if applicable. If your library does not own tripods, encourage the children to use the app's grid function, steady the iPad on a table, or balance it on their knee.

10. Release the hounds!

11. Now is the most delicious part of this recipe. Peek through the oven window and watch the children's creativity rise. You should be available to answer questions but, for the most part, relax and enjoy the ambiance.

12. As the group(s) finish, instruct the children to prepare a short verbal introduction to their film(s).

Food Styling

1. Once the films are completed, use the Stop Motion Studio app to upload the films to YouTube.

2. Arrange the chairs in your program room in theater-style seating. Invite participants, friends, and family into the screening.

3. Welcome your audience and explain the concept of stop motion filmmaking.

4. Have the group(s) present a short introduction to their film(s).

5. Serve their dish(es) and cue the applause.

6. Post the films on a variety of social media sites to afford friends and family unable to attend the premiere the opportunity to view the film(s).

One of the greatest surprises you'll find in this program is how proud the friends and family of the filmmakers are. Although the films won't be perfect, the children enjoy learning the process of filmmaking. This will likely rub off on their family and friends who may in turn be inspired to create their own films.

Variations: For younger participants, allow the children to choose a well-known fairy tale or picture book to reinterpret. You will need to take a more active role with this group, guiding them through each step. For this reason, register a smaller number of participants and consider adding additional staff. Whatever the age of the participants, serve popcorn at the premiere or make a night of it with dinner and a movie. If your budget allows, provide pizza and beverages. If not, try pot luck.

Fusion Box: If your library has a 3D printer, schedule extra time for the children to design characters, props, or set pieces and for the pieces to be printed. You may wish to recruit a group of teens to refine the designs and complete the print process.

Recipe Substitutions: Educators or media specialists may collaborate with other teachers across the curriculum with the *Stop Motion Films* program. In an art class, students learning pointillism may use their newfound skills to create scenery with paint or self-adhesive notes. In a language arts class, a creative writing unit may be devoted to developing a script for the film(s).

Garnish of Books to Be Displayed during the Program

Cassidy, John and Nicholas Berger. *The Klutz Book of Animation: Make Your Own Stop Motion Movies*. Palo Alto, CA: Klutz Press, 2010.

Horn, Geoffrey M. *Movie Animation*. Milwaukee, WI: Gareth Stevens Publishing, 2007.

Levete, Sarah. *Make an Animation!* Mankato, MN: Black Rabbit Books, 2012.

Pipe, Jim. *Make a Movie!*. Mankato, MN: Black Rabbit Books, 2012.

Shulman, Mark and Hazlitt Krog. *Attack of the Killer Video Book*. Toronto: Annick Press, 2004.

Sutherland, Adam. *Take Great Photos!* Mankato, MN: Black Rabbit Books, 2012.

17

Chalktography

How many staff members does it take to present a *Chalktography* program? Two. One to take the photo and one to hold the ladder.

Promote your library's social media with this unique photography program that presents opportunities for 'tweens, teens, and younger children to participate. Older children will create an outline of a design with sidewalk chalk on a paved work surface and act as the photographer(s). Younger children will color in the design and then pose in the photograph as a design element. If you desire, the resulting chalktography may be placed on your library's social media site(s). Friends, family, and program participants will likely want to see these photographs and will flock to your social media site(s). Take advantage of this opportunity to promote the library, the collection, upcoming programs, or whatever you desire.

Cost: The only cost that should be associated with this program is the sidewalk chalk necessary to create the designs. If your library does not own a sufficient number of photographic devices (cameras, iPads, etc.) and/or ladders or step-stools, ask the staff to lend these items to you for use in the program.

Time: You will need to plan enough time to take measurements, create a sample, make an inspirational slideshow, and make copies of your library's photo permission forms and social media location sheets. You will also need to make copies of the Design Box Instructions for 'Tweens and Teens located in Appendix C on page 216. Since the 'tweens and teens are arriving one hour before the younger participants, plan for the entire program to take at least two hours.

Early Bird Special: Fruitcake, Low Cost Program

Serving Size: Approximately five 'tweens and teens should be registered to create and photograph each design. Twelve children ages 5 to 7 should be registered to be the artists and subjects in the photographs. Upon registration, obtain written photo permission to post the children's photographs on your library's web site and other social media sites.

Staff Size: Two staff members.

Ingredients

Household ladder(s), multistep stool(s), or step stool(s)

Sidewalk chalk in a variety of colors

Tape measure(s)

Digital camera(s), iPad(s), or smartphone(s) (the higher the resolution of the device, the better the quality of the image produced)

One sheet of scrap paper

One pen or pencil

Stuffed animal or doll

One photo permission form for each registered child to be photographed

One social media location sheet listing the web address(es) for the final

photograph for each photographed child and 'tween/teen participant

Design Box Instructions for 'Tweens or Teens (see Appendix C on page 216)

(Optional) Traffic cones with which to cordon off a paved work area

Inspirational chalktography slideshow

Preheat

1. Upon registration, ask the 'tween or teen participants to arrive at the library approximately one hour before the younger children.
2. Purchase and/or gather the necessary ingredients.
3. Perform an online search for chalktography photographs to create an inspirational slideshow for the program participants. Be sure to include the sample photograph you will create. The slideshow will provide the participants with a visual explanation of chalktography and design ideas for the program.
4. It is best to plan a rain date in the event of unexpected inclement weather. Three to four days before the date of the *Chalktography* program, check the weather report for the scheduled date of the program and decide if you will hold the program on its original date or use the rain date.
5. A few days before the program, you and one other staff member should plot out the measurements necessary to plan the specific dimensions and photographic angles to ensure that your design fits into the camera frame. For consistency and to take note of the effect of natural lighting and the passing of shadows, try to plot your measurements at the same time of day the program will be held. This will avoid unwanted shadows, caused by the photographer or the ladder, encroaching upon the final product.
   a. Choose an appropriate paved location that may be cordoned off for safety. If desired, arrange traffic cones around the paved work area.
   b. Bring the ladder or step-stool, the tape measure, sidewalk chalk, stuffed animal or doll, a piece of scrap paper, and a photographic device to the paved work area.
   c. Taking into account the age of the children to be included in the photographs, release tape from the tape measure to approximate their average height and lock the tape measure.
   d. Place your locked tape measure vertically on the paved surface and mark the top and bottom, or "head" and "feet," in sidewalk chalk. Note these measurements on the piece of scrap paper. Repeat the process horizontally, atop the first mark creating a cross. This will allow you to have the option of posing the younger children either vertically or horizontally in the design. It will also determine how much of the design box will be taken up by the child and how much will be available for the chalk design.

e. Position the ladder or step-stool in a temporary testing position. You may need to adjust this position in order to find the best angle or height from which to take the photographs.

f. Bring the digital camera, iPad, or smartphone up the ladder or step stool, pausing at each step to find the optimum viewing position for your photographic device. If you are using a digital camera or smartphone with zoom, try out your zoom settings.

g. The staff member not on the ladder should place the stuffed animal or doll in the shot in the middle of the cross. This will help the photographer gauge the effects of the natural lighting and shadows on the photograph.

h. At this point, you may wish to adjust the time of day the program is scheduled to allow the best natural lighting conditions possible.

i. While you are looking through the photographic device in the optimal viewing position, the staff member on the ladder should direct the other staff member to inch toward the edge of the viewing area. Once they have reached the edge of the viewing area, the staff member should mark the position with vertical and horizontal lines creating a corner, which will eventually form a box that outlines the area that can be seen in the photograph, much like a picture frame. Measure this area and note the dimensions on the scrap paper. These dimensions will be given to the teens or 'tweens to make sure their entire design is included in the photograph.

6. Create a simple sample photograph to familiarize yourself with the process and to show to the program participants.

a. Place the stuffed animal or doll toward the bottom end of the photographic viewing area.

b. Extend the arms of the stuffed animal or doll into a position that simulates holding a small bouquet of balloons.

c. Use white sidewalk chalk to draw balloon strings extending up from the hands, leaving enough room to draw balloons at the top of the strings.

d. Before drawing the balloons, one staff member should mount the ladder or step-stool, and look through the photographic device to be sure it looks as if the stuffed animal or doll is holding the strings. Adjust your drawing or stuffed animal or doll positions, if necessary.

e. Using a variety of sidewalk chalk colors, draw balloons atop the strings.

f. Remount the ladder or step-stool and view the finished sample. If desired, make any necessary adjustments to the chalk drawing, stuffed animal, or doll or positions of the photographic device.

g. When you are satisfied with the composition of your photograph, take the photo. Be sure to include this sample photograph in the inspirational slideshow.

7. Survey your paved work area and, keeping in mind the measurements, decide how many different design boxes you have space to offer. Remember that for each design you offer, you should have an additional photographic device and ladder or step-stool. If you have a small paved work area, you may wish to offer only one design area for all the children to be photographed in.

If you have an extremely large work area, consider recruiting enough teens or 'tweens to allow each younger child to be photographed in a unique design box of their own.

8. Prepare copies of your library's photo permission form to be signed by the caregiver of each child whose photograph is to be taken.

9. Create a social media location sheet noting the web address(es) where your chalktography photos will be uploaded. Print or photocopy enough social media location sheets for both the younger and the older participants.

10. Prepare a set of directions, including the measurements to be given to the 'tween or teen artists/photographers or use the directions provided in the Design Box Instructions for 'Tweens or Teens in Appendix C on page 216.

Bake

1. On the day of the program, cordon off the paved location designated for the program.

2. If desired, arrange traffic cones around the program work area.

3. Bring all of the supplies to the paved work area.

4. Explain the concept of the program and present the inspirational chalktography slideshow to the 'tweens and teens.

5. Have one staff member bring the older participants to the outdoor paved work area, hand out the Design Box Instructions Sheets for 'Tweens or Teens Sheets and instruct the participants to begin measuring out the box(es) in which to create the design(s).

6. Ask the 'tweens or teens to decide on a theme(s) for their drawing(s).

7. Inquire if anyone is experienced in taking photographs. Choose the seemingly best candidate to photograph each design.

8. Monitor the progress of the 'tweens and teens as they measure and draw their design box(es).

9. Ask the 'tweens and teens to outline their design in the form of a coloring sheet so that the younger participants may color in the design.

10. While the 'tweens and teens are drawing, the younger participants should be arriving.

11. Gather the younger children in the program room, explain the program and their part in it, and show them the inspirational slideshow.

12. Escort the younger children to the paved work area.

13. Ask the older participants to help the younger ones color in the design(s).

14. When the design(s) is completely finished, have both staff members help the younger participants pose within the design(s). Take three or four photos of each child in the design(s) in order to avoid the inevitable closed eyes, moved arm, and so on.

15. At the completion of the program, hand out the social media location sheets to all of the program participants and/or their parents or caregivers.

16. Upload the chalktography photos to the designated social media account(s).

Make memories that children and their families will cherish forever with this special library program that provides a keepsake that can be used to create other projects. Children and/or other family members may download these photos from social media and use them to create personalized gifts and items such as holiday cards, calendars, bookmarks, mugs, etc. The photos also make the perfect addition to any scrapbook, the library's and/or the family's. The viewing of the photographs also increases the awareness and statistics of the library's social media site(s).

Variation: Consider adding this element to the *Maker Marketplace* program as a fund-raiser. You will need a printer and photograph quality paper to print out the photographs of children posing in the design boxes. Charge a fee that includes the cost of the supplies and a small profit for the library.

Leftovers: Use the sidewalk chalk to make the colorful alien landscapes in the *Project Planet* program on page 160 or the *Zen Garden* program on page 54.

Garnish of Books to Be Displayed during the Program

Ericsson, Jennifer A. *A Piece of Chalk*. New Milford, CT: Roaring Brook Press, 2007.

Hodge, Susie. *Celebrity Snapper: Taking the Ultimate Celebrity Photo*. Mankato, MN: Capstone Press, 2008.

McMillan, Sue. *How to Improve at Drawing*. New York: Crabtree Publishing Company, 2010.

Sutherland, Adam. *Take Great Photos!* Mankato, MN: Black Rabbit Books, 2012.

Thomson, Bill. *Chalk*. New York: Marshall Cavendish, 2010.

18

Fairy Tale Theater

This program enlists the help of 'tweens and/or teens to put on a theatrical production of a fairy tale starring younger children. Older children may be recruited from the library's Teen Advisory Board or from other reliable 'tween library regulars whom you have come to know. The older children will write a script based on a public domain fairy tale and create the sets. The younger children, ages 5 to 7, will become the actors in the production. If you do not have a willing group of older children, please see the "Variation" section of this recipe for instructions on how to present this program yourself.

Acting is a natural form of expression for children. Young children love to pretend. Children use acting skills on a daily basis. They heart wrenchingly plead for a puppy, cry as if the world is ending if they have to miss a favorite TV show, and act like little angels when they want to stay up past their bedtime.

Fairy Tale Theater puts all those skills to use, while at the same time producing a play providing the opportunity for children to practice public speaking, increase their vocabulary, and boost their self-esteem. In addition, the children will dress up in costumes, make new friends, and have fun. 'Tweens and/or teens will also have fun working together with their friends while at the same time increasing their own self-esteem by assisting the younger children.

Cost: The cost of the program is totally dependent on your budget. You can purchase elaborate costumes and build intricate sets or keep it simple with clothing the children already own and library furniture as set pieces. You should ask the parents or caregivers of both sets of children if they have any Halloween or dance recital costumes that would work for the characters in the chosen fairy tale. There may even be some parents who wish to volunteer their sewing or woodworking skills. It never hurts to ask.

Time: This program does require a significant time commitment by all involved. There will be separate classes for the writing of the script, creation of the sets, and each rehearsal. Not every child will be required to attend every class. If you have a good collaborative relationship with your teen librarian, he or she can supervise the script and set creations, leaving the rehearsals to you.

If you must Interlibrary Loan copies of James Howe's *Pinky and Rex and the School Play* yourself and/or choose not to use the *Pinky and Rex and the School Play* book discussion questions in Appendix A on page 199, but instead create your own set of book discussion questions, you will need to allow additional preparation time.

The older children should begin meeting first as they will need to write a script the length of a picture book based on a public domain fairy tale, making sure to include narration and simple dialogue. There should be enough speaking parts for the number of young children you plan to register. Try to keep one or two parts minimal, as there will be children who wish to be part of the group, but are hesitant to speak on stage. Do not begin rehearsing with the younger children until the script is complete and has been reviewed by a staff member.

The time involved in creating a set depends on the skills of the older children and complexity and extravagance of your plans. Tailor your set design to the number, aptitude, and experience of the older children and your time frame.

Taking into consideration the age of the actors and the picture book length of the play, the optimal class schedule includes six 45-minute long rehearsals, an hour long dress rehearsal and the performance. The dress rehearsal should be no more than two days before the performance.

Early Bird Special: Fruitcake

Serving Size: As many older children as are interested can be accommodated by this program. However, you should register no more than ten 5- to 7-year-old actors for the play.

Staff Size: Optimally this program runs best with one staff member supervising the older children and another staff member directing the younger children. One staff member can conduct this program by themselves using the directions in the "Variation" section of this recipe.

Ingredients

Printed copies of the fairy tale script for the staff member director and each of the actors (the final script should be completed prior to the first rehearsal for the young children)

Index cards (create a numbered set of index cards for each actor with one line of dialogue on each card) For an example, see the Sample Theater Dialogue Index Card for the *Fairy Tale Theater* Program in Appendix D on page 199.

Materials to create the set, including existing items to be decorated (e.g., a chair embellished to look like a throne) or new items to be created from cardboard, wood, paper, fabric, and paint.

Halloween or dance recital costumes (to save money, shop at after-Halloween sales or ask for donations from parents or staff)

Clothing stylist's frame of mind to turn what the children already own into a costume (e.g., add an apron to a floral dress to create a farm girl or to a gingham dress to create Dorothy of *The Wizard of Oz*)

Props and accessories required by your script (e.g., broom for Cinderella, apple for the Wicked Witch, glasses for an old woman)

One copy, per registered child of James Howe's *Pinky and Rex and the School Play*, or other age-appropriate book that addresses the concerns of children performing in a play

Rehearsal/Class Schedule for the *Fairy Tale Theater* Program form detailing the rehearsal dates (see Appendix B on page 203)

How to Rehearse with Your Child for the *Fairy Tale Theater* Program handout for the parents or caregivers of the actors with suggestions on how to help their child learn their lines (see Appendix B on page 205)

Audition Ratings Form for the *Fairy Tale Theater* Program (see Appendix D on page 232)

Costume Conference Letter for the *Fairy Tale Theater* Program (see Appendix B on page 204)

Smartphone with a stopwatch function or app or an actual stopwatch

(Optional) Playbill created by the older children or a staff member and pens for autographs

(Optional) Refreshments for the after-performance party, purchased or provided by the library, the older children, the actors' families, and/or staff members

Preheat (for the Older Children)

1. Choose a picture book that resembles the format of the finished product that you think would be successful and give that to the older children as a guide to pattern their script after. Good examples are Karma Wilson's *Bear Snores On* and Heather Tekavec's *Storm Is Coming*.
2. Perform an online search for a list of public domain fairy tales and print out the list for the older children to choose from.

Preheat (for the Younger Children)

1. Interlibrary Loan enough copies of *Pinky and Rex and the School Play* by James Howe or another age-appropriate title that addresses the concerns of children performing in a play to accommodate the Serving Size, plus an additional copy for the staff member.
2. Create a Rehearsal/Class Schedule form or copy the Rehearsal/Class Schedule for the *Fairy Tale Theater* Program form in Appendix B on page 203.
3. Create a How to Rehearse with Your Child for the *Fairy Tale Theater* Program handout for the caregivers of the actors with suggestions on how to help their child learn their lines or copy the "How to Rehearse with Your Child" for the *Fairy Tale Theater* Program handout provided in Appendix B on page 205.
4. Make one copy of the complete script for each actor, one for the narrator, and one for the staff member/director. In addition, create a numbered set of index cards for each actor with one line of dialogue on each card. These index cards are necessary because even if you provide each child with a script in which their part has been highlighted, it is still too confusing. With index cards, the children can concentrate on learning the lines they need to know. For an example of an actor's index card, see the Sample Theater Dialogue Index Card for the *Fairy Tale Theater* Program in Appendix D on page 233.

5. Upon registration, give the parents of the younger children the Rehearsal/Class Schedule for the *Fairy Tale Theater* Program form to be signed and returned on or before the date of the first rehearsal and a copy of *Pinky and Rex and the School Play* or the book you chose to explain the performance experience, which should be read and discussed with the children at home before the first rehearsal.

6. In order to cast the parts, assemble a collection of theater games for young children to use during rehearsals. Theater games build acting skills and provide an outlet for energy. You can find theater games through an online search or in books like those listed in the following bibliography:

> Bany-Winters, Lisa. *On Stage: Theater Games and Activities for Kids*. Chicago: Chicago Review Press, 1997.
>
> Czitrom, Nina. *Take a Bow! Lesson Plans for Preschool Drama*. Hanover, NH: Smith and Kraus, 2004.
>
> Sole, Mia and Jeff Haycock. *Theater Games for Preschool Children Ages 3–6*. Rollinsville, CO: Play-Ground Theater Company, Inc., 2009.

7. Look for music that encourages active pretending through movement and expression. Some of your story time favorites may work as well in *Fairy Tale Theater* as they do in story time. You can also find appropriate music through an online search or you may use songs like *Here Comes a Bear, I'm Me or I'm Gonna Catch You*, listed in the following bibliography:

> Bari Koral Family Rock Band. *Rock and Roll Garden*. Loopytunes, 2010.
>
> Berkner, Laurie, Brian Mueller, and Susie Lampert. *Under a Shady Tree*. Two Tomatoes, 2002.
>
> Wiggles. *Let's Wiggle*. Koch Records, 1999.

8. Create a list of book discussion questions for the book you chose to explain the performance experience or use the *Pinky and Rex and the School Play* book discussion questions in Appendix A on page 199.

Bake (for the Older Children)

1. Explain the *Fairy Tale Theater* Program and their role in it to the 'tween and/or teen participants.

2. Have them choose a public domain fairy tale in which to create a picture book length script for the younger children to perform. The script should have a speaking part for each registered actor with a selection of line counts to create some large roles, some medium roles, and one or two small roles. Instruct them that they will need to include narrative to move the plot along.

3. Show them the picture book you chose as an example of a sample format for their script.

4. Allow ample time for the participants to write the script.

5. When the script has been completed, read it to be sure it includes no inaccuracies (e.g., grammar or spelling errors, inappropriate language or actions) and has the required number and variety of parts.

6. Begin set production, allowing enough time for the type of set you will create (e.g., sets created from scratch take a longer time to build than sets created using existing materials). The sets must be complete before the dress rehearsal in case modifications are required.

7. Choose a volunteer narrator to attend one rehearsal, the dress rehearsal and participate in the final performance. This person should appear onstage with the young actors but need not be in costume. They may either memorize their lines or read them from the script.

Bake (for the Younger Children)

1. As the children arrive for the first rehearsal, collect the signed Rehearsal/Class Schedule for the *Fairy Tale Theater* Program forms and the copy of the book chosen to explain the performance experience. Give each caregiver one "How to Rehearse with Your Child" for the *Fairy Tale Theater* Program handout and explain that it is a guide to be used when helping their child rehearse.

2. Assemble the actors in a circle, either in chairs or on the floor. If you are using chairs, when setting up the chairs, be sure to leave plenty of space for the theater games. Explain to the child actors that they will be participating in a theatrical production of a fairy tale.

3. Hold a book discussion of the book chosen to explain the performance experience. Answer any questions or concerns that arise. Ask if any of the children have been cast in a play before. This may help you decide who receives the largest parts.

4. Pass out a copy of the script to each actor. If they can, instruct them to read along while you read the script aloud. Discuss the story, highlighting the important plot points.

5. Fill the rest of this first rehearsal with theater games. Include games that show:
   a. children's memorization skill
   b. their ability to represent emotion in their voice and facial expression
   c. their ability to become a character distinct from themselves
   d. their comfort level speaking and pretending in front of others
   e. their ability to focus and stay on topic
   f. their ability to project their voice loudly and clearly enough to be heard and understood by an audience
   g. their ability to follow directions and behave appropriately
   h. their ability to improvise or continue after a mistake

6. Before the children leave the first rehearsal, instruct them to take their scripts home and read or have their caregiver read them the script until they can tell the story on their own. They will be asked in the second rehearsal to help retell the story without the aid of the script.

7. Immediately after the conclusion of the first rehearsal, write down your impressions of each child's skill levels in the items listed above in Bake (for the Younger Children) 5 a–h on the Audition Ratings Form for the *Fairy Tale Theater* Program included in Appendix D on page 232. Assign each skill a number from 1 through 10 with 1 representing almost no discernible skill and 10 representing

total mastery of the skill. Add each skill number together to reach a total score. Give the largest parts to the children with the highest totals and so on until the child with the lowest score receives the smallest part.

8. When the children arrive for the second rehearsal, give the parents or care-givers the Costume Conference Letter for the *Fairy Tale Theater* Program form and schedule a time for them to come to the library to discuss their child's costume and to take a photo to be used in the optional playbill. Those using a photo in the playbill will need to obtain written permission to do so. At the costume conference, collaborate with the parents or caregivers to complete the details of the costume (e.g., if the child is playing the part of a white rabbit, ask the parent to dress the child in all white. Fleece makes an excellent sub-stitute for fur). Most parents or caregivers are very willing to either purchase or make the required costume components. If you are using purchased cos-tumes, let the parents or caregivers know what accessories you need. Instruct the parents or caregivers to bring the complete costume components to the library for you to approve *before* the dress rehearsal.

9. During the second rehearsal, let the children know which part they will play and reiterate the old adage: There are no small parts, only small actors.

10. Ask the children if they have read the script or had an adult read it to them. To reinforce the sequence of the fairy tale, retell the story as a group. Begin the story yourself and allow the children to chime in by raising their hands. Do not allow one or two children to monopolize the retelling. Don't prompt the children unless the story grounds to a halt or the retelling is incorrect.

11. Hand out the numbered index cards to the corresponding cast members.

12. Explain the layout of the stage to the children, pointing out where the audi-ence will sit and where the children will perform.

13. Physically lead each child to the spot where they will be when the play begins. Tell the children to be sure to look around and see who they are next to as they will need to know that information for the following game:
    a. Give the children 10 seconds to memorize their opening stage position.
    b. Arrange the children in a line parallel to the stage area at least six feet away from the stage area or more, if space permits.
    c. Explain to the children that when you say, "Go," they should return as quickly as possible to their opening stage position. Let the children know that this is a race and they will be timed.
    d. Repeat the race until you are certain the children know where to stand and there is no more improvement in their time. This game allows you to quickly reset the children after each run-through providing more pro-ductive rehearsal time. You'll be surprised how much time can be wasted waiting for children to transition and find their opening stage position.

14. Run-through the play in its entirety, allowing the children to use their num-bered index cards.

15. Before the children leave, instruct them to memorize their parts. Tell them to enlist the help of an older sibling or grown-up to read the narration and other parts from the script while they say their lines. This helps the children realize

that they are part of a greater production and allows them to know when to say the lines they've memorized.

16. At each subsequent rehearsal, begin with one or two theater games. This helps loosen up the children and reinforce their acting skills. Proceed with repeated run-throughs of the play.

17. Warn the children at rehearsals three and four that although they will continue to bring their index cards, they will no longer use them as of rehearsal five. (The index cards should be used only in the case of a total meltdown or the inability to recall anything.)

18. At the fourth rehearsal, introduce all of the props to give the children ample time to practice using them. The props should never leave the library.

19. Make sure all of the costumes and the scenery are ready prior to the dress rehearsal.

20. For the dress rehearsal, have the older children position the scenery and furniture as they will be set up during the performance. If possible, it is easiest to leave the scenery and furniture in place until after the performance.

21. On the day of the dress rehearsal:
    a. Do not play theater games. You will need the children's complete focus and attention.
    b. Run-through the play as many times as possible during the allotted time. Do not halt any run-through for mistakes or other interruptions. Each run-through should be conducted as if it is the final performance.
    c. Instruct the children to hold all of their questions until the completion of one full performance.
    d. Leave a small amount of time at the end of the dress rehearsal to answer any questions, allay any fears, and remind the children to practice.
    e. The last thing to be done at the dress rehearsal is to ask the children to remind their parents to bring them to the library at the specified time (usually 30 minutes before the beginning of the performance) and that they should arrive in full costume.

22. On the day of the performance:
    a. Depending on the performance space, the children should wait away from the audience, but most importantly, separate from their friends and family. This helps focus the actors and you on the task at hand.
    b. Before the proverbial curtain rises, tell the actors that they have done a great job, you are very proud of them and that they should be proud of themselves. Remind them that if they forget a line or say a line incorrectly, they should continue on. The audience doesn't have the script, so no one will know unless the actor reacts badly. They should simply smile and say it like they mean it.
    c. As you introduce the play, be sure to formally acknowledge the older children and their efforts at the performance (and in the optional playbill).
    d. A literal moment before the play begins, send the children to their opening stage positions.

23. During the performance, position yourself at the opposing side of the stage from the narrator so that both you and the narrator may feed lines to any actor who cannot recall his or her lines.
24. Break a leg!

Though *Fairy Tale Theater* may seem like a daunting process, it is actually fun and rewarding for all involved. The older children see their literary efforts come to life before their eyes. The younger children get to experience the thrill of being a star, while unwittingly increasing their verbal skills, reading comprehension, self-esteem, and learn to collaborate successfully within a group.

Food Styling

1. Arrange the chairs in your performance space in theater-style seating.
2. (Optional) As the audience arrives, hand out one playbill to each family attending the performance.
3. (Optional) At the conclusion of the performance, serve drinks and refreshments to the participants, performers, friends, and families. Refreshments may be purchased or provided by the older children, the actors' families, the library, and/or staff members.
4. (Optional) Encourage the children to autograph each other's playbills as a memento of the occasion.

Variation: To present this program with one staff member, the staff member should write the complete script before registration, making any alterations to increase or decrease the number of parts to match the number of registrants later. The sets should be minimal and representational (e.g., a chair may be used as a throne and a desk with a plastic tablecloth may be used as a dining room table). If desired, you may also schedule an additional date and time for the young actors to paint a background on butcher paper or you may purchase a background online or at a party supply store.

Fusion Box: Using the Silent Film Studio app, the older children may create a silent movie of the performance. Have an older child film the performance using an iPad. If you choose a child who was not part of the script writing group, give him or her a copy of the script so that he or she can familiarize himself or herself with it before the dress rehearsal. This familiarity will be crucial during filming. Make sure to instruct the older child to film in clips, stopping the recording after each line of dialogue and resuming filming with the next line of dialogue. (The reason for this instruction will become evident after reviewing the instructions for the *Silent Film* program on page 81). You may wish to practice this process during the dress rehearsal to find the correct position to stand, angle to shoot, etc. The lines of dialogue should be inserted on theme cards between the clips. For specific directions and filming tips, see the *Silent Film* program on page 81.

Garnish of Books to Be Displayed during the Program

dePaolo, Tomie. *Stagestruck*. New York: G. P. Putnam's Sons, 2005.
Gilman, Grace. *Dixie*. New York: Harper, 2011.
Hazen, Lynn E. *Cinder Rabbit*. New York: Henry Holt, 2008.

Hopkins, Lee Bennett. *Full Moon and Star*. New York: Abrams Books for Young Readers, 2011.

Howe, James. *Pinky and Rex and the School Play*. New York: Atheneum Books for Young Readers, 1998.

Kenney, Karen Latchana. *Cool Costumes: How to Stage Your Very Own Show*. Edina, MN: ABDO Publishing Company, 2010.

McLean, Dirk. *Curtain Up! A Book for Young Performers*. Plattsburgh, NY: Tundra Books of Northern New York, 2010.

Primavera, Elise. *Louise the Big Cheese: Diva Divine*. New York: Simon & Schuster Books for Young Readers, 2009.

Rylant, Cynthia. *Annie and Snowball and the Shining Star: The Sixth Book of Their Adventures*. New York: Simon Spotlight, 2010.

Spirn, Michele. *I Am the Turkey*. New York: Harper Collins, 2004.

19

It's All about Me

This program introduces children to the art of the self-portrait. Many artists have used representations of themselves in their works, either as the sole subject or within a larger, more complex, piece. The art methods used for self-portraiture are as varied as the artists themselves. Throughout history, artists have created self-portraits by painting, drawing, sculpting, creating collages and more. *It's All about Me* presents examples of famous and lesser-known self-portraits and offers a variety of art supplies for the participants to use in the creation of their own self-portraits.

Cost: This program may be planned to suit your library's budget. If you choose to purchase clay, you must purchase clay for sculpting. It is preferable to purchase air drying, art clay sold by school supply stores online or in craft stores, in large, economical slabs usually weighing 25 pounds. It is recommended that you purchase fishing line to divide the clay into individual portions. Most libraries have an assortment of other art supplies on hand, so all that may be necessary to purchase is drawing or watercolor paper and small mirrors. If you are unable to find suitable mirrors, see the "Variation" or "Fusion Box" sections for ideas for presenting this program without mirrors.

Time: Beyond purchasing and/or collecting the ingredients, the only preparation for this program is to pre-cut the clay into individual portions and to create a slideshow of self-portrait images for inspiration.

Early Bird Specials: Craft Closet Cleanout, Fruitcake

Serving Size: Twelve to twenty children ages 7 to 12 working independently, with a separate program for each age-appropriate group. Registration is required in order to estimate the necessary ingredients.

Staff Size: One staff member.

Ingredients

Drawing and watercolor paper*	Crayons
Pencils	Pastels
Colored pencils in a variety of colors	Paints and paintbrushes
Erasers	Small disposable foam or plastic cups or bowls for the paint and/or the water
Charcoal	
Markers	

Water to clean the paintbrushes and/or to smooth the clay

Clay

Fishing line to divide the clay into individual portions

One paper plate per registered child

Design tools (e.g., craft sticks, bamboo skewers, and plastic forks) to shape the clay

Magazines

Scissors

Glue

(Optional) Glitter glue

Embellishments (e.g., jewels, feathers, beads)

One small mirror per registered child, preferably with a stand for hands-free use (check your local dollar store)

Plastic tablecloths

One gallon size plastic bag per registered child to carry their clay self-portrait creations home in

Newspapers to carry their wet self-portraits home on

Baby wipes and paper towels (to be used in cleanup)

Inspirational self-portrait slideshow

---

*If your budget allows, consider purchasing individual canvases. In addition to art supply stores they may be available at discount chains or online stores.

Preheat

1. Create an inspirational slideshow of artist self-portraits to present to the program participants. An online image search will provide self-portraits from many different artists. Begin your slideshow with examples from famous masters, such as Rembrandt, Picasso, and Gustave Courbet. In addition to the expected painters, be sure to include a wide range of self-portraits made from other mediums such as photography, wire sculpture, and magazine collages. Children tend to gravitate toward the unusual or quirky, so don't be afraid to add creative artists like Chuck Close and Levi van Veluw and lesser-known artists such as Martin Debenham and Michael Alfano. When they are available, consider adding photographs of the artists to the slideshow to provide a side-by-side comparison of the artist and his or her work.
2. Purchase and/or gather the necessary ingredients.
3. Prior to the children's arrival:
   a. Cover the tables with the plastic tablecloths.
   b. Arrange the art supplies on the tables in groups (e.g., paintbrushes with the paint and drawing implements with the drawing paper) so that the children may more easily choose their desired ingredients.
   c. Use the fishing line to slice the clay slab into individual portions. Be sure to recover the clay after you have finished slicing the individual portions in order to keep the clay moist until the children are ready to use it. You

will place each individual portion of clay onto a paper plate as the children approach the supply table.

d. You should not create your own sample self-portrait for this program as it may inhibit the participants' creativity.

Bake

1. Present the slideshow to the participants to provide inspirational examples of self-portraiture. Allow the diversity of the images in the slideshow to speak for itself.
2. Introduce the different art supplies available to the participants for their use. Refer back to examples from the slideshow to encourage experimentation with the different mediums.
3. Instruct the children to gather their art supplies and bring them to their tables.
4. Hand one mirror to each child to aid in the creation of their self-portrait.
5. Allot the remainder of the program time to the creation of their artistic masterpieces. Let the portraits begin!

Self-portraits allow children to take a noncritical look at themselves, adding aspects of their personality into the representation of their features. In society today, children are bombarded with images of the perfect face and physique. Rather than promote perfection, this program allows children to celebrate themselves and their own uniqueness.

Variation: Upon registration, instruct the children to bring an interesting, unusual, or funny photograph of themselves to the program. They will then base their self-portrait on these photos. For this variation, you may omit the purchase of mirrors.

Fusion Box: Instruct the children to use library iPads loaded with the app Morfo 3D Face Booth to take headshots of each other. The Morfo app allows users to animate their photographs creating moving, talking self-portraits.

Leftovers: If you have purchased mirrors for use in this program, be sure to collect them at the end of the program so that you can use them in the T-shirt *Transfer*-mations program on page 122.

Garnish of Books to Be Displayed during the Program

Close, Chuck. *Chuck Close: Face Book*. New York: Abrams Books for Young Readers, 2012.
Court, Rob. *How to Draw Faces*. Chanhassen, MN: Child's World, 2005.
Henry, Sandi. *Making Amazing Art: 40 Activities Using the 7 Elements of Art Design*. Nashville, TN: Williamsonbooks, 2007.
Kohl, Maryanne F. *Great American Artists for Kids: Hands-On Art Experiences in the Styles of Great American Masters*. Bellingham, WA: Bright Ring Publishing, 2008.
Renshaw, Amanda. *The Art Book for Children*. New York: Phaidon Press, 2005.
Scieszka, Jon. *Seen Art?* New York: Viking Press, 2005.
Spilsbury, Louise and Richard Spilsbury. *Self-Portrait*. Mankato, MN: Cherrytree Books, 2010.
Temple, Kathryn. *Art for Kids: Drawing in Color*. New York: Lark Books, 2009.
Thomson, Ruth. *Look at ME Self-Portraits in Art*. North Mankato, MN: Smart Apple Media, 2006.

20

Maker Marketplace

The *Maker Marketplace* program provides participants with a real-life lesson in business. Program attendees will create four different craft projects in a succession of four classes (or you may wish to simply use one or more of these crafts in a program all its own) and then sell the products at a craft fair held in the library. If your library allows, it is best that the children keep the proceeds themselves. The following crafts are only suggestions. You can substitute any of your or your patrons' favorite crafts or ask the participants themselves ahead of time what they would like to learn to make.

Cost: These five individual programs (the four craft programs and the craft fair) will require multiple purchases and a fully stocked craft closet. Depending on the supplies you have on hand, the *Maker Marketplace* program should cost in total between $100 and $200. To lower the cost, you may wish to choose alternate craft(s) using supplies you already own.

Time: This program may require an extended shopping trip, either in a store or online. Plan an hour to an hour and a half program length for each craft, and at least two hours for the craft fair. As the children will be responsible for the promotion and display of their items and any monetary transactions, staff contributions to the craft fair are limited.

Early Bird Special: Smorgasbord

Serving Size: Each craft program should serve ten to fifteen 8- to 12-year-olds. The craft fair itself should be open to any of the attendees of any or all of the craft programs. Registration is required to estimate the necessary ingredients and to obtain allergy information to avoid serious food allergies or reactions.

Staff Size: One staff member per program.

Craft Program #1: Crafty Clay

Ingredients

As indicated by the list of suggested ingredients, this program involves the use of food and/ or edible ingredients. The ingredients included are suggestions based on a group of participants who have no known food allergies. It is your responsibility to adjust the ingredients list based on the medical needs of the participants in your program.

Measuring cups

½ cup of corn starch per registered child plus one cup to make two samples

One cup of baking soda per registered child plus two cups to make two samples

⅝ cup of cold water per registered child plus 1¼ cups to make two samples

One nonstick pot

One wooden spoon

One or two large glass bowls and one small glass bowl

Two or three damp cloths

Hot plate or stove (to be used by the staff member)

One foam or plastic disposable bowl per registered child

2 tablespoons of water to be poured into each child's disposable bowl

(Optional) Oven in which to quick-dry the "Crafty Clay"

Plastic tablecloths

Baby wipes and paper towels (to be used in cleanup)

One gallon size zippered plastic bag per registered child to carry their creations home in

Preheat

1. Purchase and/or gather the necessary ingredients. If possible, use your own, or borrow a staff member's nonstick pot, wooden spoon, large glass and small bowl, and damp cloths.
2. Libraries are notorious for having older appliances in their staff kitchens. Consider testing your hot plate or stove to ensure that it heats properly.
3. Make a small sample batch of "Crafty Clay" to familiarize yourself with the process and to avoid any mishaps due to variations in the hot plate or stove performance:
   a. Measure and pour the corn starch and baking soda into the nonstick pot.
   b. Stir this mixture together.
   c. Measure the water and pour it into the pot with the corn starch and baking soda mixture and stir until smooth.
   d. Cook on low to medium heat, stirring constantly until the mixture achieves the consistency of mashed potatoes. The cooking time may vary depending upon the intensity of the heat source and the number of batches cooked together.
   e. Transfer the clay mixture into a glass bowl.
   f. Cover the bowl with a damp cloth.
   g. Let the clay sit in the covered glass bowl until it is cool enough to handle. The larger the batch, the longer the time it will take to cool.
   h. Sculpt your clay into an object.
   i. The clay needs at least two days to air-dry. However, the drying time may be decreased by preheating an oven to its lowest setting, turning the oven off, then resting the clay object on a cookie sheet and placing it into the oven. The oven drying time may vary depending on the thickness of the clay.
4. Cover the tables in the program room with the plastic tablecloths.
5. Approximately one hour before the start of the program, make enough clay for each child to have one recipe.
6. Place the bowl(s) with the clay and damp cloth(s) on the supply tables in the program room.

7. Place the foam or plastic disposable bowls filled with water on the supply tables.
8. If you are not holding the program in your library's kitchen, set up the hot plate and ingredients on a table in the program room. You will be making one individual recipe in front of the children at the start of the program.

Bake

1. Let the children know that they will be sculpting a clay object that, when dry, may be painted at home.
2. Explain the concept of the *Maker Marketplace* program and inform the children that they may be able to sell their craft projects at the library craft fair.
3. Tell the children that if they are interested in selling their clay object(s) or other handmade items, their caregiver will need to register them to participate in the craft fair.
4. In front of the children, make the one remaining portion of "Crafty Clay" to demonstrate the process of how the clay was made. Do not give this freshly made sample to a child until it is cool to the touch.
5. Tell the children that although the clay is made with common kitchen ingredients, they should not eat this clay.
6. Give each participant a portion of the clay prepared prior to the program equal to the sample size. Instruct each child to take one disposable bowl with water from the supply table back to their work space. Explain to the children that, for a smoother clay surface, they may dip their finger into the water and gently rub the clay. Warn the children that adding too much water will damage the final product.
7. If a child is interested in becoming a vendor at the craft fair or would like to make gifts for family and friends, suggest that they use their allotted portion of clay to create smaller projects like magnets, pendants, paperweights, etc.
8. Allow the rest of the program time for the children to sculpt their chosen object(s) from the clay.
9. At the end of the program, explain the air-drying process to the children. Instruct the children that if they would like to paint their object(s) they should to wait until their object is completely dry before painting it at home.
10. Clay objects are extremely fragile. Children should be very careful when transporting their clay creations back to the library for the craft fair. Strongly suggest that the children wrap their clay objects in multiple layers of tissue paper or bubble wrap for both transportation to the library and for packaging after the item is sold.

Craft Program #2: Painted Rocks

Ingredients

One to two bags or containers of smooth, polished craft rocks (at least one 2 to 4 inch rock per registered child)

Felt-tip permanent markers or paint pens in a variety of colors

BRIGHT, BRIGHT acrylic paints in a variety of colors (did we mention bright?)

At least two foam or plastic plates per registered child

At least one paintbrush per registered child

Foam or plastic disposable bowls filled with water (to clean the paintbrushes when switching to a new paint color)

Paper towels

Newspapers

Baby wipes and paper towels (to be used in cleanup)

Inspirational pattern and design slideshow

(Optional) Hair dryer

(Optional) Clear acrylic sealer

(Optional) Adhesive magnet circles

Preheat

1. Perform an online search for images of patterns and designs such as Aboriginal or geometric art. Use these images to create a slideshow to provide inspiration for those participants who are having trouble thinking of a design suitable for placement on a rock.
2. Purchase and/or gather the necessary ingredients.
3. Create a sample to familiarize yourself with the process and to show to the children:
   a. Choose the design and colors you wish to decorate your rock with.
   b. Fill one foam or plastic disposable bowl with water.
   c. To provide a clean work surface, take one rock and place it on a foam or plastic plate.
   d. If you are using the adhesive magnet circles, apply them on the back of the rock before painting.
   e. If you desire, use the felt-tip permanent markers and/or the paint pens to outline the design on your rock.
   f. On a new foam or plastic plate, squeeze one nickel size amount of each of the brightly colored acrylic paints in your design. If the paint seems too thick, you may need to add a few drops of water to it while the paint is still on the plate palette.
   g. Use a paintbrush to paint your design onto the craft rock.
   h. Rinse your paintbrush in the water bowl and blot it dry before changing paint colors.

      i. Once you have finished painting your craft rock, you must decide upon a finish:

        1. If you choose a natural finish, simply allow your painted rock to air dry.

        2. If you wish to apply a sealer, dry the painted rock with a hair dryer. Once dry, apply clear acrylic sealer in the finish of your choice.

    4. On the day of the program, cover the tables with newspapers and arrange the craft rocks and art supplies on the supply table.

Bake

1. Introduce the *Painted Rocks* program to the participants.
2. Explain the concept of the *Maker Marketplace* program and inform the children that they may be able to sell their craft projects at the library craft fair.
3. Tell the children that if they are interested in selling their "Painted Rock(s)" or other handmade items, their caregiver will need to register them to participate in the craft fair.
4. Show the children the inspirational pattern and design slideshow and your painted craft rock sample and discuss the different ways to create a design on a rock.
5. Tell the children that they will need one paper plate to use as a work surface and another to use as an artist's palette.
6. Invite the children to visit the supply table to choose rock(s), paper plates, and art supplies.
7. If you choose to offer the option to finish the painted rocks with clear acrylic sealer, allot time to blow dry each of the children's creations and apply the sealer.
8. The participants are ready to Rock 'n Roll!

Craft Program #3: Sweet Surprise Flower Pen

Ingredients

As indicated by the list of suggested ingredients, this program involves the use of food and/or edible ingredients. The ingredients included are suggestions based on a group of participants who have no known food allergies. It is your responsibility to adjust the ingredients list based on the medical needs of the participants in your program.

Packages of inexpensive non-retractable pens (at least three to five per registered child)

Silk or plastic flowers with stems

(Optional) Wire cutters (to be used by the staff member)

Scissors

Cellophane tape

Embroidery floss in a variety of colors (may be purchased inexpensively in a variety pack)

Craft glue

One piece of small wrapped candy with a base or bottom no larger than a dime per flower pen

(Optional) Double stick cellophane tape

(Optional) Ribbon or ribbon remnants

Plastic tablecloths

Baby wipes and paper towels (to be used in cleanup)

Preheat

1. Purchase and/or gather the necessary ingredients.
2. Create a sample flower pen to familiarize yourself with the process and to show to the participants:
   a. Remove the pen cap from the pen.
   b. Using the wire cutters or scissors, cut one flower stem leaving approximately 1½ to 2 inches of stem attached to the flower.
   c. Lay the flower stem against the pen at the end opposite the pen tip. The base of the flower should be flush with the top of the pen.
   d. Anchor the flower to the pen by wrapping one strip of cellophane tape around the stem and the pen. This will make your project more manageable to work with.
   e. Continue to wrap small strips of cellophane tape around the stem and the pen until the stem is completely covered and securely fastened to the pen. Individual strips will keep the tape from clumping.
   f. Choose one color of embroidery floss.
   g. Lay approximately ½ of an inch of the cut end of the embroidery floss against the flower stem, with the cut end facing down toward the pen tip and the end that is still attached to the skein facing the flower.
   h. Using a strip of cellophane tape, anchor the embroidery floss to the stem and pen by wrapping the cellophane tape around the floss and pen.
   i. Starting at the top or flower end of the pen, carefully wind the embroidery floss in a single layer around the pen until the pen shaft is completely covered. To ensure the pen is uniformly covered, periodically slide the strands of floss back up the pen.
   j. Cut the floss from the skein.
   k. Squirt a dab of craft glue onto the cut end of embroidery floss and adhere it to the pen.
   l. Gently smooth the embroidery floss and glue with your finger. This eliminates any glue lumps and presses and secures the floss firmly onto the pen.
   m. Allow the glue to dry before replacing the cap or writing with the pen to avoid dislodging the embroidery floss.
   n. Cut a small strip of cellophane tape and roll it into a one-sided tape ring or cut a small piece of double stick tape.
   o. Place the tape ring or double stick tape against the base or bottom of one small wrapped piece of candy.
   p. Firmly press the candy into the center of the flower.
3. Cut enough flower stems, leaving approximately 1½ to 2 inches of stem attached to the flowers, so that each registered participant may choose three to five flowers.
4. Cover the tables with the plastic tablecloths.
5. Arrange the program supplies on the supply table.

Bake

1. Introduce the *Sweet Surprise Flower Pen* program to the participants.
2. Explain the concept of the *Maker Marketplace* program and inform the children that they may be able to sell their craft projects at the library craft fair.

3. Tell the children that if they are interested in selling their "Sweet Surprise Flower Pen(s)" or other handmade items, their caregiver will need to register them to participate in the craft fair.
4. Show your sample flower pen to the participants and discuss the steps used to create a flower pen.
5. Let the children know that if they make multiple flower pens within the time allotted, there is ribbon available to fashion the flower pens into a bouquet.
6. Invite the children to the supply table to choose their supplies and bring them back to their work space.
7. Allot the remaining program time to the creation of flower pens.

Craft Program #4: Pirate Loot Bag

Ingredients

One plain gift bag with handles per registered child plus one to create the sample

One skull and cross bones coloring sheet or clip art printout sized to fit the front of the bag per registered child plus one to create the sample

Copy or printer paper to print out one skull and cross bones coloring sheet per registered child plus one to create the sample

Cardboard to use to make one pirate skull and cross bones stencil per registered child plus one to create the sample

Pencil

Black acrylic or washable tempera paint

Utility or craft knife (to be used by the staff member)

One paintbrush per registered child

Three foam or plastic disposable bowls per registered child

One foam or plastic plate per registered child plus one to create the sample

One treasure map printout per registered child plus one to create the sample

One large jar of instant coffee

One tablespoon measuring spoon

One printout of a parrot coloring sheet per registered child plus one to create the sample

Black poster board in sufficient quantity to make one parrot and one flag per child plus one each for the sample

Scissors

One bottle of white glue per table

Markers, crayons, and/or colored pencils

Glitter glue

Feathers in a variety of colors

Googly eyes

One craft stick per registered child plus one to create the sample

White acrylic or washable tempera paint

Book tape and/or cellophane tape

Three bamboo skewers per registered child plus three to create the sample

One bandana or one handkerchief per registered child plus one to create the sample (the bandana or handkerchief should not have an overwhelming design)

One or two sets of fabric markers per table

Plastic tablecloths

Paper towels in a large quantity to clean off the tablecloths between "Pirate Loot Bag" components

Baby wipes and paper towels (to be used in cleanup)

Preheat

1. Purchase and/or gather the necessary ingredients.
2. Perform an online search for a skull and cross bones coloring sheet, a treasure map, and a parrot coloring sheet. Print out the coloring sheets and the treasure map. The skull and cross bones may need to be resized to fit onto your chosen bag and/or flag. The parrot may also need to be resized to appear more lifelike.
3. Make a cardboard stencil of the skull and cross bones to decorate the gift bag and flag:
   a. Cut out the skull and cross bones design from the printout.
   b. Place the design on a piece of cardboard.
   c. Trace the outline of the skull and crossbones design onto the cardboard with a pencil.
   d. Using the utility or craft knife, cut out the areas of the design that should be painted onto the bag.
4. Create a sample of the "Pirate Loot Bag" and each item inside of the bag:
   a. Pirate Gift Bag
      1. Lay one flattened gift bag face up on the table.
      2. Place the cardboard skull and crossbones stencil in the center of the gift bag.
      3. Using a paintbrush, paint black acrylic or washable tempera paint over the stencil to create the skull and cross bones image.
      4. Set aside to dry.
   b. Pirate Treasure Map
      1. Spoon one tablespoon of instant coffee into a foam or plastic disposable bowl.
      2. Add warm water and stir.
      3. Place your treasure map on a covered table.
      4. Using a paintbrush, paint the coffee and water mixture onto the treasure map making stains that will appear to antique the treasure map.
      5. Set aside to dry.
   c. Pete the Pirate's Parrot
      1. Color the parrot coloring sheet with markers, crayons, or colored pencils.
      2. Glue the coloring sheet to the poster board.
      3. Cut out Pete the Pirate Parrot.
      4. Place the Pete the Pirate Parrot face down and glue a craft stick to it.
      5. Carefully turn the parrot over.

      6. Embellish with colored feathers, glitter glue, and googly eyes.

      7. Set aside to dry.

  d. Pirate Flag

      1. Cut out black poster board in the shape of a baseball pennant.

      2. Wrap the book or cellophane tape around the top and bottom of the three bamboo skewers.

      3. Securely tape the bamboo skewer bundles to the back of the flag.

      4. Lay the pennant face up on the table.

      5. Place the cardboard skull and crossbones stencil in the center of the flag.

      6. Using a paintbrush, paint white acrylic or washable tempera paint over the stencil to create the skull and cross bones image.

      7. Set aside to dry.

  e. Pirate's Bandana

      1. Lay the bandana or handkerchief face up on the table.

      2. Using the fabric markers, create a pirate-themed design. Follow the manufacturer's directions to heat set the fabric marker design.

5. Make one photocopy of the treasure map and parrot coloring sheet for each registered child.

6. Using the skull and cross bones sample stencil created in Preheat 3a–d as a guide, make one stencil per registered child.

7. Cut one parrot size and one pennant size piece of black poster board per registered child.

8. Cover the program tables, supply table, and drying table with plastic tablecloths.

9. Arrange the supplies on the art supply table by project.

Bake

1. Introduce the *Pirate Loot Bag* program.

2. Explain the concept of the *Maker Marketplace* program and inform the children that they may be able to sell their craft projects at the library craft fair.

3. Tell the children that if they are interested in selling their "Pirate Loot Bag(s)" or other handmade items, their caregiver will need to register them to participate in the craft fair.

4. Show your sample "Pirate Loot Bag" to the participants and discuss the steps used to create each item inside the bag.

5. Beginning with the gift bag, allow 15–20 minutes for the creation of each component.

6. Invite the children to the supply table to choose enough supplies to complete one "Pirate Loot Bag" component and instruct them to bring only those supplies back to their work space.

7. Allot the remaining program time to the creation of the "Pirate Loot Bags" and the items inside them.

Craft Fair

At the conclusion of each craft program, there may be children who wish to participate in the culminating *Maker Marketplace* Craft Fair. Participants may place for sale their projects made at the library and/or additional projects created at home. Be sure to take registration for the *Maker Marketplace* Craft Fair, not only to plan the space needed for the child vendors, but also to ensure that parents and caregivers understand that the children will be creating and selling crafts. Parents should be required to remain with their children for the duration of the craft fair, providing assistance making change and executing other vendor responsibilities.

Ingredients

One table for each child vendor (For the short duration of this program, you may wish to reserve tables normally used by patrons.)

Maker Marketplace Craft Fair Parent/Caregiver Information Handout (see Appendix B on page 206)

Preheat

1. Photocopy the *Maker Marketplace* Craft Fair Parent/Caregiver Information Handout (see Appendix B on page 206)
2. Decide whether you wish to reserve a specific table for each child or whether the tables will be allotted on a first-come, first-served basis.
3. Reserve the vendor tables. Make sure to include time for the vendors to set up beforehand and clean up their tables afterward.
4. Upon registration, give each parent or caregiver a copy of the *Maker Marketplace* Craft Fair Parent/Caregiver Information Handout.

Bake

1. Lead the children to the vendor tables reserved specifically for them or instruct the children to choose from among the reserved tables.
2. Welcome the people who have come to the library specifically to shop at the *Maker Marketplace* Craft Fair and encourage other library patrons and staff members to attend the craft fair as well.
3. Periodically check in on each vendor to answer questions, address any concerns, and gauge shopper reactions to the different projects to help decide what types of projects to create for next year's *Maker Marketplace* Craft Fair.

The *Maker Marketplace* program introduces participants to the idea that children can make money and have fun doing it. It provides a safe opportunity in which to learn life skills and fosters a feeling of independence. In addition to the benefits to the participants, there are benefits for the library. Because this is a program not traditionally associated with a library, it will attract new visitors and encourage people, both patrons and staff, to think about what other nontraditional activities the library may offer.

Variations: Though *Maker Marketplace* can take place at any time of the year, consider changing it to a Holiday Craft Fair and swapping out one or more of the craft projects for holiday-themed crafts. You may also use this program outline to hold a teen *Maker Marketplace* by substituting age-appropriate, interest-appropriate crafts.

Recipe Substitutions: Hold the *Maker Marketplace* program as a school fund-raiser with the crafts made by the children and/or the Parent Teacher Association or similar organization members. You may wish to team with a math teacher for a lesson in accounting and business math. After the craft fair, examine what was and wasn't sold for an economic lesson on supply and demand.

Garnish of Books to Be Displayed during the Programs

Bernstein, Daryl. *Better than a Lemonade Stand: Small Business Ideas for Kids*. New York: Aladdin, 2012.

Enz, Tammy. *Build Your Own Mini Golf Course, Lemonade Stand, and Other Things to Do*. Mankato, MN: Capstone Press, 2011.

Hansen, Mark Victor. *The Richest Kids in America: How They Earn It, How They Spend It, How You Can Too*. Newport Beach, CA: Hansen House Publishing, 2009.

Holt, Kimberly Willis. *Piper Reed Gets a Job*. New York: Henry Holt and Company, 2009.

Kenney, Karen Latchana. *Super Simple Clay Projects: Fun and Easy-to-Make Crafts for Kids*. Edina, MN: ABDO Publishing Company, 2010.

Limos Plomer, Anna. *Pirate Ship Adventure Crafts*. Berkeley Heights, NJ: Enslow Publishers, 2011.

Paulsen, Gary. *Lawn Boy*. New York: Wendy Lamb Books, 2007.

Oldham, Todd. *Kid Made Modern*. Los Angeles: Ammo Books, 2009.

Scheunemann, Pam. *Cool Odds and Ends Projects: Creative Ways to Upcycle Your Trash into Treasure*. Minneapolis, MN: ABDO Publishing Company, 2013.

Scheunemann, Pam. *Cool Stuff for Family & Friends*. Edina, MN: ABDO Publishing Company, 2012.

21

My, What Big Claws You Have

Paleoartists use art and science to create visual representations of prehistoric creatures and their environments. Footprints, fossils, and speculation combine to create stunning examples of nature's diversity. As the science of paleontology evolves, so too does our understanding of what dinosaurs and other prehistoric animals looked like.

In the 1850s, Sir Richard Owen and Benjamin Waterhouse Hawkins created the first life-sized sculptures of dinosaurs. Charles R. Knight built upon their work and refined the images, painting some of the world's most renowned works featuring dinosaurs and prehistoric life. Owen, Hawkins, and Knight would be astounded by today's technological innovations that allow for the creation of walking, life-sized dinosaurs in films such as *Jurassic Park* and in museum exhibits like the *Sports Run Exhibit* at the Perot Museum of Nature and Science in Dallas, Texas.

Dinosaurs are not the only creatures that have left evidence of their existence. Modern-day animals do as well. Forests and fields are full of animal tracks. They are used by scientists to track migration patterns and identify species. The children will become animal track reconstructionists and will make assumptions using the characteristics of the tracks to create a visual representation of what they think the animal looks like. The *My, What Big Claws You Have* program provides the participants with a selection of printed, unidentified, life-sized animal tracks because, unlike dinosaurs, we know exactly what contemporary animals look like. At the end of the program, the participants will be given a factsheet with a photo revealing information about the animal that made the tracks they chose.

Cost: This program has only one required expense. You must purchase clay for sculpting. It is preferable to purchase air-drying clay in economical slabs, usually weighing 25 pounds each, at online school supply or craft stores. It is recommended that you purchase fishing line to divide the clay into individual portions. Most libraries have an assortment of art supplies in their craft closet, which may be used to complete this project.

Time: In addition to purchasing and/or gathering the ingredients, preparation for this program includes creating a slideshow of paleoart images and/or film clips for inspiration, finding, and printing out animal tracks, and creating animal factsheets. This program should last approximately one hour.

Early Bird Specials: Craft Closet Cleanout, Fruitcake

Serving Size: Ten to fifteen children ages 5 to 12, working individually with a separate program for each age-appropriate group. Registration is required in order to estimate the necessary ingredients.

Staff Size: One staff member.

Ingredients

Animal tracks handouts (five copies of each of the four to six different animal tracks for the children to choose from)

Animal factsheets

Clay

Fishing line to divide the clay into individual portions

Paper plates

Design tools (e.g., craft sticks, bamboo skewers, or plastic forks) to shape the clay

Drawing and watercolor paper (for those who do not want to use clay)

Pencils and/or colored pencils

Erasers

Charcoal

Markers

Crayons

Pastels

Paints in a variety of colors

Paintbrushes

Small foam or plastic cups or bowls for the paint and/or the water

Water to clean the paintbrushes or smooth the clay

Scissors

Glue

Design elements (e.g., jewels, feathers, beads)

Plastic tablecloths

Newspapers and/or gallon size plastic bags to carry their creations home in

Baby wipes and paper towels (to be used in cleanup)

Inspirational paleoartist and/or dinosaur animation slideshow

---

Preheat

1. Create a slideshow of paleoartists and/or dinosaur animations to present to participants. An online search will provide images and videos from many different artists and filmmakers. Don't forget to include works and information by and about Sir Richard Owen, Benjamin Waterhouse Hawkins, and Charles R. Knight. If you do include animal tracks in your slideshow, do not include those you are giving to the children in the art portion of this program so that the children come to their own conclusions about the tracks they are given.
2. Prepare the animal tracks handouts:
   a. Locate four to six examples of life-sized animal tracks online.
   b. Print out these examples for the children to choose from on the day of the program.

    c. Double-check that your examples do not contain the name of the animal or any identifying wording about the animal that the tracks represent. Ideally, the printout should contain just the animal tracks.

    d. Print five copies of each of the four to six tracks to provide a variety for the children to choose from.

3. Create an animal factsheet containing a photo and information about the animal corresponding to each set of tracks for the big reveal. Make at least five copies of each animal factsheet.

4. Purchase and/or gather the remaining ingredients.

5. Prior to the children's arrival, cover the tables with the plastic tablecloths. Arrange the art supplies on the tables in like groups (e.g., paintbrushes with the paint, drawing implements with the drawing paper) so that children may more easily choose the proper supplies.

6. Use the fishing line to slice the clay slab into individual portions. Be sure to recover the clay after you have finished slicing the individual portions in order to keep the clay moist until the children are ready to use it. You will place each individual portion of clay onto a paper plate as the children approach the supply table.

Bake

1. Present the paleoart slideshow to the participants to provide inspiration. Let the children know that they will use the same techniques as paleoartists to reconstruct contemporary animals from the life-sized representations of their tracks.

2. Hold up an example of each of the animal tracks from which the children will choose.

3. Allow time for the children to choose one set of animal tracks each.

4. Ask the children to examine their chosen set of animal tracks. The participants should ask themselves questions about what type of animal might have made the tracks. You might wish to prompt the children with the following questions:

    a. How big are the tracks?

    b. How far apart are the tracks?

    c. Judging by the tracks, do you think the animal is tall or short, big or small?

    d. Do the animal tracks include claws? If so, what do you think the animal uses the claws for?

    e. Do the animal tracks appear to come from a web-footed animal? If so, what do they use their webbed feet for?

    f. What kind of climate do you think the animal lives in?

    g. Ask the children if they can think of any other questions that could be asked to help identify their animal tracks.

5. Introduce the different forms of art supplies available for their use.

6. Instruct the children to gather their chosen art supplies and bring them to their tables.

7. Let the children explore their tracks and create their vision of the animal that made their tracks.

8. Encourage the children to share among the group what animals they think their animal tracks came from and why they think so.
9. After all the projects are complete, it is time for the big reveal. Give each child the animal factsheet that corresponds to the set of animal tracks they chose. Provide the children with a small amount of time to share their discoveries. Ask the children if their thoughts have changed regarding the difficulties faced by paleoartists of the past and present.
10. If the children have chosen to use clay, help them carefully place their animal in a gallon size plastic bag for cleaner, easier transportation home. Any other art may be transported home atop newspaper.

The *My, What Big Claws You Have* program teaches children to think independently and reach their own conclusions. The combination of art and animals appeals to most children's natural interests. Rather than memorizing a set of facts about an animal or mimicking an art technique, the children learn how to investigate, create, and deduce on their own.

Variations: If the participants' interest in dinosaurs is very high, conduct an online search for dinosaur tracks and let the children see if they can create the dinosaur that made them or use the dinosaur tracks and add the *My, What Big Claws You Have* program to a book discussion of *The Dinosaurs of Waterhouse Hawkins* by Barbara Kerley.

For a younger audience, remove any potentially frightening images or video clips from your inspirational slideshow and consider pairing this recipe with an age-appropriate dinosaur-themed book such as *Chalk* by Bill Thomson.

Fusion Box: For a fun addition for older children, try the inexpensive iPhone app, Animal Tracks Quiz. This app includes actual photos of animal tracks. For younger children who may not have the skill or attention span to create elaborate animal representations, consider adding the Paint for Cats iPad app. This app is intended for cats to paint works of art with their paws. The children can use stuffed animal paws or their own hands to imitate cat behavior and create animal track paintings of their own. If you are offering either of these apps, you may wish to add 15 minutes to the program length.

Recipe Substitutions: This program lends itself to collaboration with the science department. Present this program to any class in conjunction with a unit on dinosaurs or the scientific method. If an art teacher wishes to participate in the collaboration, he or she may have some additional techniques and insight into this program.

Garnish of Books to Be Displayed during the Program

Arndt, Ingo. *Best Foot Forward: Exploring Feet, Flippers and Claws*. New York: Holiday House, 2013.

Arnosky, Jim. *Wild Tracks! A Guide to Nature's Footprints*. New York: Sterling Publishing Co., Inc., 2008.

Kerley, Barbara. *The Dinosaurs of Waterhouse Hawkins*. New York: Scholastic, 2001.

Levine, Lynn. *Mammal Tracks and Scat: Life-Size Tracking Guide.* East Dummerston, VT: Heartwood Press, 2008.

Levine, Sara. *Bone by Bone Comparing Animal Skeletons.* Minneapolis, MN: Lerner Publishing Group, 2013.

Sloan, Christopher. *Bizarre Dinosaurs: Some Very Strange Creatures and Why We Think They Got That Way.* Washington, DC: National Geographic, 2008.

Thimmesh, Catherine. *Scaly Spotted Feathered Frilled: How Do We Know What Dinosaurs Really Looked Like?.* Boston: Houghton Mifflin Books for Children, Houghton Mifflin Harcourt, 2013.

Zoehfeld, Kathleen Weidner. *Dinosaur Tracks.* New York: Collins, 2007.

22

T-shirt *Transfer*-mations

Turn everyday wear into a work of art using a few simple ingredients. T-shirts are a staple in every child's closet. This program teaches children how to transfer their own artwork onto a T-shirt, creating a unique fashion statement. Once the children learn this easy method, they can reproduce this technique at home with the help of an adult.

Cost: The cost of this program depends on your budget. The cost will be significantly reduced if you ask each registered child to bring in one white T-shirt. This also avoids any sizing difficulties; one size rarely fits all. If you are determined to provide the T-shirts, check the local dollar store for the best prices. The only other cost is sandpaper, which should be priced between $1 and $2 per sheet.

Time: Beyond purchasing and gathering any necessary ingredients and creating a sample, there is no preparation time for this program. The program should last 45 minutes to one hour.

Early Bird Specials: Fruitcake, Time Saver

Serving Size: Twelve to twenty 5- to 12-year-olds, with a separate program for each age-appropriate group. Registration is recommended, especially if you are providing the T-shirts.

Staff Size: One staff member.

Ingredients

Crayons

At least two 1 inch paintbrushes

One piece of fine sandpaper per child, plus one for the sample T-shirt and a few extra pieces for the inevitable mistakes

(Optional) One white cotton or polyester cotton blend T-shirt per registered child

Two white cotton or polyester cotton blend T-shirts to be used to create the samples

One piece of flat cardboard that has never been split or folded per registered child (the piece of cardboard should be slightly larger than the sheet of sandpaper)

Iron (to be used by the staff member)

Ironing board

Paper towels

Masking tape

Scrap paper

Pencils

T-shirt *Transfer*-mations Handout
   (see Appendix B on
   page 207)

(Optional) Fabric markers in a variety
   of colors

(Optional) Mirrors

Preheat

1. Purchase and/or gather the necessary ingredients.
2. Bring in your own or borrow an iron and ironing board.
3. Every iron is different. Create a sample T-shirt using the instructions outlined below. This will familiarize you with the process and help you judge the proper iron setting and the correct amount of ironing time. Be sure to use the same brand of crayons and colors and the same grade of sandpaper in the creation of your sample as you will provide for the children. This will ensure consistent results for the program participants.
   a. Place the piece of sandpaper on your work surface textured side up.
   b. Create a colorful design or picture on the textured side of the sandpaper with the crayons. Do not use crayons that are the same color as the T-shirt as they will not transfer (e.g., clouds colored with white crayons will not show up on a white T-shirt). Any writing must be done backward as it will be reversed when the transfer process is complete. You will need to press down hard when coloring, to leave enough crayon on the sandpaper to clearly see the design. For more vibrant results, go over the design multiple times, creating as thick a coating of crayon as possible.
   c. Preheat the iron on the cotton setting.
   d. When your design is finished, use the 1 inch paintbrush to brush off any excess crayon wax from the areas of the sandpaper that are not part of the design. This prevents any stray wax from being transferred onto the T-shirt.
   e. Slide the T-shirt onto the ironing board with the front of the T-shirt lying flat, face up on the ironing board and the back of the T-shirt beneath the ironing board so that the back of the T-shirt does not accidentally receive any of the crayon transfer. However, if you want to place the design on the back of the T-shirt, reverse the T-shirt's placement on the ironing board.
   f. Place the piece of cardboard between the ironing board and the underside of the front of the T-shirt. The cardboard should be centered under the T-shirt where the design will be transferred.
   g. Center the sandpaper design crayon side down on top of the T-shirt and cardboard.
   h. Place two paper towels over the sandpaper.
   i. Iron on the paper towel for 30 seconds.
   j. Without moving the T-shirt, carefully lift up one corner of the sandpaper to make sure that your design has transferred. If your design has not fully transferred, iron in 10-second increments, checking between each, until the

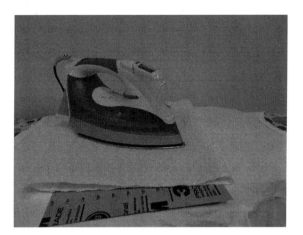

transfer process is complete. After the first 30 seconds, if the color has not transferred at all, you may wish to adjust the iron's setting.

k. Remove the paper towels and sandpaper and place two new paper towels on top of the design now transferred to the T-shirt and iron to remove any excess wax.

l. Although the T-shirt looks ready to wear, the color must be set before wearing. To set the color, the T-shirt must be placed in the dryer for 20 minutes.

4. Color a second design on sandpaper to provide a demonstration for the beginning of your T-shirt *Transfer*-mations program.

5. Arrange the supplies on tables in order of use: T-shirts, sandpaper, crayons and, if desired, fabric markers to add further elements to the areas of the T-shirt not included in the transfer.

6. Designate one area of the room as your ironing station and set up the iron, ironing board, and cardboard there. Place a piece of masking tape on the floor a few steps back from the ironing board to provide a safe area from which the children may watch.

7. Photocopy one copy of the T-shirt *Transfer*-mations Handout in Appendix B on page 207 per registered child and fill in the fabric marker setting directions in the blank provided according to your fabric marker manufacturer's suggestions.

Bake

1. Explain the T-shirt *Transfer*-mations program to the participants.

2. Create a second sample, using the pre-colored design on sandpaper and the directions in Preheat 3a–l, in front of the children. Explain each of the steps as you demonstrate. Have the children help by counting off the ironing time out loud as a group.

3. Be sure to explain that the image transferred to the T-shirt will be reversed. Any lettering would have to be written backward in order to be read. Hand out scrap paper to the participants to allow them to practice writing backward. If you desire, you may also provide them each with mirrors (or they may share one or more mirrors) to check the accuracy of their backward-writing attempts.

4. Instruct the children to take one white T-shirt (if you are providing them), one piece of sandpaper, and a selection of crayons from the art supply table back to their work area.

5. Ask the children to place their piece of sandpaper on their work area textured side up and begin coloring their designs.

6. Once the children have started to color, preheat the iron on the cotton setting (or the setting that worked best on your sample T-shirt).

7. As they finish their designs, invite the program participants to line up near the iron station. The children will want to see the transfer process, but in order to

avoid an accident, ask the children to stand behind the piece of masking tape on the floor. If the children enjoyed counting off the ironing time as a group, ask them to do so again individually.

8. Reiterate that although the T-shirt looks ready to wear, it must be placed in the dryer for 20 minutes to set the color. Let the participants know that you will send home a letter to their parents or caregivers with instructions for finishing the process of setting the color.

9. If you are using the optional fabric markers, allow the children to add designs or lettering to their T-shirts with the fabric markers. Instruct the children to follow the specific directions provided in the T-shirt *Transfer*-mations Handout to heat set the portion of the design made with the fabric markers.

T-shirt *Transfer*-mations is a program that lends itself to so many uses. Why not send a copy of the entire set of directions and some suggestions for usage (e.g., birthday party, family reunion, vacation souvenir) to the parents or caregivers. The directions and suggestions are included in the T-shirt *Transfer*-mations Handout in Appendix B on page 207.

Variations: There are multiple variations for T-shirt *Transfer*-mations. You needn't choose just one. You can use this project to have children create book bags to be sold with the proceeds benefiting the library or the Friends of the Library. You would need to purchase blank cloth book bags without a coating of any kind. Before investing in large quantities, purchase one blank bag and test to be sure that your image transfers properly. This program may also be added or served as a substitution for one of the projects in the *Maker Marketplace* program on page 106.

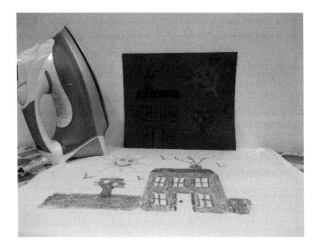

A parent-child book group would be a great place to present this program. The duos can create matching or individual looks. Your chess club can make matching T-shirts. As a bonus, when the kids wear them to school, or the parents wear them around town, the library will receive free advertising.

Leftovers: If you have purchased mirrors for use in this program, you may use them in the *It's All about Me* program on page 103.

Garnish of Books to Be Displayed during the Program

Hantman, Clea. *I Wanna Make My Own Clothes*. New York: Aladdin Paperbacks, 2006.

Scheunemann, Pam. *Cool Fabric Projects: Creative Ways to Upcycle Your Trash into Treasure*. Minneapolis, MN: ABDO Publishing Company, 2013.

Sirrine, Carol. *Cool Crafts with Old Jeans: Green Projects for Resourceful Kids*. Mankato, MN: Capstone Press, 2010.

Warwick, Ellen. *Injeanuity*. Toronto: Kids Can Press, 2006.

23

Do Play with Your Food

Children are told not to play with their food. This program offers a creative opportunity for children to do just that. What may outwardly look like simply making a mess is actually a sensory art experience. There will be three food art exploration stations: food collage, pie crust clay, and paintsicles. The children will rotate among the stations in small groups. Be warned, art can be messy and food art can be *really* messy. Make sure everyone, including you, dresses for a mess.

Cost: This program should cost less than $100.

Time: Beyond purchasing and/or gathering the ingredients, the only preparation for this program is creating an inspirational slideshow of the work of food artists.

Early Bird Special: Fruitcake

Serving Size: This hour-long program works best with 12 children ages 5 to 10, with a separate program for each age-appropriate group. To accommodate more children, add one staff member for every four additional participants. Registration should be required for this program in order to estimate the necessary ingredients and to obtain allergy information to avoid serious food allergies or reactions.

Staff Size: Two staff members.

Ingredients (Listed by Station)

As indicated by the list of suggested ingredients, this program involves the use of food and/or edible ingredients. The ingredients included are suggestions based on a group of participants who have no known food allergies. It is your responsibility to adjust the ingredients list based on the medical needs of the participants in your program.

For this program, you will create three unique food art stations. Each station should have its own table with all the food art supplies arranged so that children can serve themselves.

In addition to the individual ingredients listed by station below, you will need:

One disposable foil lasagna pan or empty cardboard shipping box per registered child
Marking pen
Self-adhesive labels
Plastic tablecloths
Baby wipes and paper towels (to be used in cleanup)
Inspirational slideshow of food artists

Food Collage Station

White poster board
White frosting (two cans for every 12 children)
Plastic knives
Dry food (e.g., cereal, beans, pasta, candy)
Disposable foam, paper or plastic bowls

Pie Crust Clay Station

Tubes or boxes of ready-made pie crusts found in your grocer's refrigerator
    case (½–1 single pie crust per registered child)
Knife (to be used by the staff member)

Paintsicles Station

Three ice cube trays
Plastic wrap
One sharp knife (to be used by the staff member)
36 craft sticks
Light or clear liquid or juice (e.g., water, white grape juice, lemonade)
Food coloring
Spoons (one spoon for each food coloring combination)
One piece of white paper per registered child

Preheat

1. Create a slideshow of food artists and their works to provide inspiration for the children in their culinary creations. Examples of artists to include in your slideshow are Jason Mecier, Jim Victor, and Carl Warner. Mecier is famous for his food mosaic portraits of celebrities, Victor sculpts with butter, chocolate and cheese, and Warner creates detailed foodscapes.

2. Purchase and/or collect the necessary ingredients.

3. To create the Paintsicles:
    a. Pour the water, white grape juice, apple juice, or lemonade into the ice cube trays. Be sure not to completely fill the individual compartments before adding the food coloring as the water from full compartments will spread, ruining any color combinations you may create with the food coloring.
    b. Add a tiny drop of food coloring into each cube compartment. To increase the variety of colors offered, mix your food coloring (e.g., blue and yellow

to create green) on a spoon and add half the mixture into one cube. Be sure to include a variety of colors in each ice cube tray. NOTE: You may need to add more red food coloring than other colors to create a true red or to create the proper mix for the other colors.

c. Cover the ice cube trays with plastic wrap.

d. In the center of each ice cube compartment, insert the tip of the sharp knife into the plastic wrap to make a small hole.

e. Insert one craft stick into the hole of each ice cube compartment, creating a paintbrush-like handle.

f. Carefully place the ice cube trays into the freezer. If you have trouble getting your craft sticks to stand straight and tall, let the ice cube tray freeze for 15 to 30 minutes and straighten the craft sticks. Check the ice cube tray periodically during the freezing process and straighten any craft sticks that may have fallen.

4. Cut the white poster board into pieces no larger than 8½ inches by 11 inches. This allows the children to create a manageable work of art in the time allotted.

5. With the marking pen, write each child's name on one self-adhesive label and affix it to one disposable foil lasagna pan or one empty cardboard shipping box.

6. Arrange the tables with ample room between stations. Cover the tables with the plastic tablecloths.

7. Use one table per station, one table for replacement supplies, and two tables to place the disposable foil lasagna pans or empty cardboard shipping boxes upon. These pans or boxes will hold the children's drying artwork while they move from station to station.

8. Pour the dry food for the food collages into the disposable bowls. Use one bowl for each item.

9. If desired, cut the individual pie crusts in half.

10. Put the correct supplies on each station's table.

11. Remove one ice cube tray at a time 15 minutes before each group arrives for their turn at the Paintsicle station. The ice cubes need to be wet, not melted, in order provide a fluid stroke of paint.

Bake

1. Present the food artist slideshow to the participants to provide inspiration.

2. Explain the different activities to be found at each station.

3. Divide the children into small groups so that they may rotate easily among the stations.

4. Directions by station (children should spend approximately 15 minutes at each station):

a. "Food Collage"—Give each child one piece of white poster board. Instruct each child to spread white frosting on the poster board. The frosting will act as glue. Have the children decorate the poster board with the dry food. Instruct them to lightly press the dry food into the frosting. Have the children place their artwork in their labeled pan or box on the designated drying tables before moving on to the next station.

b. "Pie Crust Clay"—Give each child ½ or 1 pie crust. Let their imaginations guide their sculpting experience. Have the children place their artwork in their labeled pan or box on the designated drying tables before moving on to the next station.

c. "Paintsicles"—Give each child a piece of white paper. Carefully lift the plastic wrap off the ice cube tray. Ask the children to choose the colors they wish to paint with and hand out the "Paintsicles" accordingly. Instruct the children to use the "Paintsicles" as if they were paintbrushes. Have the children place their artwork in their labeled pan or box on the designated drying tables before moving on to the next station.

The *Do Play with Your Food* program is the perfect activity in which children discover that art supplies are not only found in the art store. This program strengthens participants' observational skills, allowing them to view the world around them as a place of beauty and providing them with a new perspective of limitless means of expression.

Variations: Choose your favorite food art station and pair it with a book for a deliciously artistic book discussion. For the younger crowd, choose a book like Freymann's *How Are You Peeling?*. For older children, consider pairing this program with a book discussion of *The Candymakers* by Wendy Mass. Book discussion questions for *The Candymakers* are available in Appendix A on page 200.

Fusion Box: To add a taste of technology, try the app Snackerdoodle. This app allows users to choose from 150 kinds of food to create their own tasty masterpieces. You can even use the Snackerdoodle app to decorate your own photo with macaroni. This app can be used alone, as an additional food station, or paired with one of the books suggested in the "Variations" section for another delicious book discussion program.

Recipe Substitution: Use the Snackerdoodle app recommended in the "Fusion Box" section in conjunction with a unit on nutrition. Instruct the children to make healthy food masterpieces to reinforce the concepts introduced in the unit. Be sure to add Guiseppe Archimboldo, an Italian painter best known for creating portraits composed of fruits and vegetables, to your inspirational slideshow.

Garnish of Books to Be Displayed during the Program

Bloch, Serge. *You Are What You Eat and Other Mealtime Hazards*. New York: Sterling, 2010.

Bredeson, Carmen. *Weird but True Food*. Berkeley Heights, NJ: Enslow Publishers, 2012.

Freymann, Saxton. *How Are You Peeling? Foods with Moods*. New York: Arthur A. Levine Books, 1999.

Gutman, Dan. *Mrs. Yonkers Is Bonkers!* New York: HarperTrophy, 2007.

Silverstein, Alvin, Virginia B. Silverstein, Laura Silverstein Nunn, and Gerald Kelley. *Chocolate Ants, Maggot Cheese, and More: The Yucky Food Book*. Berkeley Heights, NJ: Enslow Publishers, 2011.

Speck, Katie and Paul Rátz de Tagyos. *Maybelle and the Haunted Cupcake*. New York: Henry Holt, 2012.

Warner, Carl. *A World of Food*. New York: Abrams Books for Young Readers, 2012.

24

Fondant Game

Knead up a tasty twist for your book discussion of *The Candymakers* by Wendy Mass, with a recipe of no-bake fondant dough and a dash of creativity. Children will design and create working mazes out of fondant dough and use chocolate-covered malted milk balls as marbles to navigate through their mazes. The *Fondant Game* program is sure to stir up a batch of fun.

Cost: The most expensive part of this program is the purchase of the listed food ingredients. Since food prices vary by region and retail establishment, expect this program to cost between $100 and $125.

Time: Most of the preparation time will be split between reading *The Candymakers*, preparing the fondant maze sample and pre-cutting the *Fondant Game* cardboard, wax paper pieces and, if desired, poster board. If you must Interlibrary Loan copies of the book yourself and/or choose not to use the discussion questions in Appendix A on page 200, but instead create your own set of book discussion questions, you will need to allow additional preparation time. The program should last 45 minutes to one hour.

Serving Size: Twelve to fifteen 8- to 12-year-olds. Registration is required in order to obtain the correct number of copies of *The Candymakers*, to obtain allergy information to avoid serious food allergies or reactions and to estimate the necessary ingredients.

Staff Size: One staff member.

Ingredients to make one individual 3 pound portion of fondant dough

As indicated by the list of suggested ingredients, this program involves the use of food and/ or edible ingredients. The ingredients included are suggestions based on a group of participants who have no known food allergies. It is your responsibility to adjust the ingredients list based on the medical needs of the participants in your program.

One copy of the book *The Candymakers* for each registered child to be available at the time of registration plus an additional copy for the staff member

One cup of light corn syrup per registered child plus one additional cup to create the sample

One cup of shortening per registered child plus one additional cup to create a sample

One half of a teaspoon of salt per registered child plus an additional half of a teaspoon to create the sample

One teaspoon of clear vanilla extract or water per registered child plus one additional teaspoon to create the sample

One 2 pound bag of confectioners' sugar per registered child plus an additional 2 pounds to create the sample

(Optional) One large zippered plastic bag per registered child to be used if you are purchasing the confectioner's sugar in any quantity other than 2 pounds

One extra large mixing bowl per registered child

One wooden or metal spoon per registered child

Two 1 cup measuring cups

One ½ teaspoon measuring spoon

One 1 teaspoon measuring spoon

One roll of wax paper

One plastic knife per registered child

One bamboo skewer per registered child

One metal spoon per registered child

One foam, paper or plastic plate per registered child

One disposable rectangular or circular disposable foil pan per child plus one additional pan to create the sample

One cardboard rectangle or circle cut neatly to fit inside the rectangular or circular disposable foil pan per registered child plus one additional piece of cardboard to create the sample

Cellophane tape

Utility knife or box cutter (to be used by the staff member before the program)

One bag, box, or carton of chocolate-covered malted milk balls to provide at least one to each registered child plus one additional chocolate-covered malted milk ball for the sample

(Optional) Food coloring

One piece of poster board cut to the size of the disposable rectangular or circular foil pan per registered child plus one additional pre-cut poster board for the sample

Pencils and erasers

One pair of scissors per registered child

Plastic tablecloths

Baby wipes and paper towels (to be used in cleanup)

(Optional) One piece of tracing paper per registered child

(Optional) One ruler per registered child

Inspirational maze design slideshow

Preheat

1. Interlibrary Loan enough copies of *The Candymakers* to accommodate the Serving Size, plus an additional copy for the staff member.
2. Photocopy the list of *The Candymakers* book discussion questions provided in Appendix A on page 200 or create your own list of questions.
3. Research maze designs either online or in books to provide the children with examples of successful maze line placement.
4. Create an inspirational slideshow showcasing a variety of simple maze design images.

5. If desired, choose a few examples of simple maze designs from books or print several online examples for participants to trace if they are unable or do not wish to create their own designs.

6. Purchase and/or gather the necessary ingredients.

7. If you do not choose to use a stencil to create your maze design, skip to Preheat 9.

8. If you wish to create a stencil to use to make your maze, sketch a maze design the size of the disposable foil pan onto the poster board. A ruler may be used to help create a more precise, sharper line. Be sure the maze design lines are larger than the width of the chocolate-covered malted milk balls. To simplify the process, you may trace a maze design found in a book or printed online onto a piece of tracing paper. Affix the tracing paper to the poster board with loops of cellophane tape in the four corners of either the tracing paper or the poster board. Cut out the inside of the maze design lines on the tracing paper and/or the poster board in order to create a stencil to place on top of the fondant dough.

9. Create a sample fondant maze to familiarize yourself with the process and to show to the program participants:

    a. In an extra large mixing bowl, stir together one cup of light corn syrup and one cup of shortening.

    b. Mix in ½ teaspoon of salt and one teaspoon of clear vanilla extract or water.

    c. Gradually add the 2 pounds of confectioners' sugar and mix until the fondant dough is stiff. If stirring becomes too difficult, you may wish to switch to kneading the mixture with your hands halfway through adding the confectioners' sugar.

    d. If you are using food coloring, add a few drops in and mix. If the color is too light, add more food coloring, one drop at a time, mixing between additions, until you achieve the desired color.

    e. Knead the mixture with your hands. If the fondant dough is too sticky, knead in more confectioners' sugar.

    f. Continue kneading for six to eight minutes, until the fondant dough is smooth.

    g. Cover one pre-cut cardboard rectangle or circle with a piece of wax paper slightly longer than the cardboard. Fold the excess wax paper underneath the cardboard and secure the wax paper to the underside of the cardboard with cellophane tape. Sprinkle the wax paper with confectioners' sugar.

    h. Place the fondant dough onto the confectioners' sugar dusted wax paper and spread it evenly with your hands so that it covers the entire surface of the wax paper. To create a smooth look, hold two fingers out flat and rub them across the fondant dough. The fondant dough should be at least ½ inch high in order to contain the chocolate-covered malted milk ball marble within the maze.

    i. If you do not choose to use a stencil to create your maze design, roll a chocolate-covered malted milk ball on the fondant dough to create the outline of your maze design.

    j. If you are using a stencil, place the poster board maze design stencil atop the fondant dough.

k. Using the plastic knife, follow the outlines of the path of the chocolate-covered malted milk ball or stencil to mark the lines of the maze design in the fondant dough. If you make a mistake in the creation of your maze design, temporarily remove the stencil and smooth the fondant dough with your fingers, the knife, and/or spoon.

l. Once the outline of the maze design is cut into the fondant dough, scoop out the fondant dough in between the maze design lines. The fondant dough may peel out all in one piece. If this does not happen, dig out the middle of the maze design line with the spoon, then switch to the knife to cut off a precise wall in the edges of the fondant dough.

m. Transfer the removed fondant dough to one foam, paper or plastic plate. Save this extra fondant dough in case you need to make any adjustments to the maze at a later time.

n. Place the cardboard with the fondant dough maze on top of it into one disposable rectangular or circular foil pan.

o. Add the chocolate-covered malted milk ball marble to the starting point and test your maze to be sure that the marble runs smoothly through the design. Make any necessary adjustments to the fondant dough maze by squeezing the dough in any areas that are too tight for the chocolate-covered malted milk ball to travel through or by adding extra fondant dough to any area which is not tall enough to contain the chocolate-covered malted milk ball.

p. Store any unused fondant dough in an airtight container either at room temperature or in the refrigerator.

10. If you have purchased confectioners' sugar in any quantity other than two pounds, for each registered child, measure out 2 pounds of confectioners' sugar and place it into a zippered plastic bag.

11. On the day of the program, cover the tables in the program room with plastic tablecloths.

12. Arrange the ingredients on the supply table in like groups, with the dough creation ingredients on one end of the table and the maze design ingredients on the other.

13. Place a pre-cut poster board rectangle or circle, a pencil, and a pair of scissors at each participant's work station.

Bake

1. Gather the children in your favorite book discussion formation.
2. Explain the components of the program to the participants.
3. Hold *The Candymakers* book discussion.
4. Present the inspirational maze design slideshow.
5. Discuss the steps used to create the maze. Ask the children to sketch a rectangular or circular maze design onto the poster board. Be sure the maze design lines are wider than a chocolate-covered malted milk ball. If any of the participants are unable to create their own maze design, offer them the tracing paper and a choice of maze design examples to copy. Have the children cut

out the inside of the maze design lines in order to create a stencil to place on top of the fondant dough. Allow 10 to 15 minutes of the program time for the participants to complete their maze design stencils.

6. Instruct the children to take one extra large mixing bowl and one metal spoon from the supply table.
7. Fill each child's bowl with one cup of corn syrup and one cup of shortening. Instruct the children to return to their work station and stir the mixture until it is well blended.
8. The children should then come back to the supply table. Place the ½ teaspoon of salt and 1 teaspoon of clear vanilla extract or water into each child's bowl. Instruct the children to take the bowl, spoon, and one bag of confectioners' sugar back to their work station.
9. Ask the children to follow the steps in Preheat 9c–o as a group.
10. Walk around the room, answering any questions that may arise.
11. Near the end of the program, explain to the children that they should store their fondant dough games in the refrigerator.

Throughout history, mazes have been constructed from bushes, hay bales, bricks, books, crops, cardboard and bamboo skewers, and/or plastic drinking straws (see *Cardboard aMAZEment* on page 25) and now, fondant dough. Because navigating a marble through a maze requires concentration, the *Fondant Game* program is truly food for thought!

Fusion Box: Provide examples of successful maze line placement design using maze apps on your library's iPad(s). Mouse Maze, Fairytale 123 Maze, and Magic Maze are examples of interesting maze designs from which the children may take inspiration.

Leftovers: Use the Mouse Maze, Fairytale 123 Maze, and Magic Maze from this program's "Fusion Box" section in the *Cardboard aMAZEment* program on page 25.

Garnish of Books to Be Displayed during the Program

Mass, Wendy. *The Candymakers*. New York: Little, Brown, 2010.

Maurer, Tracy Nelson. *Cupcakes, Cookies and Cakes*. Vero Beach, FL: Rourke Publishing, 2010.

Munro, Roxie. *Amazement Park*. San Francisco: Chronicle Books, 2005.

Munro, Roxie. *Ecomazes: Twelve Earth Adventures*. New York: Sterling Publishing Company, Inc., 2010.

Nilsen, Anna. *Mousemazia: An Amazing Dream House Maze*. Cambridge, MA: Candlewick Press, 2000.

Tuminelly, Nancy. *Cool Sugar-Free Recipes: Delicious and Fun Foods without Refined Sugar*. Minneapolis, MN: ABDO Publishing, 2013.

25

Food Detectives

While a bloodhound uses his sense of smell to sniff out clues, the participants in the *Food Detectives* program will use their senses of taste, sight, and smell to decode the ingredients of a balanced meal. Besides the opportunity to eat dessert first, the children will learn about vegetarian and vegan food choices, and about the differences between conventionally grown and organically grown foods.

Cost: The purchase of the listed food ingredients is the most expensive part of the cost of this program. Since food prices vary by region and retail establishment, expect this program to cost between $100 and $150.

Time: The bulk of the preparation time for this program will be spent purchasing and preparing the food products for consumption. The program should last approximately 60 minutes to 90 minutes.

Serving Size: Twelve to sixteen 9- to 12-year-olds. Registration should be required in order to obtain allergy information to avoid serious food allergies or reactions and to estimate the necessary ingredients. In order to present this program to include children ages 7 and 8, see the "Variation" section at the end of this recipe.

Staff Size: One to two staff members.

Ingredients

As indicated by the list of suggested ingredients, this program involves the use of food and/ or edible ingredients. The ingredients included are suggestions based on a group of participants who have no known food allergies. It is your responsibility to adjust the ingredients list based on the medical needs of the participants in your program.

An assortment of popular candy bars

Two foam, paper or plastic plates per registered child

Kitchen knife (to be used by the staff member before the program)

One plastic knife

(Optional) Slideshow of the cross-sections of popular candy bars

Blenders (at least one blender for every four registered children. If you are unable to borrow multiple blenders, see the "Variation" section at the end of this recipe)

One plastic scraper for every four registered children

One large box of bathroom-size disposable cups containing at least 75 cups

Four ripe bananas plus two extra for the inevitable "unappealing" bruises and fingerprints

Four 6 to 8 ounce containers of vanilla or plain cow's milk yogurt

Four 6 to 8 ounce containers of vanilla or plain soy milk yogurt

Four 6 to 8 ounce containers of vanilla or plain almond milk yogurt

1 quart of cow's milk

1 quart of soy milk (refrigerated only; not shelf stable)

1 quart of almond milk (refrigerated only; not shelf stable)

12 large foam, paper, or plastic disposable cups

Six cups of frozen fruit (use packages containing individual fruits, not one large package containing a mixture of fruits)

One ½ cup measuring cup for every four registered children

One ¼ cup measuring cup for every four registered children

Four plastic lined garbage bins

Two foam, paper or plastic bowls per registered child, half of which should be one color or design and the other half another color or design

A variety of in-season salad ingredients, pre-washed and conventionally grown

The same variety of in-season salad ingredients, pre-washed and organically grown

One large bowl for each conventionally grown salad ingredient and another for each organically grown salad ingredient

Serving spoons and/or forks for each salad ingredient

A selection of two to three salad dressings

At least one plastic fork per registered child

Microwave oven(s)

16 chicken nuggets

16 vegetarian "chicken" substitute nuggets

Two heavy-duty microwavable paper plates or microwave safe dinner plates large enough to hold 16 nuggets each

Two napkins per registered child, half of which should be one color and the other half another color

One commercially filled plastic water bottle per registered child

Plastic tablecloths

Napkins of any color or design except those used at the nugget station

Baby wipes and paper towels (to be used in cleanup)

One copy of the *Food Detectives* Score Sheet you created or the *Food Detectives* Score Sheet (see Appendix C on page 218) per registered child

Four copies of the Secret Smoothie Recipe for the *Food Detectives* Program (see Appendix C on page 218), laminated, if possible

Pencils with erasers

Scrap paper

One permanent marker

Preheat

1. Research vegetarianism and veganism, and conventionally versus organically grown foods so that you can explain these concepts to the children as they move through the stations.

2. Decide if you want to offer actual candy bars for the children to taste or if you will perform an online search for the cross-sections of a variety of candy bars to be used in a candy bar guessing game slideshow or if you will use a combination of the two. The slideshow is not only cost-effective but also eliminates the necessary accommodations for children with some food allergies. Today, peanut allergies are very common. To avoid peanut allergies, consider placing the peanut-filled candy bars you'd like to include in the program in the slideshow and using actual candy bars that do not contain nuts for taste-testing purposes.

3. Create your own Food Detectives Score Sheet or use the *Food Detectives* Score Sheet provided in Appendix C on page 218, Photocopy or print at least one *Food Detectives* Score Sheet per registered child.

4. If you not providing physical sample of all of the candy bars, create a numbered slideshow of cross-sections of a variety of candy bars. Either reveal the answers in the slideshow or fill out a master *Food Detectives* Score Sheet with the answers so that you may verbally reveal the correct answers to the program participants.

5. Purchase and/or gather the necessary ingredients.

6. Photocopy and, if possible, laminate four copies of the Secret Smoothie Recipe for the *Food Detectives* Program in Appendix C on page 218.

7. Using the permanent marker, write the name of each registered child onto the label of one commercially filled plastic water bottle. Next, write the words "cow's milk" onto 4 of the 12 large foam, paper or plastic disposable cups. Repeat the process for "soy milk" and "almond milk."

8. On the day of the program:
    a. Cover the supply tables with plastic tablecloths.
    b. Place the napkins of any color on each of the tables at each food station.
    c. If you are using actual candy bars, place an identical selection of candy bar slices on a plate for each registered child. If the name of the candy bar is etched into the chocolate, use a plastic knife to scrape off the name.
    d. Put one pre-labeled water bottle, one *Food Detectives* Score Sheet and the pencils with erasers for each registered child on the candy bar table. If you are only using the candy bar slideshow, arrange the water bottles on the first station at which the children will eat. NOTE: If you are not starting the program at the candy bar table, arrange the water bottles, *Food Detectives* Score Sheets, and the pencils with erasers on the first station at which the children will eat.
    e. Position the blenders on sturdy tables close to electrical outlets.
    f. Place one ½ cup measuring cup, one ¼ cup measuring cup and one Secret Smoothie Recipe by each blender. Arrange the plastic lined garbage bins near each blender table. The participants will scrape out the remnants of one Secret Smoothie into these plastic lined garbage bins before creating

another. Place one cup labeled "cow's milk," one cup labeled "soy milk," and one cup labeled "almond milk" onto each blender station table.

g. Place each type of salad ingredient in its own large bowl. Put each of the bowls into a refrigerator. Be sure to note which bowls contain organically grown ingredients and which bowls contain conventionally grown ingredients.

h. Place the microwave oven(s) in the program room. Put the heavy-duty microwavable paper plates or microwave safe dinner plates and two stacks of the different colored napkins on the table next to the microwave oven(s).

9. Moments before the program begins:
a. If you have decided to use actual candy bars, place the plates with the cross-sections of the candy bars onto the candy table.

b. Bring in the Secret Smoothie ingredients and divide them so that each blender table has all types of milk, poured into the appropriately labeled cups, yogurt, two choices of frozen fruit, and one banana.

c. Arrange two distinctly separate salad tables buffet style. One table should offer all of the organically grown ingredients and another table all of the conventionally grown ingredients so that the children will be able to distinguish which type of ingredients were in their salad bowls at the time of the big reveal. Place all of the red bowls (or any other color or design) on the table with the organically grown ingredients and all of the blue bowls (or any other color or design) on the table with the conventionally grown ingredients.

d. Arrange the plastic forks and salad dressings on each salad table. Place at least one serving spoon and/or fork into each ingredient bowl. You will instruct the children to fill their salad bowl with salad ingredients from the table from which they took their bowls.

e. Remove both the chicken nuggets and the vegetarian chicken substitute nuggets from the freezer and set them by the microwave oven(s). Place the nuggets onto the microwavable plates, one type of nugget per plate, and remove the labeled boxes from the program room.

Bake

1. Introduce the *Food Detectives* program and explain to the program participants what they will do at each of the four food stations.

2. Distribute a pencil with an eraser and one *Food Detectives* Score Sheet to each registered child. Instruct the children how to keep track of their conclusions for each of the food stations.

3. Gather the children around the candy bar table.
a. Present the candy bar guessing game slideshow and/or give the children the pre-prepared plates of candy bar slices.

b. Instruct the children to use their senses of sight and smell before sampling each candy bar.

c. Ask the children to take a sip from the water bottle labeled with their name between candy bars slices in order to cleanse their palates.

d. Remind the children to record their results on the *Food Detectives* Score Sheet before moving on to the next food station.

4. Ask the children to divide into groups of four with each group gathering around one blender.

   a. Explain to the children that they will be making Secret Smoothie Recipes for each other using the Secret Smoothie Recipe on the laminated card located at each blender table.

   b. Instruct the participants that while one group member turns his or her back, the remaining three group members will choose a type of milk, a type of yogurt, and a type of frozen fruit and use these ingredients, in addition to the banana pieces, to create a unique Secret Smoothie.

   c. The three group members will then record the ingredients used to make the Secret Smoothie on a piece of scrap paper.

   d. Once the Secret Smoothie is blended, the group member with his or her back turned will taste the Secret Smoothie, deduce which specific ingredients were used, and write the ingredients on their *Food Detectives* Score Sheet.

   e. After guessing, the remaining group members will reveal the actual ingredients used to make the Secret Smoothie.

   f. The person who has guessed the ingredients will compare his or her answers to what was used in the actual Secret Smoothie and record the number of correct answers on their *Food Detectives* Score Sheet.

   g. Repeat this process until each group member has tasted the Secret Smoothie concocted just for them.

   h. Between each new Secret Smoothie, instruct the children to use a plastic scraper to empty the Secret Smoothie residue left in the blender into the plastic lined garbage bins located near each blender station.

   i. Remind the children that before moving to the next station, they should cleanse their palettes with a sip of water.

5. Ask the children to create two salads, each made from the ingredients of their choice, but emphasize that they should be careful to take each salad bowl from the table from which they take their ingredients.

   a. Explain to the children the reason it is important to take the ingredients from the table from which they chose their bowl is because this will allow them to determine whether the ingredients are organically grown or conventionally grown.

b. Allot the children ample time to taste their salads and record their conclusions on their *Food Detectives* Score Sheets. Remind the children to cleanse their palates with a sip of water between tasting the two salads.
6. Gather the children around the microwave oven(s) and cook the chicken nuggets or vegetarian chicken substitute nuggets.
   a. While the nuggets are cooking, tell the children that one of the nuggets they will be eating is made from chicken and one is not.
   b. Explain that they must guess which nugget is chicken and which nugget is made from a vegetarian chicken substitute.
   c. Place samples of the first nuggets on one color of napkin.
   d. While the children are sampling the first batch of nuggets and recording their conclusions, cook the second batch of nuggets.
   e. Repeat the tasting and recording process with the second batch of nuggets on the second color of napkins, reminding the children to take a sip of water to cleanse their palates in between nuggets.
7. Instruct the participants to tally their *Food Detectives* Score Sheets to receive their official results. Compare their results to find out who is the "Greatest Food Detective."

The participants of the *Food Detectives* program will have fun while learning about food options they may not have been previously exposed to. The child detectives will be surprised how good almond milk and other nontraditional foods actually taste.

Variation: If you are unable to borrow more than one blender or are presenting this program to a younger audience who should not operate blenders themselves, consider presenting this program in a game show format. Children may compete individually or in teams of Food Detectives. Since you will only be creating one Secret Smoothie that all the children will taste, you may wish to add an additional food station. For example, have the children try to discern which small piece of bread is traditional white bread and which is white whole grain bread. This variation eliminates the need for the *Food Detectives* Score Sheets as you will be announcing the answers as you go. You may, however, wish to keep track of the participants' scores on a piece of paper, an easel, or project the scores from a computer screen.

Recipe Substitution: Partner with a health or home economics teacher on a nutrition unit.

Leftovers: If you have selected cherry tomatoes or baby carrots to offer in your salads, you may use the leftovers in *The Very Healthy Butterfly* program on page 172.

Garnish of Books to Be Displayed during the Program

Eamer, Claire. *The World in Your Lunch Box: The Wacky History and Weird Science of Everyday Foods*. Toronto: Annick Press, 2012.
Tuminelly, Nancy. *Cool Nut-Free recipes: Delicious and Fun Foods without Nuts*. Minneapolis, MN: ABDO Publishing Company, 2013.
Wagner, Lisa. *Cool World Cooking: Fun and Tasty Recipes for Kids!* Minneapolis, MN: Scarletta Junior Readers, 2013.
Whitmore, Courtney Dial. *Candy Making for Kids*. Layton, UT: Gibbs Smith, 2012.
Witherspoon, Jack. *Twist It Up: More than 60 Delicious Recipes from an Inspiring Young Chef*. San Francisco, CA: Chronicle Books, 2011.

26

Pet Spa

Help children change their pet's day from *ruff* to *purr-fect* with the creation of dog treats, cat toys, and/or a stuffed animal carrier. Children, working at their own pace, may choose to complete as many of the three projects they desire. Participants of the *Pet Spa* program may become their pampered pet's "top dog" or "cat's pajamas."

Cost: The three individual crafts included in this program may require multiple purchases and a fully stocked craft closet. The cost of food, fabric, and carrying boxes varies by geographic location, but the total cost for the program should not exceed $100. To lower the cost, you may wish to choose an alternate craft(s) made from supplies you already own.

Time: Most of the preparation time for this program will be spent purchasing, gathering, and preparing the necessary ingredients. This program is lengthier than most, approximately 60 minutes to 90 minutes, due to the multiple offerings and the option for the children to complete more than one project during the allotted program time.

Early Bird Special: Smorgasbord

Serving Size: Twelve to fifteen 8- to 12-year-olds. Registration is recommended in order to estimate the necessary supplies and to obtain allergy information to avoid serious food allergies or reactions.

Staff Size: Three staff members, each one facilitating a single project.

Craft Project #1: **Trail Mix Dog Treats**

Special thanks to Pastries 4 Pets, an award-winning dog bakery in Stafford Springs, Connecticut, for sharing its "Trail Mix Dog Treats" recipe for this program. Pastries 4 Pets' contribution to this program is an example of a library-community partnership. Is there a local business you can think of to partner with?

Ingredients

As indicated by the list of suggested ingredients, this program involves the use of food and/or edible ingredients. The ingredients included are suggestions based on a group of participants who have no known food allergies. It is your responsibility to adjust the ingredients list based on the medical needs of the participants in your program.

One cup old-fashioned rolled oats (not instant) per registered child plus one cup to create the sample

¼ cup unsweetened coconut (if you cannot find unsweetened, you may substitute with sweetened coconut)

per registered child plus ¼ cup to create the sample

¼ cup dried cranberries (do NOT substitute with cranRAISINS) per registered child plus ¼ cup to create the sample

¼ cup finely chopped unsalted peanuts per registered child plus ¼ cup to create the sample

¼ cup honey per registered child plus ¼ cup to create the sample

½ cup peanut butter per registered child plus ½ cup to create the sample

One tablespoon cinnamon per registered child plus one tablespoon to create the sample

One medium-size plastic bowl per registered child

One wooden or metal spoon per registered child

One roll of wax paper

Plastic wrap and/or zippered plastic bags

Baby wipes and paper towels (to be used in cleanup)

Plastic tablecloths

One self-adhesive notepad

Writing utensils

(Optional) One pair of disposable latex or rubber gloves per registered child

Preheat

1. Purchase and/or gather the necessary ingredients.
2. Create a sample batch of the "Trail Mix Dog Treats" to familiarize yourself with the process.
   a. Pour all of the ingredients into one medium-size plastic bowl.
   b. Using the wooden or metal spoon, mix the ingredients together.
   c. Divide the dog treat dough into eight portions. For cleanliness and/or easier cleanup, you may wish to don a pair of latex or rubber gloves before dividing the dough.
   d. Roll each portion into a ball.
   e. Flatten each ball into a 1 inch cookie shape.
   f. Place the treats onto a piece of wax paper and refrigerate for 15 minutes.
3. On the day of the program, fill one medium-size plastic bowl with 1 cup rolled oats, ¼ cup unsweetened coconut, ¼ cup dried cranberries, ¼ cup finely chopped peanuts, ¼ cup honey, ½ cup peanut butter, and 1 tablespoon cinnamon for each registered child.
4. Cover the ingredient filled bowls with plastic wrap and set aside.
5. Cover the tables in the program room with plastic tablecloths.
6. Place the ingredient filled bowls, spoons, wax paper, plastic wrap and/or zippered plastic bags, baby wipes and/or paper towels, self-adhesive notepad, writing utensils, and disposable gloves, if using, on the "Trail Mix Dog Treats" table.

Bake

1. Let the children know that they will be making "Trail Mix Dog Treats."
2. Instruct the children how to make their "Trail Mix Dog Treats" using the steps in Preheat 2a–e.

3. Ask the children to write their name on one sheet of self-adhesive note paper and place it on the edge of a piece of wax paper large enough to accommodate all eight "Trail Mix Dog Treats." Have the participants place the cookies onto the piece of wax paper and refrigerate the cookies for 15 minutes.
4. Tell the children in order to keep the "Trail Mix Dog Treats" fresh they should wrap each cookie in plastic wrap or place them into a zippered plastic bag.
5. Instruct the children to store any uneaten "Trail Mix Dog Treats" in their refrigerator.

Craft Project #2: **Catnip Mouse Cat Toy**

Ingredients

3 to 3½ yards of velour, fleece, or fur fabric purchased either by the yard or in remnants

Felt scraps

Thread to match the color of the chosen fabric

One sewing needle per registered child

One large bag of craft stuffing

(Optional) Embroidery floss to create noses and whiskers

One knee-high stocking per registered child

One 4 ounce container of catnip

One set of mouse pattern pieces

One box of straight pins

Scissors

Preheat

1. Purchase and/or gather the necessary ingredients.
2. Perform an online search to find a suitable mouse pattern. Print out one copy of the pattern and cut out the pieces.
3. Follow the directions on the pattern to construct the mouse. Here are some tips to use when sewing ANY mouse pattern:
   a. When pinning the mouse ears to the head, make sure the ears are facing in the same direction.
   b. Leave an opening in the mouse's tummy large enough to fit the craft stuffing and catnip-filled stocking.
   c. Cut the felt scraps to sew on top of the mouse head or body to add depth to the ears, nose, or tummy.
   d. If you are using the optional embroidery floss, sew on a nose and whiskers to the mouse.
4. If the pattern you've chosen does not include directions for adding catnip:
   a. Use less craft stuffing in the mouse's tummy.
   b. Insert a small amount of catnip into one knee-high stocking.
   c. Knot the knee-high just above the catnip.
   d. Cut off the excess hosiery above the knot.
   e. Insert the knotted stocking into the tummy of the mouse.
   f. Fill any remaining space in the mouse's tummy with craft stuffing.

5. Once you have worked out any pattern idiosyncrasies discovered in the creation of the sample, print out a set of (adjusted) pattern pieces to use as a guide when cutting the children's fabric.
6. Lay out and pin one complete set of pattern pieces onto the fabric. This will reveal the specific amount of fabric you will need to cut for each mouse. Cut the remaining fabric into individual portions using your complete set of pinned pieces as a guide.
7. Pin one complete set of mouse pattern pieces to each individually portioned piece of fabric or to save time, pin one set of pattern pieces to multiple layers of the individually portioned pieces of fabric. Cut out the pieces.
8. On the day of the program, place a complete set of pre-cut fabric pieces at each registrant's work space.
9. Arrange the sewing accessories (thread, floss and felt of different colors, needles, etc.) in the order of their use on the "Catnip Mouse Cat Toy" table.

Bake

1. Let the children know that they will be hand sewing a "Catnip Mouse Cat Toy."
2. Without actually sewing, provide an overview of your pattern's steps.
3. Demonstrate how to thread a needle and make a knot in the thread.
4. Send the children to the supply table to choose their accessories.
5. The children may begin constructing and sewing their mice.
6. Walk around the work space area to answer questions and help with any problems that may arise.

Craft Project #3: **Stuffed Animal Carrier**

Ingredients

One white cardboard carrying box with handles per registered child, plus one additional white cardboard box to embellish in front of the children
Crayons, markers, colored pencils, etc.
Craft glue
Glitter glue
Craft embellishments (e.g., sequins, beads, ribbon, pom-poms)
(Optional) Stickers
Scissors
Plastic tablecloths
Baby wipes and paper towels (to be used in cleanup)

Preheat

1. Purchase and/or gather the necessary ingredients.
2. Cover the tables to be used for the creation of the "Stuffed Animal Carriers" with plastic tablecloths.

3. Arrange the art supplies on the "Stuffed Animal Carrier" supply table according to like groups (e.g., crayons with markers, pom-poms with ribbon and scissors)

Bake

1. Gather the children around the "Stuffed Animal Carrier" supply table.
2. Explain to the children that they will create their own "Stuffed Animal Carriers."
3. Take one white cardboard carrying box and quickly draw a pattern with crayons or markers onto the box. Adhere a few design elements to the box. Point out to the children that they may want to use many more design elements and/or art supplies than you have used and that they are free to use any supplies that they wish.
4. Invite the children to choose their art supplies from the supply table and bring them to their work space.
5. Allow the participants as much time as they wish to complete their "Stuffed Animal Carrier."

Kids will have so much fun creating these items for their pets; you'll be the "Best in Show!"

Leftovers: Use the leftover pre-cut ingredients from the "Catnip Mouse Cat Toy" project as an additional or substitute craft for the *Maker Marketplace* Craft Fair on page 106.

Garnish of Books to Be Displayed during the Program

Friday, Megan. *Pet Crafts: Everything You Need to Become Your Pet's Craft Star!* Laguna Hills, CA: Walter Foster Publishing, 2009.

Gratz, Wendi and Jo Gratz. *Creature Camp: Make Your Own 18 Softies to Draw, Sew & Stuff*. Concord, CA: C&T Publishing Inc., 2013.

Green, Gail D. *The Kids' Guide to Projects for Your Pet*. North Mankato, MN: Capstone Press, 2012.

Plumley, Amie Petronis and Andria Lisle. *Sewing School: 21 Sewing Projects Kids Will Love to Make*. North Adams, MA: Storey Publishing, 2010.

Price, Pamela S. *Cool Pet Treats: Easy Recipes for Kids to Bake*. Edina, MN: ABDO Publishing Company, 2010.

27

Unheavy Metal

The 'tween and teen years are transitional times. 'Tweens and teens want to move away from the childish elements of home décor and have their surroundings reflect their interests. Out go the pink ruffles and teddy bears; out go the blue stripes and toy cars. Their new spaces will likely include elements of science fiction, fantasy, Steampunk, and/or Gothic references. *Unheavy Metal* takes this aesthetic into account and gives the participants an opportunity to create a unisex aluminum foil "metal" wall hanging. The program attendees will create their own designs to be embossed onto the "metal."

Cost: Assuming that you have enough design elements and craft glue or white school glue in your craft closet, the heavy-duty aluminum foil, cotton swabs, wooden dowels, and black shoe polish should total $50 or less.

Time: You will need time to purchase supplies, gather the design elements, and create a sample. This program should last 45 minutes to one hour.

Early Bird Specials: Craft Closet Cleanout, Low Cost Program, Time Saver

Serving Size: Twelve to twenty 9- to 12-year-olds. Registration is required in order to estimate the necessary ingredients.

Staff Size: One staff member.

Ingredients

Thin cardboard or poster board of any color

Heavy-duty aluminum foil

Design elements (e.g., adhesive-backed foam shapes, craft jewels, yarn, leaves, feathers, and/or any lightweight three-dimensional objects)

One bottle of craft glue or white school glue per registered child

Cotton swabs

Pencils with original erasers

Hole punch

Hole reinforcers

(Optional) Craft sticks

Scissors

12 inch to 16 inch wooden dowels

Black scuff or shoe polish with a sponge applicator (one bottle for every four registered children)

Paper towels

Raffia, yarn, or metallic ribbon

Newspapers

Baby wipes and paper towels (to be used in cleanup)

Preheat

1. Purchase and/or gather the necessary ingredients.
2. Create a sample metal wall hanging to familiarize yourself with the process and to show to the participants:
   a. Cut the thin cardboard or poster board into one 8½ inch by 11 inch piece.
   b. Cut one 20 inch piece of heavy-duty aluminum foil.
   c. Use the craft glue or white school glue to adhere design elements to the 8½ inch by 11 inch thin cardboard or poster board piece.
   d. Once the design elements have been fastened to the thin cardboard or poster board, choose whether your metal will have a smooth or crushed texture. For a smooth finish, use the heavy-duty aluminum foil as is. For an antiqued texture, gently crinkle the foil with your fingertips. Do not crush the foil into a ball as it may be too difficult to unfold without tearing the foil. After you have crinkled the foil, unroll it and thoroughly flatten it on the table.
   e. Apply the craft glue or white school glue on top of the thin cardboard or poster board and design elements. Spread the glue lightly with your fingertips or a craft stick so that the glue is evenly distributed taking care not to dislodge the design elements.
   f. Find the center of the heavy-duty aluminum foil and carefully place it, dull side down, on top of the center of the thin cardboard or poster board and design elements, leaving an overhang on all sides. Press very lightly on the top of the foil to adhere the foil to the base and reveal the design elements.
   g. Using a cotton swab, carefully trace around the outlines of the design elements so that they are more visible. If the cotton swab does not produce the desired result, try gently repeating the process with the eraser end of a pencil or your fingertips.
   h. Fold the foil overhang around the back of the thin cardboard or poster board.
   i. Using the sponge applicator, dab the surface of the metal wall hanging with the black scuff cover or shoe polish.
   j. Wipe off any excess polish with a clean paper towel.
   k. Using the hole punch, make two holes in the top of the metal wall hanging. Each hole should be approximately 2 inches from each edge. Adhere hole reinforcers around the holes on the unfinished side of the project.
   l. Cut two pieces of yarn, raffia, or ribbon about 8 inches in length each. Use the smaller edge of the 8½ inch by 11 inch thin cardboard or poster board as a guide. Thread one piece of yarn, raffia, or ribbon through each hole. Place the wooden dowel along the top of the metal wall hanging. Tie a knot or bow around the wooden dowel with the yarn, raffia, or ribbon to attach the metal wall hanging to the wooden dowel.
3. Cut the thin cardboard or poster board into one 8½ inch by 11 inch piece per registered child.
4. Cut one 20 inch piece of heavy-duty aluminum foil per registered child.

5. Cover the work tables with newspaper.
6. Arrange the art supplies and design elements on the tables in order of their use.

Bake

1. Introduce the *Unheavy Metal* project and show your sample metal wall hanging to the group.
2. Talk the children through the steps used to create a metal wall hanging in Preheat 2c–j with the participants.
3. Instruct each participant to take one thin piece of cardboard or poster board and one piece of pre-cut heavy-duty aluminum foil from the art supply tables back to their work space. Have the program attendees return to the art supply tables to choose their design elements and a bottle of craft glue or white school glue.
4. Allot the rest of the time to the creation of the metal wall hangings.
5. Walk around the room answering any questions that may arise.

Interior design is a safe way for teens and 'tweens to express themselves. This project creates a unique look by utilizing supplies that are not normally associated with arts and crafts. The result produces an edgy, age-appropriate, individualized piece of home décor.

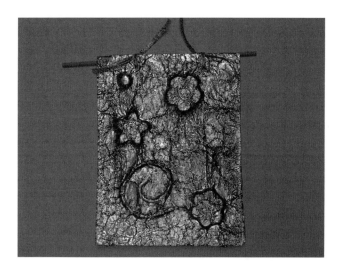

Variation: If your craft closet or budget are running low, have the children sketch a design in pencil on the thin cardboard or poster board. Trace over the pencil design with craft glue. Allow the glue to dry COMPLETELY. Resume the project directions in the original recipe from Preheat 2d.

Recipe Substitution: Consider collaborating with a history teacher on a unit on the Middle Ages. Cut the thin cardboard or poster board in the shape of a shield. An online search will provide many templates. Use the design elements in the original recipe or use the instructions from the "Variation" section to create the designs on the shield.

Leftovers: Use the leftover foil in the *Project Planet* program on page 160.

Garnish of Books to Be Displayed during the Program

Hantman, Clea. *I Wanna Re-Do My Room*. New York: Aladdin Paperbacks, 2006.

Llimós Plomer, Anna. *Medieval Castle Adventure Crafts*. Berkeley Heights, NJ: Enslow Publishers, 2011.

Scheunemann, Pam. *Cool Stuff for Your Room: Creative Handmade Projects for Kids*. Minneapolis, MN: ABDO Publishing Company, 2012.

Warwick, Ellen. *Stuff for Your Space*. Toronto: Kids Can Press, 2004.

Weaver, Janice and Frieda Wishinsky. *It's Your Room: A Decorating Guide for Real Kids*. Toronto: Tundra Books, 2005.

IV

Desserts

These recipes are fun, feel good, lower-tech programs for young children.

28

Our Maker Neighborhood

Most people assume it's too hard to present a Maker program for the youngest of children. After all, they can't really MAKE anything. In actuality, preschoolers are often the most creative and open to new ideas. For this age group we recommend a program that offers a variety of choices for individual exploration.

Preschoolers are very curious about their neighborhoods and about the people and entities that comprise their community. They often pretend to be firefighters, letter carriers, and chefs because play is their work. *Our Maker Neighborhood* builds on these moments by transforming a library space into a simulated street with stations representing different sectors. If your neighborhood has a unique flavor or distinct attribute, consider adding it to your rendition of *Our Maker Neighborhood*.

Cost: This program may cost as little or as much as you are able to invest. You can use existing materials or purchase additional ingredients. You may often obtain donations of blocks, toys, or puppets by posting a sign in your library. This may help lower the cost of the program.

Time: Once the basic framework is established, little preparation time is required. The optimal length of this program is one hour, and it may be run once or on a weekly or monthly basis.

Early Bird Special: Low Cost Program, Smorgasbord, Time Saver

Serving Size: This program is intended for children ages 1 to 5, each attending with an adult caregiver. This program should be held as a drop-in. However, if your ingredient supplies are limited, registration may be necessary.

Staff Size: One staff member.

Ingredients (Listed by Station)

For this program, you'll create activity stations representing different areas of a neighborhood—such as retail stores, restaurants, and construction sites. Use your imagination and the resources you have on hand to create the stations. You may need to purchase or have a staff member make some of the items listed below, but keep in mind that everything is optional. Most of these items are available online, at superstores, or discount stores.

As indicated by the list of suggested ingredients, this program may involve the use of food and/or edible ingredients. The ingredients included are suggestions based on a group of participants who have no known food allergies. It is your responsibility to adjust the ingredients list based on the medical needs of the participants in your program.

The Garment District

Lace-up or sewing activities to promote fine motor skills

Paper dolls

Learn to dress materials (e.g., dolls, vests, and novelty books to practice dressing skills, such as learning how to button, zip, and tie laces)

Construction Junction

Plastic tools (e.g., hammers and screwdrivers)

Toy trucks

Building blocks made from cardboard, wood, or plastic

Plastic interlocking building blocks large enough to avoid posing a choking hazard

Creation Station

Art and craft projects

Sensory art materials (e.g., clay, and potatoes and paint to create potato prints)

Everyday art supplies (e.g., crayons and coloring sheets)

Baby wipes and paper towels (to be used in cleanup)

Plastic tablecloths

Act Your Age Stage

Costumes (e.g., hats, boas, crowns, and robes)

Puppets

Toy musical instruments

Scarves, plastic eggs, bells, etc.

Maker Market or Restaurant

Toy food

Toy pots and pans and plastic dinnerware

Play kitchen (A book cart with hand-drawn burners on the top shelf makes an excellent stove. Use the bottom shelf to bake!)

Toy cash register

Play money

(Optional) Touch-a-Tech

iPad(s)

Maker apps (e.g., Grandpa's Workshop, Grandma's Kitchen, Toca Builders, Playart, Art Maker, ColART, Leo's Pad, Pettson's Inventions (1 & 2), Morton Subotnick's Pitch Painter, Play Lab, Doodlecast, Bamba Toys and Wombi Helicopter)

Other stations might include the library, post office, pet shop, garden center, grocery store, and any other community destinations you wish to include.

Preheat

1. Decide which stations your neighborhood will include and what each station will offer. Plan your program according to the number of available staff, the size of the room, and the usual number of children who attend your drop-in programs. Six stations should accommodate up to 50 children. We recommend one extra station for every nine additional children expected.
2. Purchase, gather, and/or prepare the ingredients, including craft supplies, toys, costumes, art and craft projects, etc.
3. If you are planning to include a "Touch-a-Tech" station, purchase and install the iPad app(s).
4. It is best to designate one table for each station. Arrange the tables around the perimeter of the room leaving ample space in the center of the room for patrons to comfortably move between stations.
5. Cover the "Creation Station" tables with plastic tablecloths.
6. Scatter chairs around the perimeter of the room so that adults may sit while the children play.
7. Clearly designate each station with a sign explaining what the station represents, the choices available at that station, and what the children will learn as they play.
8. If directions are required to complete an art or craft project, they should be displayed prominently.
9. Place the created, purchased, and/or gathered ingredients at their proper stations. You may wish to arrange the puppets, musical instruments, costumes, eggs, scarves, and building blocks on the floor instead of tables so that children may easily reach them.

Bake

1. Welcome the attendees to the *Our Maker Neighborhood* program.
2. Explain what each station represents and the activities available at that station.
3. Invite the parents and caregivers to explore the stations along with their children.
4. Walk around the room answering questions and offering encouragement and positive reinforcement.

Allow the children to wander from station to station, exploring as they wish. Some may want to visit all the stations, while others may focus on only one or two. The children should take home any art they create except that which represents a collaborative effort. Any artistic collaborative efforts should be placed on display at the library.

Variation: To combine all the "neighborhood" elements into one activity, find a large, empty cardboard box (e.g., a refrigerator or furniture box). Next, cut holes in the box for windows and doors. Let the children decide what type of structure it will become (e.g., house, library, post office). Provide art supplies for children to decorate their new building.

Recipe Substitutions: Preschool teachers can extend community helper units by using the existing framework and creating additional stations such as the hospital, police station, or bank. If an iPad(s) is available, the Community Helpers Play & Learn: Educational App for Kids is perfectly suited to this program.

Leftovers: Borrow the costumes from this program to use in the *Fairy Tale Theater* program on page 94.

Garnish of Books to Be Displayed during the Program

Brown, Don. *A Wizard from the Start: The Incredible Boyhood & Amazing Inventions of Thomas Edison*. Boston: Houghton Mifflin Books for Children, 2010.

Chwast, Seymour. *Get Dressed!* New York: Abrams Appleseed, 2012.

Dall, Mary Doerfler. *Little Hands Create! Art & Activities for Kids Ages 3 to 6*. Nashville, TN: Williamson Books, 2004.

McLean, Dirk. *Curtain Up! A Book for Young Performers*. Plattsburgh, NY: Tundra Books of Northern New York, 2010.

Rinker, Sherri Duskey. *Goodnight, Goodnight, Construction Site*. San Francisco: Chronicle Books, 2011.

Zalben, Jane Breskin. *Mousterpiece*. New York: Roaring Brook Press, 2012.

29

Preschool Drum Corps

From the time they are babies, children love music and any type of musical sound or rhythm. The *Preschool Drum Corps* program provides participants the opportunity to create their own musical instruments and play them for a crowd in a drum line parade.

Cost: This program is designed to be of little or no cost. Ask staff members to save their empty cylindrical oatmeal containers. These will be used to create the drums. If you do not have yarn or ribbon in your craft closet, you will need to purchase enough to create straps for each drum. Raiding your craft closet should produce enough materials for the children to decorate their drums.

Time: You will need time to purchase or collect the ingredients, choose the music- or parade-themed book(s) and marching music, and create a sample drum to familiarize yourself with the process and to show to the program participants. This program should last 45 minutes to one hour.

Early Bird Specials: Craft Closet Cleanout, Low Cost Program

Serving Size: This program works best with twelve children ages 4 to 6.

Staff Size: One staff member. To accommodate more children, add one staff member for every four to eight additional participants.

Ingredients

One empty cylindrical oatmeal container with plastic lid per child plus one to create a sample
(Optional) Box cutter (to be used by a staff member before the program to cut down the empty cylindrical oatmeal containers, if desired)
Hole punch or awl
Yarn or ribbon in a large quantity (to create straps for the drums)
Crayons or markers
(Optional) An assortment of stickers from your craft supply closet
Two unsharpened pencils per child
Newspapers
Music- or parade-themed picture book(s)
Marching music or song(s)

Preheat

1. Purchase and/or gather the necessary ingredients.
2. Select the music- or parade-themed book(s) to read aloud.
3. Select the marching song(s) for the children to practice their marching skills.
4. Create a sample drum to show to the participants:
   a. Peel the label off of the empty cylindrical oatmeal container.
   b. If you wish, the drums may vary in height. Decide whether or not you want to cut down your oatmeal container to make a smaller drum or whether you'd like to keep it the size it is. If desired, remove the plastic lid and, using the box cutter, cut down the oatmeal container to the chosen size, taking care to cut evenly so the lid may be replaced securely.
   c. Replace the lid onto the top of the empty cylindrical oatmeal container. Using a pencil, mark one hole on either side of the container 1 inch from the bottom of the lid.
   d. Remove the lid once again. With the awl or Phillips head screwdriver, make one hole through each of the measured pencil marks.
   e. Measure a length of the yarn or ribbon long enough to make a strap for the drum. The drum strap should be long enough to hang comfortably around the neck of a child.
   f. Insert one length of the yarn or ribbon into each hole and knot each end inside of the container.
   g. Decorate the drum with crayons, markers, and/or stickers.
   h. Replace the lid onto the oatmeal container.
   i. Use the pencils, eraser side down, as drumsticks and await your marching orders.
5. Peel the labels off of the remaining empty cylindrical oatmeal containers.
6. If desired, cut down the remaining oatmeal containers to the chosen size following the directions in Preheat 4b.
7. Make holes in each of the remaining oatmeal containers following the directions in Preheat 4c–d.
8. Measure, cut, and attach the yarn or ribbon to the remaining oatmeal containers following the directions in Preheat 4e–f.
9. Arrange the ingredients on the supply table.

Bake

1. Seat the children on the floor in your favorite story time configuration. Read the selected music- or parade-themed book(s) to the group.
2. Ask the children if any of them have ever participated in a parade. Discuss the various types of musical instruments that might be played in a parade and perhaps some of the children's favorite songs.
3. Play the marching song(s) and practice marching with the children.
4. Ask the children to return to their story time seating positions.
5. Explain to the children that they will be making drums to use in a drum line parade.
6. Show your sample drum to the children and discuss the steps involved in creating their own drums.
7. Have each child choose a work area on the floor.

8. Hand out newspapers and instruct the children to cover their work areas.
9. Once their work areas are covered, invite the children to take one prepared empty cylindrical oatmeal container with its lid back to their work areas.
10. Instruct the children to gather their art supplies from the supply table and bring them to their work areas.
11. Ask the participants to remove the lids and demonstrate that they may find it easier to embellish their containers if they insert one hand into the container and decorate with the other. Of course, some children may find it easier to simply place their container directly onto the newspaper.
12. Allow enough time for the children to embellish and decorate their drums. But remember to leave at least 15 minutes for the drum corps to march in parade formation. At regular intervals, gently remind the children how much time remains before the parade of drums marches throughout the library.
13. When it is time for the drum line parade, ask the children to return all of their art supplies to the supply table.
14. Have the children replace their lids onto their oatmeal containers.
15. Instruct the children to place the yarn or ribbon over their heads so that the drum hangs in front of them.
16. Give each child two pencils. Demonstrate to the children how the two pencils, eraser side down, may be used as drum sticks.
17. Just prior to the drum corps parade:
    a. Assemble the children in parade formation.
    b. Lead the children to the place where their parents and caregivers usually wait while their children attend a program.
    c. Bring your drum line parade to a quick rest stop to provide a photo op for their parents and caregivers.
    d. Continue your parade throughout the library.

The combination of the physical act of drumming and the creation of a musical sound tolerable to most parents and caregivers gives the *Preschool Drum Corps* program a snappy beat you can happily dance to. Parents and caregivers may appreciate this idea so much that they will gladly put away the pots, pans, and spoons (or use them to make dinner) and get the whole family drumming!

Variation: In addition to the drums, each child could create a tambourine or other musical instrument. An online search will produce a number of instructions for the creation of different instruments.

Leftovers: Use any leftover empty cylindrical oatmeal containers in the *Transportation Station* program on page 164 to create smokestacks.

Garnish of Books to Be Displayed during the Program

Black, Michael Ian. *A Pig Parade Is a Terrible Idea*. New York: Simon & Schuster Books for Young Readers, 2010.
DK Publishing. *Let's Make Music*. London: DK Publishing, 2005.
Geringer, Laura. *Boom Boom Go Away!* New York: Atheneum Books for Young Readers, 2010.
Newton, Jill. *Crash Bang Donkey!* Chicago, IL: Albert Whitman and Company, 2010.
Roosa, Karen. *Pippa at the Parade*. Honesdale, PA: Boyds Mills Press, 2009.
Salzmann, Mary Elizabeth. *What in the World Is a Drum?*. Minneapolis, MN: ABDO, 2012.

30

Project Planet

The existence of other worlds and planets has always fascinated people of all ages. Most people will not be fortunate enough to have the opportunity to experience the physical elements of another planet firsthand. However, *Project Planet* allows children to create a three-dimensional representation of an alien landscape. The children can create their own imaginary celestial world or base their projects on scientific data.

Cost: The cost for this program is minimal. Fine, white sand may be purchased from a garden or craft store; however, if you're heading to the beach, bring an extra pail and it's free! Depending on the availability and price of fine, white sand, table salt may be a less expensive alternative. You may buy polished rocks or go outside and collect them. Empty egg cartons, empty cylindrical oatmeal containers, and empty paper towel tubes may be donated by staff members, family, or friends. Ask the cataloging or acquisitions department to save empty cardboard shipping boxes from book orders. If aluminum foil and sidewalk chalk in a variety of colors are not already in your craft closet, you will need to purchase them.

Time: Most of the preparation time for this program is spent cutting the cardboard boxes to the specified height, cutting rings from the empty cylindrical oatmeal containers and the paper towel tubes and cutting out the individual egg cups from the empty egg cartons. You will also need time to gather or purchase the remaining ingredients. The recommended length of this program is 45 minutes to one hour.

Early Bird Special: Fruitcake

Serving Size: Twelve 3- to 8-year-olds, with a separate program for each age-appropriate group. Registration is required in order to estimate the necessary ingredients. Younger children may be offered basic scientific facts from a space-themed picture book, but the emphasis will be on creating a sensory art experience. Older children may be presented with more in-depth material about the solar system, but will also benefit from the creative process.

Staff Size: One staff member.

Ingredients

As indicated by the list of suggested ingredients, this program may involve the use of food and/or edible ingredients. The ingredients included are suggestions based on a group of participants who have no known food allergies. It is your responsibility to adjust the ingredients list based on the medical needs of the participants in your program.

One empty rectangular cardboard shipping box per registered child plus one to create the sample

Box cutter (to be used by a staff member before the program)

Scissors (to be used by a staff member before the program)

Masking tape or book tape

Heavy-duty aluminum foil (The foil will be used to cover the bottom and the 3½ to 4 inch sides of the empty cardboard shipping boxes. The longer the boxes you choose, the more foil you will need.)

Three empty cylindrical oatmeal containers

Four cardboard paper towel tubes

Six empty dozen egg cartons

(Optional) Rocks (for little ones, be mindful of the choking hazard presented by small rocks or pebbles)

Fine, white sand (approximately nine cups of sand per registered child, depending on the size of the empty cardboard box) or an equivalent amount of table salt and nine additional cups to create the sample

One foam, paper or plastic disposable bowl per registered child plus one to create the sample

One ¼ cup measuring cup

Sidewalk chalk in a variety of colors (the brighter the chalk, the more vivid your final result will be)

(Optional) Glitter in a variety of colors

Newspapers

Baby wipes and paper towels (to be used in cleanup)

Space-themed picture book(s)

Preheat

1. Purchase and/or gather the necessary ingredients.
2. Using the box cutter, cut down the empty rectangular cardboard shipping boxes to a height between 3½ to 4 inches.
3. If the box is taped or glued on the bottom, reinforce the closure with masking or book tape to support the weight of your *Project Planet* creation and to prevent sand or salt from escaping.
4. Line the bottom and sides of the cut cardboard boxes with the heavy-duty aluminum foil.
5. Using the box cutter or a pair of scissors, slice rings no larger than ½ inch in width from the empty cylindrical oatmeal containers and the cardboard paper towel tubes. These will be used to represent craters on the planet's surface.
6. Cut out the individual egg cups from the empty egg cartons. The individual egg cups need to be shortened in height by cutting off approximately half from the top or open end of the cup. The egg cups will be used to create hills and valleys on the planet's surface.
7. Make a small batch of colored sand or salt:
    a. Scoop ¼ cup of sand or salt into a foam, paper or plastic disposable bowl.
    b. Choose a piece of colored chalk, insert it into the sand or salt, and alternate between a stirring motion and a grinding technique similar to using

a mortar and pestle. Be sure to scrape the bottom of the bowl with each stir. The longer you mix the chalk and sand or salt, the greater the color saturation.

    c. Periodically shake the bowl to evenly distribute the pigment.

    d. If you are using glitter, sprinkle the glitter into the bowl and stir and/or shake to distribute the glitter as evenly as possible.

8. Create a simple *Project Planet* sample containing one large crater, one small crater, one hill, and one rock, if desired, to show to the participants. Younger children will need this visual to understand the concept and mechanics for this program.

9. Choose a space-themed picture book(s) to share with the children.

10. Arrange the ingredients on the table in order of use.

Bake

1. Invite the children to sit on the floor in your favorite story time configuration.

2. Read aloud your chosen space-themed picture book(s).

3. Discuss space travel and the solar system with the children. Ask the children what they know about our universe. Highlight the differences among the planets, for example, size, climate, surface color.

4. Show your sample *Project Planet* to the participants. Remove the oatmeal container ring and paper towel tube ring to show the children what you've used to create craters. Remove the egg cup to show the children what you've used to create hills and valleys.

5. Demonstrate how to make colored sand or salt using the steps in Preheat 7a–d.

6. Instruct the children to choose a work space on the floor and cover it with newspaper.

7. Give each child one prepared cardboard box.

8. Have the children choose a selection of oatmeal container and paper towel tube rings and egg cups. They should take some time to arrange these elements on the bottom of their cardboard boxes before they begin to color their sand or salt.

9. Have each child choose one piece of colored sidewalk chalk.

10. Scoop or pour ¼ cup of sand or salt into a foam, paper or plastic disposable bowls and give one bowl to each child.

11. If the children choose to make colored sand for their planetary surface, reiterate the steps in Preheat 7a–d. When they are satisfied with the color of their sand or salt, they can pour it over their oatmeal container rings, paper towel tube rings, and egg cups. They should repeat this process until the bottom of the box is covered. The children may create additional colors, add glitter, and/or use uncolored sand or salt at any time.

12. When the participants feel they have the proper amount of sand or salt covering their planetary surface, if desired, they may add rocks as an additional geological feature.

13. At the end of the program, tell the children that they may continue to add elements to their project once they have brought it home. Suggest using toy cars and trucks as planet rovers; action figures may explore the surface as astronauts and toy monsters may represent alien life forms.

Project Planet is an artistic introduction to astronomy. Young participants may be part of a generation that routinely travels the galaxy. You may be the one to help propel their aspirations out of this world!

Fusion Box: The Dr. Seuss app There's No Place Like Space makes a great addition to this program when it is presented to participants ages 5 and up. The app is likely too lengthy for those younger than 5 years of age. If your library is fortunate enough to own multiple iPads, give one iPad to each child. If not, one iPad may be shared with the group. If you choose to add the app to the recipe as written above, you should add at least 15 minutes to the length of the program or simply substitute the app for the space-themed picture book(s).

Leftovers: Use the leftover heavy-duty aluminum foil in the *Unheavy Metal* program on page 146, the leftover sand and colored sidewalk chalk in the *Zen Garden* program on page 54, and the leftover colored sidewalk chalk in the *Chalktography* program on page 89.

Garnish of Books to Be Displayed during the Program

Boekhoff, P. M. *Nifty Thrifty Space Crafts*. Berkeley Heights, NJ: Enslow Elementary, 2008.

Cousins, Lucy. *Create with Maisy*. Somerville, MA: Candlewick Press, 2012.

Dall, Mary Doerfler. *Little Hands Create! Art & Activities for Kids Ages 3 to 6*. Nashville, TN: Williamson Books, 2004.

Kelly, Mark E. *Mousetronaut: Based on a (Partially) True Story*. New York: Simon & Schuster Books for Young Readers, 2012.

Llimós Plomer, Anna. *Space Adventure Crafts*. Berkeley Heights, NJ: Enslow Elementary, 2011.

O'Brien, Patrick. *You Are the First Kid on Mars*. New York: G.P. Putnam's Sons, 2009.

31

Transportation Station

Babies love a toy steering wheel with a squeaky horn. Toddlers yearn for their first tricycle. Preschoolers can't wait to ride the school bus. Children are fascinated by the various modes of transportation and the freedom and independence they represent.

There is no need to reinvent the wheel with a complicated program. Here is a simple idea for preschool-aged children featuring the universally loved theme of transportation. After reading a transportation-themed story or stories and discussing the different modes of transportation, the children will create their own vehicles out of cardboard boxes. To cap off the program, the participants will showcase their vehicles for friends and family in a convoy throughout the library.

Cost: This program is designed to be of little or no cost. Ask the cataloging or acquisitions department to save larger empty cardboard shipping boxes from book orders. In addition, ask staff members to save their empty cylindrical oatmeal containers. These may be worn as hats to represent train and boat smokestacks, truck whistles, etc. You will need elastic, cut rubber bands or ribbon to secure the smokestacks. Gather crayons, markers, and glitter glue to decorate the vehicles. Add anything else you have in your craft closet (e.g., paper plates, feathers, pom-poms, sequins, stickers, tissue paper, streamers) so that the children may accessorize their vehicles.

Time: You will need time to collect the ingredients, choose a transportation-themed book(s) to share with the group, cut the bottoms off of all of the empty boxes, and create a smokestack for each child. Due to the simplistic nature of the project in this program, there is no need to create a sample unless you believe it is necessary. The length of this program is one hour. Remember to leave 15 minutes at the end of the program for the library convoy.

Early Bird Specials: Craft Closet Cleanout, Low Cost Program

Serving Size: This program works best with 12 children ages 4 to 6.

Staff Size: One staff member. To accommodate more children, add one staff member for every four to eight additional participants.

Ingredients

Transportation-themed book(s)

One large empty rectangular cardboard shipping box per child (look for something big enough for the children to stand in, but light enough for them to carry)

Box cutter (to be used by a staff member before the program)

One empty cylindrical oatmeal container per child

Hole punch or awl (to be used by a staff member before the program)

Crayons

Markers

Glue

Glitter glue

Cellophane, book, and/or masking tape

Elastic, cut rubber bands or ribbon

Embellishments (e.g., paper plates, heavy-duty aluminum foil, adhesive-backed foam shapes, feathers, pom-poms, sequins, stickers, tissue paper, streamers, and anything else you may have in your craft closet)

Newspapers

Baby wipes and paper towels (to be used in clean up)

Preheat

1. Choose your favorite transportation-themed book(s).
2. Gather the empty cardboard shipping boxes. Cut out the bottom of each box with the box cutter. This will allow the children to step into their boxes.
3. Gather the empty cylindrical oatmeal containers:
   a. Using the hole punch or awl, make one hole on either side of the open end of the container.
   b. Insert one elastic, cut rubber band or ribbon into each hole and knot the end inside the container. These will be tied underneath the child's chin to secure the smokestack hat.
4. Gather the art supplies.
5. Just prior to the children's arrival:
   a. Place the cardboard shipping boxes and cylindrical oatmeal container hats in an area that will not provide a distraction for the children (e.g., under a table, behind the chair in which the staff member will be seated).
   b. Arrange the art supplies on the tables in like groups (e.g., crayons with markers and glue with pom-poms and feathers)

Bake

1. Seat the children on the floor in your favorite story time configuration.
2. Read the selected transportation-themed book(s) to the group.
3. Discuss the many different modes of transportation with the children (e.g., train, boat, car, bus, construction vehicle, farm vehicle, airplane). Be sure to elicit as much input from the children as possible.
4. After a rousing discussion, let the children know they will create their own custom vehicle. Ask the children to take a moment to decide what type of vehicle they would like to make.
5. Have each child choose a work area on the floor.
6. Hand out newspapers and instruct the children to cover their work areas.

7. Once their work areas are covered, invite each child to take one prepared cardboard box and one prepared oatmeal container back to his or her work area.

8. Instruct the children to gather their art supplies from the supply table and bring them back to their work areas. The children should be allowed to make their choices independently, but you may wish to offer suggestions as to the use of the different ingredients. For example, paper plates make great headlights or wheels and aluminum foil gives the smokestacks a metallic look.

9. Allow enough time for the children to create their embellished vehicles and decorate their smokestack hats, but remember to leave at least 15 minutes for the library convoy. At regular intervals, gently remind the children how much time remains before the convoy.

10. When it is time for the convoy, ask the children to return all of their art supplies to the supply table.

11. Demonstrate how to step into the cardboard vehicle, pulling up on the sides before walking. Allot some time for the children to practice "driving" their vehicles.

12. Just prior to the convoy:
    a. Help the children secure their smokestack hats.
    b. Assemble the children in parade formation.
    c. Lead the library convoy to the place where the parents and caregivers usually wait while their children attend a program.
    d. Bring your convoy to a quick rest stop to provide a photo op for parents and caregivers.
    e. Continue your convoy throughout the library.

13. 10–4 Good Buddy!

It is important to provide children with safe opportunities in which to assert their independence. The *Transportation Station* program allows them to make choices to

exercise their creativity but, unlike drawing with crayons on a freshly painted wall, these decisions will be met with parental applause.

Variation: Cardboard boxes may represent many different concepts. Instead of transportation, choose a book focused on the home. Ask the children to create a home they would like to live in. They might make a castle, farmhouse, doghouse, RV, igloo, etc. After the children's home construction is complete, invite the parents to tour the "neighborhood" and have each child describe the type of house they have created and why they want to live there. Add music and refreshments and you have created a block party.

Recipe Substitution: Collaborate with first- and second-grade teachers in a history lesson on the American Revolution. Change the name of the program to *One if by Land, Two if by Sea*. Collect empty cardboard shipping boxes large enough to accommodate two children. The children will create horses from these boxes by using art supplies, accessories, and their imaginations. You can cut a window hole in each empty cylindrical oatmeal container and place a poster board candle inside to create a lantern. Bring history to life with a flash mob performance of Paul Revere's famous midnight ride.

Leftovers: Use any leftover empty cylindrical oatmeal containers in the *Preschool Drum Corps* program on page 157.

Garnish of Books to Be Displayed during the Program

Hubbell, Patricia. *Airplanes: Soaring! Diving! Turning!* New York: Marshall Cavendish, 2008.
Kuklin, Susan. *All Aboard! A True Train Story*. New York: Orchard Books, 2003.
LaReau, Kara. *Otto: The Boy Who Loved Cars*. New York: Roaring Brook Press, 2011.
Lyon, George Ella. *Planes Fly!* New York: Atheneum Books for Young Readers, 2013.
McMullan, Kate. *I'm Fast*. New York: Balzer +Bray, 2012.
Rinker, Sherry Duskey. *Steam Train, Dream Train*. San Francisco: Chronicle Books, 2013.
Singer, Marilyn. *I'm Your Bus*. New York: Scholastic Press, 2009.

32

Happy Campers

Bring the best of summer to any season and fill your room with happy campers. The participants, or campers, will each build their own tent, create their own paper campfire, share campfire stories complete with shadow puppets, and make and enjoy no-cook s'mores. They will do all of this without mosquitoes, poison ivy, or extreme temperatures but with the luxury of indoor plumbing.

Cost: To minimize the cost, ask staff members to donate empty cardboard paper towel and toilet paper tubes and lend tarp substitutes (e.g., towels, tablecloths, sheets, lengths of fabric) and flashlights. You must purchase the ingredients to make the s'mores: graham crackers, chocolate bars, and marshmallow fluff. If you do not have an ample supply of paper plates, napkins, or plastic knives on hand, you will need to purchase these as well. Your craft closet will likely already contain tissue paper, glue, and markers.

Time: Because you are borrowing so many items, you will need to plan well in advance to remind the staff members of their contributions. A trip to the grocery store will also be required. It should take only a small amount of time to gather the necessary art supplies and either choose a book to read or memorize a story to tell. This program should last 45 minutes to one hour.

Early Bird Special: Low Cost Program

Serving Size: Twelve children ages 4 to 6. Registration should be required for this program in order to estimate supply quantities and to obtain allergy information to avoid serious food allergies or reactions.

Staff Size: One staff member. To accommodate more children, add one staff member for every four to eight additional participants.

Ingredients

As indicated by the list of suggested ingredients, this program involves the use of food and/ or edible ingredients. The ingredients included are suggestions based on a group of participants who have no known food allergies. It is your responsibility to adjust the ingredients list based on the medical needs of the participants in your program.

Two to four chairs per child to use as the foundation for the tent

Tarp substitutes (e.g., towels, tablecloths, sheets, lengths of fabric)

Empty cardboard paper towel or toilet paper tubes (at least three paper towel tubes or six toilet paper tubes per registered child plus one additional set of tubes to create the sample)

Scissors (to be used by the staff member)

Markers

Paper plates (at least two plates for each registered child plus additional plates to hold the ingredients of the s'mores)

Yellow, orange, and red tissue paper

One glue stick per registered child

Picture books, including characters that may easily be represented by shadow puppets (e.g., a hopping two-fingered peace sign becomes a bunny, horizontally flipped clapping hands create a chomping alligator)

Flashlight(s)

Graham crackers

Chocolate bars

Two jars of marshmallow fluff

Plastic knives

Napkins

Newspapers

Baby wipes and paper towels (to be used in cleanup)

Preheat

1. Make sure you have acquired all the staff donations and purchased and/or gathered the other ingredients.
2. Be sure to have access to two to four chairs per registered child to serve as the inner structure of their tents.
3. If you are using cardboard paper towel tubes, cut each tube in half.
4. Create a paper campfire to familiarize yourself with the process and to show to the children:
   a. Choose no more than six cardboard tubes. Decorate the cardboard tube "logs" with tree knots or wood grain.
   b. Glue the logs onto a paper plate.
   c. Tear off pieces of the yellow, orange, and red tissue paper and glue them on top of and, if desired, inside the logs creating the look of a fire.
5. For the paper campfire, each child uses one paper plate. In order to prevent a mix up when it is time to take their crafts home, write the first name and first initial of the last name of each registered participant on the bottom of one paper plate.
6. Choose a story to share. You may choose a book to read or memorize a story to tell. Remember to choose a story that features characters easily translated into shadow puppets.
7. Arrange the art supplies on the supply table.
8. Keep the ingredients for the s'mores out of the view of the children until it is time to eat.

Bake

1. Welcome the children to camp! Ask if anyone has ever been camping. Discuss the different activities campers might participate in.
2. Explain to the children that they will build their own tents using two to four chairs as a foundation and the tarp substitutes as the tent coverings. Give the children free reign to build whatever kind of tent they choose.
3. After the tents are pitched, tell the children that night will soon be coming, and they need to build a fire to provide light and warmth. Instruct the children to create a work space inside or in front of their tent by placing newspaper on the floor.
4. Show the children the example of the paper campfire you have created.
5. Allow each child to choose no more than six prepared cardboard tube logs. Have the children bring the cardboard tube logs and a selection of markers to their work space. Discuss tree knots, wood grain, and texture with the children, but allow them to decorate their cardboard tube logs with any design they wish.
6. Hand out the correctly labeled paper plate, one sheet each of orange, red and yellow tissue paper, and one glue stick to each camper.
7. Instruct the children to complete their campfires following the steps in Preheat 4b–c.
8. Now that the fires are lit, it is time for a story. While their paper campfires dry, gather the children around the sample paper campfire you created. Turn on the flashlight(s) and turn off the lights. Instruct the children how to make simple shadow puppets and ask them to project their shadow puppets onto the wall into the flashlight projection as you read the book or tell the story.
9. Is anyone hungry yet? It's finally time to let the children know that they will be making s'mores. Explain that a s'more is a delicious sandwich consisting of chocolate and marshmallow filling between two graham cracker "bread" slices. Lay out the graham crackers and chocolate bars on paper plates and place them on a table. Place two jars of marshmallow fluff and several plastic knives at the end of the table where you will be standing so that you may more closely supervise and assist with the children's use of the plastic knives. Give each child a paper plate and a napkin. Have each child take two graham crackers. They will then spread marshmallow fluff onto one cracker and place a piece of chocolate on top of the marshmallow fluff. Place the remaining graham cracker on the chocolate to finish the sandwich. They may take their s'mores back to their tent or sit by their fires and enjoy. Baby wipes and paper towels should be at the ready to aid in cleanup.

Happy Campers is a fun program that provides the children an opportunity to construct their own domains, enjoy stories, create art, and eat a yummy snack. Consider presenting this program during the height of winter when everyone wants to enjoy the outdoors, but simply can't.

Fusion Box: To add to your program or to act as a substitute for the actual food portion, purchase the Happy Campfire App for .99. In this app, you can make virtual s'mores, hear campfire songs and stories, create constellations, and even stoke a fire. If you wish to retain all the original elements of the program and add the Happy Campfire app, consider adding 15 minutes to the length of the program. If your library is fortunate enough to own multiple iPads, use one iPad per child. This app may also be enjoyed by a group taking turns with one iPad.

Garnish of Books to Be Displayed during the Program

Carlin, Patricia. *Alfie Is Not Afraid*. New York: Disney/Hyperion Books, 2012.

DiPucchio, Kelly S. *Sipping Spiders through a Straw: Campfire Songs for Monsters*. New York: Scholastic Press, 2008.

Hooks, Gwendolyn. *The Noisy Night: A Pet Club Story*. Mankato, MN: Stone Arch Books, 2011.

Mader, Jan. *Let's Go Camping!* Mankato, MN: Pebble Plus Books, 2007.

O'Byrne, Nicola. *Open Very Carefully*. Somerville, MA: Nosy Crow, 2013.

Stills, Caroline. *The House of 12 Bunnies*. New York: Holiday House, 2012.

Studelska, Jana Voelke. *Camping for Fun!* Minneapolis, MN: Compass Point Books, 2008.

Watt, Mélanie. *Scaredy Squirrel Goes Camping*. Toronto: Kids Can Press, 2013.

33

The Very Healthy Butterfly

Preschoolers, like butterflies, experience a significant period of growth and change. They shed their infantile dependence like a cocoon and grow into independent individuals who are learning to fly solo. *The Very Healthy Butterfly* program subliminally encourages healthy eating habits while allowing preschoolers to explore the life cycle of the butterfly.

Cost: Since food prices vary by region and retail establishment, expect this program to cost approximately $60 to $75. The cost of this program may increase if you decide to purchase organic ingredients.

Time: Most of the preparation time for this program is spent shopping and creating the sample. This program should last 45 minutes to one hour.

Serving Size: Twelve to fifteen children ages 4 to 6. Registration should be required in order to estimate the necessary ingredients and to obtain allergy information to avoid serious food allergies or reactions.

Staff Size: One staff member.

Ingredients

As indicated by the list of suggested ingredients, this program involves the use of food and/ or edible ingredients. The ingredients included are suggestions based on a group of participants who have no known food allergies. It is your responsibility to adjust the ingredients list based on the medical needs of the participants in your program.

One pre-divided heavy-duty paper or plastic plate per registered child plus one to create the sample

One fine-tipped permanent marker

One 3-mm bamboo skewer per registered child plus one to create the sample (If you do not intend to use the leftover bamboo skewers in another project, the diameter size may be irrelevant)

Scissors (to be used by the staff member)

One wooden clothespin per registered child plus one to create the sample

One snack size–zippered plastic bag per registered child plus one to create the sample

Washable markers in a variety of colors

One pipe cleaner per registered child plus one to create the sample

Ten golden raisins per registered child plus an additional 10 to create the sample

Five to seven average-size green seedless grapes per registered child plus an additional five to seven to create the sample

One baby carrot per registered child plus one to create the sample

½ cup of whole grain fish-shaped crackers plus an additional ½ cup to create the sample

Five to ten small cherry tomatoes per child plus an additional 5–10 to create the sample

Eight foam, paper, or plastic disposable bowls per table

Picture book(s) about butterflies and/or the life cycle of the butterfly

Instrumental music to fly to or the song "The Caterpillar" by Margie La Bella from the *Move! Move! Sing! Play Along and Learn!* CD

Plastic tablecloths

Baby wipes and paper towels (to be used in cleanup)

Preheat

1. Purchase and/or gather the necessary ingredients.
2. Choose the picture book(s) about butterflies and/or the life cycle of the butterfly.
3. Choose instrumental music to play in the background while the participants act out the life cycle of a butterfly or use the song "The Caterpillar" by Margie La Bella from the *Move! Move! Sing! Play Along and Learn!* CD.
4. Using the fine-tipped permanent marker, write the first name and the first initial of the last name of each registered child on the bottom of one pre-divided plate.
5. Create a sample to familiarize yourself with the process and to show to the children:
    a. If the heavy-duty paper plates you have purchased are not divided into four sections, or are divided into fewer than four sections, use the permanent marker to create four divisions. Label the divisions of the heavy-duty paper plate: "Eggs," "Caterpillar," "Chrysalis," and "Butterfly."
    b. Add 10 golden raisins to the division of the paper plate labeled "Egg."
    c. Bamboo skewers are difficult to cut with scissors. For this step you should snap the bamboo skewer with your hands and trim the excess strands with scissors. Snap one bamboo skewer in a length long enough to thread five to seven green seedless grapes onto. Thread the grapes onto the skewer to create a caterpillar. Place the caterpillar in the "Caterpillar" division of the paper plate.
    d. Place one baby carrot chrysalis into the section of the paper plate labeled "Chrysalis."
    e. Decorate the top of the clothespin with markers to create a colorful butterfly thorax or body.
    f. Attach the decorated wooden clothespin to the middle of one unzipped snack size plastic bag.
    g. Fill slightly less than ½ of the snack bag with whole grain fish-shaped crackers and push the crackers to one side off the snack bag. Repeat this

process with the cherry tomatoes. Leave the remaining space in the middle of the snack bag for the clothespin. Zip the bag closed and attach the clothespin.

   h. Bend one pipe cleaner in half and clip the bent portion in between the clothespin pincers. Shape both ends of the pipe cleaners to resemble insect antennae.

   i. Place the butterfly onto the "Butterfly" section of the plate.

6. Snap and trim one bamboo skewer for each registered child.

7. Bend one pipe cleaner in half for each registered child.

8. Cover all the tables with plastic tablecloths.

9. Decide how many children will be seated at each table. This will determine the appropriate amount of food to place in the foam, paper or plastic disposable bowls. Into each of the eight bowls per table, place the determined amount of individual items: golden raisins, pre-prepared bamboo skewers, green seedless grapes, baby carrots, whole grain fish-shaped crackers, cherry tomatoes, clothespins, and pre-folded pipe cleaners. Do not place these bowls onto the children's work tables. Keep these bowls on the supply table.

10. Place a selection of markers in a variety of colors on each of the children's work tables.

Bake

1. Gather the children in your favorite story time configuration.

2. Read aloud the picture book(s) about butterflies and/or the life cycle of the butterfly. Discuss the different stages of the life cycle of the butterfly with the children.

3. Reinforce the science of the life cycle of the butterfly by prompting the children to act it out. Cue the music. Instruct the children to curl up into the smallest size they can and pretend to be eggs. The children should then pretend to break out of their eggs and crawl along the floor like caterpillars. Ask the children to wrap their arms around their bodies to cocoon themselves into chrysalises. Prompt the butterfly children to slowly emerge from their chrysalises. Ask them to first poke one wing out, then another, then their heads and legs. Let the butterfly children fly and soar around the room.

4. Once again, gather the children into the story time configuration. Explain the edible butterfly life cycle project they will create and show them *The Very Healthy Butterfly* sample.

5. Ask the children to choose a work space at a table and be seated.

6. Hand each child his or her pre-labeled plate.

7. Place one bowl of golden raisins on each table and instruct the children to place 10 raisins into the portion of the plate labeled "Eggs." Some children may need help identifying the different portions of the plates. Walk around the room reinforcing the life cycle concept aloud with the group and help children individually.

8. Remove the raisin bowls on each table and replace them with one bowl of pre-cut bamboo skewers and one bowl of grapes. Instruct the children to thread the grapes through the bamboo skewers to create their caterpillars.

Have the children place their caterpillars on the section labeled "Caterpillar" on their plates.

9. Once everyone has put their caterpillars onto their plates, place one bowl of baby carrots onto each table and remove the bowls of grapes and bamboo skewers. Continue talking about the life cycle of butterflies and offering assistance where needed.

10. Remove the bowls of baby carrots and place the bowls containing the clothespins, cherry tomatoes, fish-shaped crackers, and pipe cleaners along with the correct with the correct number of snack size–zippered plastic bags onto each table.

11. Instruct the children to use the markers on the table to create colorful butterfly thoraces or bodies. Walk around the room and as children finish coloring their clothespin butterfly bodies, attach their clothespin to the middle of their snack size unzipped plastic bag. Instruct the children to fill the bags with whole grain fish-shaped crackers and cherry tomatoes.

12. Ask the children to raise their hands when they are finished filling their snack bags. The staff member should remove the clothespin, zip up the snack bag, and replace the clothespin. Have each child choose one pre-bent pipe cleaner from the bowl. Open the clothespin, insert the bent portion of the pipe cleaner into the clothespin, and reclose the clothespin over the pipe cleaner to secure it. Ask the children to shape the pipe cleaners into butterfly antennae. The children should place their completed butterfly onto the "Butterfly" section of the plate.

13. The children are now ready to spread their wings and fly home, but they may need help carrying their projects back to their parents or caregivers.

This program is a model for teaching preschoolers in an active, rather than passive, fashion. Hands-on learning for this age group is likely to allow the children to understand the concept rather than merely memorizing it.

Variation: To emphasize nutrition, add an additional 15 minutes to the length of this program. Discuss the health benefits obtained from making healthy choices, for example, incorporating the food components from the butterfly life cycle project into the children's diets.

Leftovers: Use the leftover bamboo skewers in the *Off to the Races* program on page 20 and the *Maker Marketplace's* "Pirate Loot Bag" on page 106. Any leftover cherry tomatoes or baby carrots may be used in the *Food Detectives* program on page 135.

Garnish of Books to Be Displayed during the Program

Carle, Eric. *The Very Hungry Caterpillar*. New York: Philomel Books, 1983.
Foley, Greg E. *Don't Worry Bear*. New York: Viking, 2008.
Kalman, Bobbie. *Caterpillars to Butterflies*. New York: Crabtree Publishing Company, 2009.
McNamara, Margaret. *Butterfly Garden*. New York: Simon Spotlight, 2012.
Middleton, Charlotte. *Nibbles' Garden: Another Green Tale*. New York: Marshall Cavendish Children, 2012.
Salzmann, Mary Elizabeth. *Fluttering Butterflies*. Minneapolis, MN: ABDO Publishing Company, 2012.

Appendix A: Book Discussion Questions

Alternate Reality Book Discussion Questions Ages 7–10
Da Wild, Da Crazy, Da Vinci *by Jon Scieszka*

1. In *Da Wild, Da Crazy, Da Vinci*, what country are Sam, Joe, and Fred "visiting?" How did they get there? Why did they wish to go to Italy?
2. Leonardo da Vinci hides some of his secrets by writing in a special language. What is it? Do you think you could write or even speak backward?
3. Leonardo da Vinci seems to have quite a sense of humor. Can you name any of the jokes he invented in this book?
4. Who is Captain Nassti? Do you think his name suits him? Why or why not?
5. What is "the power drain?" Who does Joe use the power drain on and why?
6. Lord Borgia "does not ask. He commands!" What does Lord Borgia command Sam, Joe, and Fred to do?
7. Why do you think Leonardo gives the boys the last name "da Brooklyn?" Does this give you a clue to how Leonardo got his last name?
8. Fred used a piece of cheese to block a stream of water heading toward his sandwich (soggy sandwiches are gross!). After Leonardo saw this, it inspired him to create what invention that helped Lord Borgia to take over the city of Urbo?
9. Joe says that it is too hard to describe what it feels like to time travel. He compares it to trying to describe the taste of chocolate ice cream to someone who had never tasted it before. Can you describe the taste of chocolate ice cream?
10. Sam wants to return to Italy to talk more with Leonardo. Joe isn't sure. Would you want to spend more time with Leonardo or move on to a new time warp adventure?
11. If you could be a time traveler like Sam, Joe, and Fred, what time period would you like to travel to? Where would you want to go? Who would you want to meet while you are there?

Alternate Reality Book Discussion Questions Ages 9–12
The Templeton Twins Have an Idea *by Ellis Weiner*

1. Professor Elton Templeton was a respected engineer and inventor. What happened in his office at Elysian University on the day his twins Abigail and John were born?
2. A tragic event occurred in the Templeton family when the twins were 12 years old. What was the event, and how did it affect the twins and their father?
3. The book's Narrator repeated that he was being forced to tell the story of the Templeton twins. Do we learn who the Narrator was? Do we learn who was forcing him to tell the story and/or why? Do you enjoy writing? Why or why not? If you do like to write, do you create stories, poems, songs, or something else?
4. Abigail and John each had hobbies and interests that helped save their lives. What were they? Do you have any interests or hobbies?
5. What was John's favorite quote to say, and what does it mean?
6. Abigail and John wanted to get a dog. They knew they needed to devise an unusual way to ask their father for one. What was their plan and were they successful? Have you ever asked for a pet?
7. What is unusual about the illustrations in the book? How do they relate to the interests and talents of the characters?
8. What was the FACAPPTWCOM and how did it work? Who was it designed to be used by?
9. Professor Templeton took a new position at the Tickeridge-Baltock Institute of Technology. What was the nickname of the school?
10. What was Professor Templeton's most recent invention?
11. Who interrupted Professor Templeton's speech at the university? Describe the appearance of this individual. What is this person's reason for confronting Professor Templeton? Professor Templeton said, "'What matters is not what ideas you have, but what you do with your ideas.'" What do you think he meant? Do you agree or disagree?
12. Who was Nanny Nan?
13. What are some of Professor Templeton's inventions? Would you use any of them? Do you think he would have been successful if he had sold them to the public?
14. Do you like meatloaf? Would you make the meatloaf recipe the Narrator included in the book? What is your favorite food? What is your least favorite food?
15. What is a cryptic crossword puzzle? Do you think you would enjoy solving this type of puzzle?
16. Dan D. Dean is Dean D. Dean's twin brother. Is he an identical twin or a fraternal twin? Is there a difference?
17. Did you like it when the Narrator stopped telling the story to address the reader personally? Did you find his comments distracting, or did they add to the story?
18. Dean D. Dean kidnaped Abigail and John so Professor Templeton would give him the Personal One-Man Helicopter. What was Dan D. Dean's reason for helping his brother kidnap the twins?

From *The Maker Cookbook: Recipes for Children's and 'Tween Library Programs* by Cindy R. Wall and Lynn M. Pawloski. Santa Barbara, CA: Libraries Unlimited. Copyright © 2014.

19. Abigail knew that "the words you use to think about something can determine how much success you have in dealing with it." What do you think she meant?
20. Was Dean D. Dean successful in his attempt to steal the Personal One-Man Helicopter?
21. What do you think happened to Dean D. Dean and his twin brother Dan D. Dean after the story ended? Do you think the Templeton family has seen the last of them?
22. At the conclusion of the story, Professor Templeton told Abigail and John that he had an idea for a new invention. What do you think his new invention was and/or what invention would you like to see him design?

Balloon Zip Line Book Discussion Questions Ages 7–10
The Curse of the Bologna Sandwich *by Greg Trine*

1. According to Headmaster Spinner, what is a superhero's greatest weapon?
2. Who is Superhero Carl? Do you think he is worthy of the title "superhero?"
3. What two superhero activities does Melvin have trouble accomplishing?
4. After graduation, to what town is Melvin sent? In this town, they haven't had a superhero since Kareem Abdul-Jabbar. Do you know who Kareem Abdul-Jabbar is? Do you think famous sports stars are like superheroes? Why or why not?
5. What's the first rule of the superhero code? Why do you think this is important enough to be the number-one rule?
6. Melvin took an unusual flight to Los Angeles. What was so unusual about it? If you could do it safely, would you want to fly this way?
7. Melvin likes math. He even uses word problems to relax. Do you like math? What do you do to relax?
8. What is Melvin's favorite cartoon? What is your favorite cartoon and why?
9. What is Melvin's superhero weakness? If you were a superhero, what do you think your weakness would be?
10. What character does Candace Brinkwater play in the school play?
11. From where does Melvin derive his superhero powers? How did you find out that his superhero powers come from his cape?
12. Since Melvin and Candace couldn't both wear the cape at the same time, what solution did the two teammates find?
13. What was the one thing that everyone noticed first about the McNasty family? The sense of smell can be very powerful. Is there something that other people like, but you don't enjoy the smell of?
14. Since Melvin and Candace share the same superhero cape, they have the same superhero weakness. How do the McNasty brothers find out Melvin and Candace's superhero weakness?
15. How are Melvin and Candace able to escape from being held hostage by the McNasty brothers?
16. What is Melvin and Candace's favorite snack? What is your favorite snack?
17. Why does Melvin turn down Headmaster Spinner's offer to become the superhero for the beautiful island of Fiji? If you were Melvin, would you have turned it down?

Balloon Zip Line Book Discussion Questions Ages 9–12
Powerless *by Matthew Cody*

1. At the start of the story, 12-year-old Daniel Corrigan and his family are moving to Noble's Green, Pennsylvania. Why is the family making this move? What is the town of Noble's Green known as?
2. Daniel thinks, "The only thing worse than your first day in a new town . . . is your first day in a new school in a new town." Have you ever had the experience of moving to a new town? If so, where did you come from, and where did you move to? Describe what it was like to start at a new school. Are there any advantages in moving to a new town?
3. Daniel considers Sherlock Holmes to be his hero. By his estimation, a better detective than Holmes could never be found. Do you have a hero, detective, or otherwise, of your own that you look up to?
4. What is your impression of Mr. Snyder, Daniel's new homeroom teacher? Would you like to have Mr. Snyder as one of your teachers?
5. Who are the Supers of Noble's Green? What special powers do they each exhibit? If you could have one of their superpowers, which would it be and why? Do you wish you had a superpower that was different from those of the Supers of Noble's Green? Is there a superpower you know that you would *not* like to have and why?
6. Do all of the children who live in Noble's Green have superpowers? Do any of the adults exhibit superpowers? Are the Supers born with these abilities, or do the powers appear at another time?
7. Children with special powers have lived in Noble's Green for many years. What are the four rules that have been passed down through the generations of Supers?
8. Describe the secret tree fort the Supers use as a hideout and meeting place.
9. What significant event happens to each one of the Supers on his or her 13th birthday?
10. Explain the differences between the person who is Jonathan Noble and the legend of Johnny Noble. What do the Supers of Noble's Green think he was able to do that no other super-child has done since? Do they think it may be possible for another super-child to achieve this same goal? What is Eric's theory about why the world does not know of Johnny Noble's existence?
11. The Supers learn and theorize about Johnny Noble through comic books. Do you read comic books or graphic novels? If so, what are your favorite books, series, characters, and/or authors?
12. Who are Clay Cudgens and his sidekick, Bud? What are their super strengths and weaknesses? Because they are not friends with the Supers, they do not visit the tree fort. Where do they prefer to hang out instead?
13. Daniel watches Clay and Bud destroy old cars in the junkyard for no reason. He observes that it is a waste for them to have special powers while other people who might use these powers for good do not have super powers. Do you agree or disagree with this statement? Do you think people always use all their talents for good?
14. Do you think someone necessarily needs to have superpowers to accomplish good and/or heroic deeds in the world? Can you think of any examples, either from world events or among the people you know, of heroic acts being performed?

15. Why is Mollie so concerned about Eric turning 13-years-old? Why does Mollie think Daniel is the only person who can save the Supers from the Third Rule and what is her plan for attempting to do so? Is her plan successful?

16. Describe the shadow figure Daniel sees in Simon's room. Is there a name for this character?

17. Rohan believes in destiny and fate—that what's meant to happen will happen and you can't fight it. Do you agree or disagree with this statement?

18. Who is Herman Plunkett? Describe his appearance and demeanor during his and Daniel's first meeting.

19. One book in particular in Plunkett's reading room library appeals to Daniel. What is the title, author, and/or lead character of this book? What term does Plunkett refer to Daniel as because of his interest in this book?

20. Herman Plunkett wrote and illustrated the Fantastic Futures, Starring Johnny Noble comics that the Supers use as their guidebooks. What is the explanation he gives to Daniel as his inspiration for using Johnny Noble as the main character?

21. Do you like to write and/or draw? If so what type of writing do you prefer—stories, poems, songs, etc.? If you like to draw, do you have any favorite themes or art supplies that you like to use?

22. Herman Plunkett gives Daniel a portfolio containing original penciled drawings for the Fantastic Futures comics. Among the pages is a cover from one of the issues. What is the significance of this cover?

23. Who do Mollie and Daniel encounter in the Old Quarry?

24. Daniel returns to Herman Plunkett's reading room to confront him with the suspicion that Plunkett himself is the Shroud. Who does Plunkett point to as the true identity of the Shroud, and what are the clues he gives to Daniel to back up his claim?

25. Daniel and Rohan break into Eric's house looking for evidence as to his true identity. What exactly are they looking for? Do they find it? Are there any consequences to their actions?

26. Daniel learns a few things about his Gram while flipping through her old scrapbook. Not only was she adopted when she was 10 years old, but she was also one of the surviving orphans from the St. Alban's fire. What else does he learn about her? Who was also a surviving St. Alban's orphan?

27. Who is enlisted to help save Eric from the Shroud? What is his or her reason for going along with this plan? Why does Daniel blame himself for the predicament Eric and all of the Supers are in?

28. Why is Herman Plunkett so bitter about the night of the St. Alban's fire and the powers given to Jonathan Noble and the other orphans? What is his justification for taking the powers away from the other super-children? Who does Plunkett choose to be his successor? Does that person accept Plunkett's offer?

29. At various points throughout the story, different characters may have felt helpless in their own situations. Why do you think each of the following characters had a reason to feel that way:
    a. Daniel
    b. Daniel's mother
    c. Eric
    d. Mollie

    e. Gram

    f. Clay

    g. Herman Plunkett

30. Describe the final epic battle that takes place at the Old Quarry. What does the outcome mean for the futures of the Supers?

31. Who does Rose claim helped Eric wake up from a state of unconsciousness in the cave? Are there any other clues as to where else this character may have appeared throughout the story?

32. What rests in a hollowed out book on a shelf in Daniel's room?

33. The surviving orphans of the St. Alban's fire took on superpowers which were passed down to future generations within their families. Who appears to be the newest member of Daniel's family to exhibit super strength?

34. What do you think happens to the characters after the story ends?

35. Would you read the book *Super*, the sequel to *Powerless*?

36. Do you think this book should be made into a movie? If so, should it be animated or live action?

37. Do you think this book should be turned into a graphic novel or have a comic book adaptation?

Off to the Races Book Discussion Questions Ages 7–10
Barfing in the Backseat: How I Survived My Family Road Trip *by Henry Winkler and Lin Oliver*

1. Have you ever gone on a family road trip? How did you decide where to go? Where did you want to go and why? Did you get to go where you wanted to go? What do you think of Papa Pete's solution for deciding where to go?
2. Have you ever worked on a crossword puzzle? Would you consider a crossword puzzle tournament a fun thing to do for your vacation?
3. Hank wants to go to the Colossus Coaster Kingdom. Has anyone ridden a real colossal roller coaster, like the Bizzaro in the Six Flags amusement park in Massachusetts or Millennium Force at Cedar Point amusement park in Ohio?
4. Why do you think Hank got assigned a homework packet to complete during his vacation? Has this ever happened to you?
5. Chapter six contains a list of the worst places to go on a road trip. What do you think is the worst place to go on a road trip?
6. Hank and his sister Emily each get to choose a best friend to bring on the road trip. Who do they choose? Did you think they chose wisely?
7. Frankie, Hank's best friend, helps him out of a lot of sticky situations. What other qualities do you think a best friend should have?
8. Frankie's parents gave him a cell phone to use for emergencies. What did Frankie and Hank use the phone for? Do you think Frankie's parents will be mad when they find out?
9. At the Science Museum in Virginia, Emily finds a lab that allows kids to add "all kinds of flavors to 250 different candies." What is your favorite candy? Would you add any flavor to it if you could or would you want it to remain just as it is?
10. Mrs. Zipzer wanted to visit Buzz Haven Honey Farm. Would you want to go to a bee farm? Why or why not?
11. Where did Frankie choose to go on the road trip? Why did he give up his road trip choice? If you were Frankie, would you have given up your trip to Chapel Hill, North Carolina?
12. Did Hank finish his homework packet in time to go to Colossus Coaster Kingdom? What could he have done to have made sure his homework packet was completed on time?
13. After Mr. Zipzer found out Hank had not completed the homework packet, what did he do? If you were Mr. Zipzer, what would you have done?
14. People sometimes say things work out for the best. Do you think this was the case for Hank and his winter vacation road trip? Why or why not?

Off to the Races Book Discussion Questions Ages 9–12
A Whole Nother Story *by Dr. Cuthbert Soup*

1. Mr. Ethan Cheeseman is a scientist and inventor. He knows his latest, nearly completed device, the Luminal Velocity Regulator (or LVR) may be used for either good or evil. What is the LVR, and what does Mr. Cheeseman intend to use his invention for?
2. Many different people and organizations want to steal the LVR and use it for their own purposes. Mr. Cheeseman knows the only means of ensuring the LVR's safety is to keep the device solely in his own possession and disappear until it can be perfected. What has been his method of attempting to protect the device for almost two years and who else is affected by this decision?
3. What was the term Mr. Cheeseman called the people pursuing him and his family?
4. Mr. Cheeseman has three children. What are their names? "Steve" is also considered a member of the Cheeseman family. Describe Steve's appearance and personality. Does he serve a purpose for one of the Cheeseman children in particular? How did Steve come to be a member of the family?
5. Pinky, the Cheeseman family dog, has developed unusual psychic abilities that allow her to protect the family. What are these abilities, how did she acquire them, and how do they benefit the Cheeseman family?
6. How do the Cheeseman children feel about being constantly on the move?
7. What unique hobby or interest does each one of the Cheeseman children have? How do these hobbies or interests help them during the course of their adventure?
8. The author of *A Whole Nother Story*, Dr. Cuthbert Soup, argues that the wheel is the greatest invention ever created. Do you agree or disagree with his statement? Is there another invention you would deem to be the greatest? If so, what is it? Why?
9. Throughout the course of the story, the author offers pieces of advice on a variety of topics. Did you find one particular piece of advice from the book held special meaning for you or that you simply found particularly amusing?
10. Gerard claims that chewing on his big wad of flavorless bubble gum helps him think better. If you like to chew, do you have a brand and/or flavor that is your favorite?
11. The Cheeseman children do take one pleasure from moving around a lot. What is it and in what way are they each changed by it? If you could do this yourself, would you? What would your new name be and why?
12. Why did Mr. Cheeseman teach his son Jough to drive when he was 12 years old? Does this skill become important at some point in the story? At what age do you think a person should legally be allowed to drive and why? If you were allowed to drive now, where would you go and why?
13. Representatives from the Plexiwave company offered Mr. Cheeseman a job with a $2 million per year salary, great benefits, a beautiful home on a tropical island, with wonderful schools and no crime.
    a. What types of different products does the Plexiwave company manufacture?
    b. Did the Mr. Cheeseman accept the Plexiwave job offer?
    c. Would you have accepted such a job offer even if you did not agree with the principles of the company?
    d. What were the consequences, if any, from the outcome of this meeting?

From *The Maker Cookbook: Recipes for Children's and 'Tween Library Programs* by Cindy R. Wall and Lynn M. Pawloski. Santa Barbara, CA: Libraries Unlimited. Copyright © 2014.

14. Mr. 5 sports an odd tattoo on his left wrist, 3VAW1X319. If read in the reflection of his mirrored sunglasses, what would it read?

15. What is the reason Mr. Cheeseman is having such a difficult time finishing the LVR?

16. Who are Captain Jibby and the members of his Traveling Circus Sideshow? How did Captain Jibby lose his right hand and what was it replaced with? Where were they heading to when their black and white school bus broke down and what are they hoping to accomplish once they get there? How do they repay the Cheeseman family for fixing their school bus?

17. Before stopping to help Captain Jibby fix his broken-down school bus, Mr. Cheeseman said, "'We must never allow our own circumstances to become an excuse for not helping others in need.'" Can you think of any examples in the story where the Cheeseman's help other characters?

18. What is special about Jough's earmuffs and what does he do with them after he no longer needs them?

19. Nearly every member of Jibby's Traveling Circus Sideshow is experiencing some sort of physical ailment. For example, Jibby himself has lost his right hand while Sammy the strong man has a sore back. What is the explanation given to account for their physical misfortunes?

20. Dr. Cuthbert Soup believes that dogs are the best animals to have for a pet. Do you agree or disagree with this statement? If you disagree, what animal do you believe is the best choice for a pet? Do you have any pets?

21. During the course of their travels, the Cheeseman family finds themselves spending the night at Coral's Bed-and-Breakfast. After midnight, a mysterious being visits Maggie. Who, or what, is this visitor, and what did it mean when it said, "Fraud, fraud, it's not the dog"?

22. Dr. Cuthbert Soup considers himself the Advisor to the Ill-Advised at the National Center for Unsolicited Advice. What event occurred that caused him to pursue this occupation? Do you know what type of career you would like to pursue? If so, what is it and what types of qualifications are necessary to enter this field? Do you have a back story or reason for finding this field of particular interest?

23. The Cheeseman family finally settles down in a small pink house in yet another new town. The children easily make new friends and Mr. Cheeseman can now concentrate on cracking the code to the LVR. Coincidentally, what new factory is being constructed in their new town?

24. Who does Jough call when he learns his father and Gerard have been kidnapped?

25. How is the second half of the LVR's code discovered, and what is the code in its entirety? Do you think this is a good piece of advice?

26. Captain Jibby and Juanita turn out to be ancestors of the Cheeseman family. What is their relationship to the Cheeseman's?

27. What year do Jibby and the members of his Traveling Circus Sideshow come from? What was their profession? What is their solution for undoing the curse of the White Gold Chalice?

28. What do Agents Aitch Dee and El Kyoo find in the white moving van in the Plexi-wave warehouse?

29. What do you think becomes of the Cheeseman family and Captain Jibby and his crew?

30. Would you be interested in reading the sequel to this book, *Another Whole Nother Story*?

31. *A Whole Nother Story* is filled with action, adventure, comedy, and a quirky cast of characters. Do you think this book would make a good movie? Would you watch it if it was? Can you think of any actors that you would cast in specific roles in the movie?

Cardboard aMAZEment Book Discussion Ages 7–10

Judy Moody & Stink: The Mad, Mad, Mad, Mad Treasure Hunt *by Megan McDonald*

1. Where are Stink and Judy Moody vacationing? Have you ever been to the Outer Banks in North Carolina?

2. Stink and Judy wonder if the famous pirate Christopher Moody could be one of their ancestors. Can you name any other famous real-life pirates?

3. Stink mentions that one of the "Pirate Rules" is that no girls are allowed to board a pirate ship. Why do you think this was? Was this rule always followed? If you could add a rule to Stink's list of "Pirate Rules," what would it be?

4. Who is Cap'n Weevil and what exciting information does he tell Judy and Stink?

5. Judy and Stink argue about whether or not the first clue leads to the flagpole or the church, but neither is correct. Where does the first clue lead? Stink astonishes his sister Judy with all the facts he knows about lighthouses. Do you know any facts about lighthouses? Have you ever visited a lighthouse? If so, where was it, and what was it like?

6. Stink has a survival kit. What is his survival kit? One of the things in his survival kit is a Morse code decoder. Do you know what Morse code is? Can you decode the following Morse code phrase?

   .__ .... ._ .. _ _ .... _ ... ._ ._ .... ?

7. Judy figures out that the answer to clue #3, "sign of the pirate," is an acrostic on the sign for the art shop "Ye Artful Eye." What is an acrostic?

8. Stink, Judy, and their parents go on the town Ghost Walk? Would you want to go on a ghost walk? If so, would you rather go in the daytime or at night?

9. How does Stink solve the hourglass clue? Do you think Stink did the right thing, or do you think he cheated?

10. Who are Tall Boy and Smart Girl? Why do you think Judy and Stink decide to share their prizes with them? If you had won the treasure hunt, would you have shared your prize?

Cardboard aMAZEment Book Discussion Questions Ages 9–12
The Gollywhopper Games *by Jody Feldman*

1. The Golly Toy and Game Company is celebrating its 50th anniversary by holding a competition called the Gollywhopper Games. Explain the concept of the Gollywhopper Games and the prizes the winner will receive.

2. What is Gil Goodson's entire first name? Does he like his name? What nickname is Gil given in the story and by whom is it given? Do you have a nickname? If so, how did you acquire it?

3. Gil's father was the vice president of the Golly Toy and Game Company. He had been arrested for allegedly attempting to steal money from the company by reprogramming the computer system to divert $25,000 per week from an account accessible only to the company's president and his attorneys.
   a. Even before the trial began, how was Gil treated by his classmates and friends at school?
   b. Gil had once enjoyed participating in sports. Did he find support in his teammates? Name the character that was particularly mean to Gil.
   c. What was the verdict in Mr. Goodson's trial? Did it change the way people felt about the Goodson family?

4. Describe some of the ways in which Gil and his family's lifestyle has changed as a result of "The Incident."
   a. Is Mr. Goodson now employed?
   b. What activity seemingly takes all of Mr. Goodson's other time and concentration?
   c. What do Gil and his family decide they will do if Gil wins the Gollywhopper Games?

5. What are some of the benefits children of the Golly Toy and Game Company employees receive?

6. Like Gil, each of the competition contestants on Gil's team has a personal reason for entering the Gollywhopper Games. What are the reasons for the following characters:
   a. Bianca LaBlanc
   b. Thorn Dewitt-Formey
   c. Lavinia Plodder
   d. Rocky Titus
   Did they find what they were looking for at the Gollywhopper Games, or did they find something different?

7. Bianca tells Gil, "You have to have a story. Everyone has a story, at least that's what Oprah said." Do you agree or disagree that each person has a unique story?

8. How has Gil been preparing for the Gollywhopper Games? How does Gil feel about Bianca wanting to use his notebooks? Why does he let her? How would you have responded to Bianca?

9. The Golly Toy and Game Company is the largest toy company and boasts more than 800 products available for purchase. Many different toys and games are mentioned throughout the course of the story, for example, the collapsible car track, and the glowing volleyball. Can you name other toys and/or games from the story? Which would you like to play with? Do you have your own favorite game or toy?

From *The Maker Cookbook: Recipes for Children's and 'Tween Library Programs* by Cindy R. Wall and Lynn M. Pawloski. Santa Barbara, CA: Libraries Unlimited. Copyright © 2014.

10. While Gil's father still worked for the Golly Toy and Game Company, Gil would go to work with his father on Saturdays and test new toys. Is this something you would like to do? Do you have an idea for a toy or game that you would like to see developed?

11. Once Gil and his father make it into University Stadium, contestants are treated to a concert by Skorch, a popular rock star. Who is your favorite musician or band? Have you ever seen them live in concert?

12. Who cheats on the very first question of the Gollywhopper Games? Is that the only cheating scandal in the competition? Why does Gil need to stop the cheating before the competition starts?

13. Gil finds a lucky penny on the football field near the track. Do you have an object that you feel provides you with good luck, for example, a shirt you always wear on the day of a test to ensure a good score?

14. Who is Carol and why does she want Gil's team to win?

15. In the course of the Gollywhopper Games, puzzles of logic are followed by physical stunts. Of all of the puzzles and stunts from the story, which one was your favorite? Which kind of games would you rather compete in?

16. Each person on Gil's team has both strengths and weaknesses. What are they and how do they add to or detract from the team's mission? Do you think this is true of any team? Are you on any teams, either sports or academic? Can you think of any examples of how your teammates help one another?

17. Who is Bert Golliwop? Why does he ask Gil to forfeit his spot on the team in return for the consolation prizes and a lot of money? Does Gil accept his offer? What would you have done?

18. The winners of the team challenge must then compete against each other as individuals. Do you prefer working together with others toward a single goal or alone on a solitary project? Do you think one way of working is better than another? What are the advantages or disadvantages to both methods of working?

19. What is Rocky's "guarantee" and what does he whisper in Gil's ear right before the third puzzle of the final games? Why do you think he chose that moment to tell Gil? What distressed Gil most about Rocky's "guarantee"? Is Rocky's plan successful?

20. Some of the members of Gil's team are given a second chance during the finals. Describe the circumstances regarding this development and who was involved.

21. Who is ultimately the winner of the Gollywhopper Games? Who is the runner up? Do you think the right people won?

22. Who really stole the money from the Golly Toy and Game Company? What were their reasons? Do you feel any differently toward Rocky as a result?

23. How does the Golly Toy and Game Company compensate the Goodson family for all they have endured as a result of the stealing allegations? What project has Mr. Goodson really been working on?

24. Do you think Gil and his family will go through with the plan they discussed now that they know Gil has won the competition?

The *Fake Spill* Book Discussion Questions Ages 7–10
The Get Rich Quick Club *by Dan Gutman*

1. What is the mission of the Get Rich Quick Club? How do they propose to achieve this goal?
2. What does Gina Tumolo love so much that she even dreams about it? What is her goal in life, and why does she think this is so important to her?
3. Who is Rob Hunnicutt and what type of animal does he keep as a pet?
4. On their first day of summer vacation, Rob and Gina discuss attending summer camp. Did they go to summer camp this year? Do you attend a camp, class, or other organized activity during the summer? If so, what sorts of events do you take part in?
5. Why does Gina say, "Man, I could listen to Quincy talk all day"?
6. What do Eddie and Teddy Bogle collect? Do you maintain a collection of any kind?
7. How did the friends come up with the name the Get Rich Quick Club?
8. While brainstorming money-making ideas for their company, Rob and Gina discuss and agree on the "fact" that UFOs do not exist. Do you agree with Rob and Gina? Or do you think there may be the possibility of life on other planets? If so, what forms of life do you think may exist and do you believe the Earth will ever discover and/or connect with them?
9. Which newspaper finally agrees to publish the fake UFO photo? Did the Get Rich Quick Club receive $1 million asking price they had hoped for?
10. After the newspaper prints the fake UFO photo, a TV news crew interviews the friends for information regarding their encounter. Who gives the news team a description of the sighting and what is their story? What do they claim the aliens said to them?
11. After their ridiculous story of the UFO encounter appears on the news, do people believe their tale? What happens in their town as a result of the publicity?
12. Who knew all along that the UFO photo and story were a hoax? Why do you think they did not tell on their friends?
13. At any point, does it appear as though the Get Rich Quick Club may actually get rich? What do each of the kids propose they will do with the millions of dollars in endorsements they expect to receive? What would you do with the money if you suddenly made millions of dollars?
14. The friends debate the merits of several different kinds of candy bars. What is your favorite candy bar and/or candy and why? What is your least favorite candy bar and/or candy and why?
15. Why does Gina assume Eddie and Teddy Bogle were the ones who told the newspaper the entire story is a hoax? Who finally told the truth and why?
16. Late in the story, a UFO does, in fact, visit the friends. Describe the UFO and alien. Why does the alien want to take a picture of the kids? Why do Eddie and Teddy give it their box of dryer dust? When asked by Rob to reveal the secret of the universe, what is the alien's reply?
17. At the conclusion of the story, Rob has another one of his money-making ideas. What sorts of adventures do you think the friends will find themselves in next?

The Fake Spill Book Discussion Questions Ages 9–12
Pickle: The (Formerly) Anonymous Prank Club of Fountain Point Middle School *by Kim Baker*

1. Who are the League of Pickle Makers? When and where does the organization meet? Are the members of the club really interested in making pickles or is the club a cover for another, more secretive purpose?

2. Ben Diaz answers an advertisement from Pete's Pizza, a local restaurant, for free ball-pit balls for any person who would come to the restaurant and take them. What does Ben do with the 12 garbage bags and several nets full of ball-pit balls? What is the worst part of the ball-pit balls that lingers even after the balls are gone?

3. Ben and his best friend Hector live in the same apartment building. Who is Hector's grandmother, and why does Hector try so hard to stay out of trouble?

4. What is "The Graffiti Incident" and why does it make Ben hesitant to trust Hector's ability to keep a secret?

5. Ben's family owns a Mexican restaurant called Lupe's. Ben works in the restaurant as a dishwasher, busboy, and/or in whatever other capacity he is needed. Do you think it would be fun to work in the restaurant or another family business? What are the advantages and/or disadvantages to working in a family business?

6. Ben knows he will need help if he wants to pull pranks bigger than filling his homeroom with ball-pit balls. Oliver, Frank, and eventually Bean (the original Pickle Makers) are recruited for the individual talents they could bring to the organization. What are each of their contributions?

7. Fountain Point Middle School offers a wide diversity of clubs and extracurricular activities. Are you a member of a school organization, club, or team?

8. Ben must start a club that other students would not want to be a member of, but adults would think kids might want to join. How does Ben decide upon the name the League of Pickle Makers? What name would you have given to the club?

9. For one year, the teachers of Fountain Point Middle School have been planning a Pioneer Fair featuring historical reenactments, livestock, foods of the era, contests, and games. Is this an event you or your school would be interested in attending and/or hosting? What sorts of events either would be or are popular at your school?

10. Ben's homeroom teacher, Ms. Ruiz, volunteers to be the faculty advisor to the League of Pickle Makers. She assumes the club wants to enter the Pioneer Fair's preserving and pickling contest. She gives Ben one of her pickling cookbooks and activity money from the fund to the club so they may begin making pickles. What do the club members decide to do with some of the money instead?

11. What is Bean Lee's real name? Do you have a nickname? If so, how did you earn it?

12. What do you think is the most important to each of the members of the League of Pickle Makers—pulling pranks, making new friends, or feeling as though they belong to a group?

13. How does it make Ben feel to distance himself from his best friend Hector in order to be in the League of Pickle Makers? How does it make Hector feel to watch Ben spending time with his new friends?

14. Food plays a large role in the story—the delicious offerings at Lupe's restaurant, the diet Hector's grandmother places him on, Oliver's love of baking, the pickling competition, and Lupe's chef, Diego, teaching Ben and Oliver to cook. Do you like to cook? If so, what types of food do you prefer to make?

15. Why do you think Ben told Hector the activities the League of Pickle Makers were actually working on?

16. What is Principal Lebonsky's response to the cricket prank ruining the Pioneer Fair? Who does she punish? Do you think her solution to ending the pranks at Fountain Point Middle School is fair?

17. How do the students protest the principal's punishment following the nutrition assembly? Are they successful in having their club and team privileges reinstated?

18. Why does Hector tell his grandmother that he, along with Ben, is responsible for the pranks taking place at Fountain Point Middle School? Is she convinced Hector was really involved in the shenanigans? How do the other members of the League of Pickle Makers feel about Hector taking the blame? Do they allow Ben to be solely responsible for shouldering the punishment of the pranks?

19. The students at Fountain Point Middle School wanted the freedom to choose the types of organizations and clubs they joined. One classmate, Leo Saylor, even protested that he was *too* involved in extracurricular activities, by quitting two sports teams without telling his father. He found that he finally had the time to read and/or relax. How many extracurricular activities are you involved in? Do you think kids today participate in too many activities, not enough activities, or the just the right amount? How do you balance school, homework, clubs, hobbies, and relaxation?

20. Of all the pranks pulled by Ben and the League of Pickle Makers, which one was your favorite and why?

From *The Maker Cookbook: Recipes for Children's and 'Tween Library Programs* by Cindy R. Wall and Lynn M. Pawloski. Santa Barbara, CA: Libraries Unlimited. Copyright © 2014.

Meteorite Strike Book Discussion Questions Ages 7–10

How to Save Your Tail: If You Are a Rat Nabbed By Cats Who Really Like Stories about Magic Spoons, Wolves with Snout-warts, Big, Hairy Chimney Trolls . . . and Cookies, too *by Mary Hanson*

1. There were two things that Bob the rat really loved. What were they? Which one of those things led to the trouble that starts off this book?

2. Who are Brutus and Muffin? What first distracts Brutus and Muffin from making a meal of Bob?

3. Do you think that you would like a cookie recipe that had "double butter with cream cheese filling and a sinful blend of spice, mint, chips, and sugar"?

4. What is your favorite cookie? Do you prefer to bake your own cookies, or do you like the taste of store bought cookies better?

5. Do you think it is Brutus or Muffin who likes Bob's stories the best?

6. If you were a cat who ate mice, would you rather have eaten Bob or heard one of his stories?

7. What kind of stories did Bob tell? Do you think these stories really happened to his ancestors? Why or why not?

8. In Bob's story, Sherman and the Beanstalk, what was Sherman's favorite food (besides cookies)? What kind of cookies did Sherman smell wafting down from atop the Beanstalk? What was different about the cook's spoon? What kind of animals were the Giant and Justine? What happened to Jack and the others? At the end of Sherman and the Beanstalk, a question is posed: are cookies any good without milk? What do you think?

9. What fairy tale does Bob's story The Three Rats pose a sequel to? What new characters are added? The three rats want to convince the warthog to marry Elsie. How do they do it? Do you think it would be fun to really see the future or would you prefer not to know some things?

10. Bob's story The Chimney Troll starts out much like the original Rumplestilskin, but then things take quite a different turn. What are the differences between Rumplestilskin and Bob's The Chimney Troll? Do you think you could take care of 13 babies? Do you think that the Chimney Troll regretted saying, "a deal is a deal?"

11. In Bob's story The Wood Fairy, why do you think the wood fairy gave Griselda the ability to spit out jewels as she spoke? What would you do if you could suddenly manufacture precious gems just by speaking? What "gift" did the wood fairy give Griselda's stepsister and why?

12. Bob's story Bob's Slipper is a retelling of what classic fairy tale? In Bob's story, the fairy godmother is scared away by a witch. This leaves Bob, using a spell from a book, to get Cindy ready for the ball. Do things go according to plan? What happens?

13. Does Bob eventually escape Brutus and Muffin? If so, how? Do you think they all lived happily ever after?

Meteorite Strike **Book Discussion Questions Ages 9–12**
Wonderstruck *by Brian Selznick*

1. What do we learn about Ben at the start of the story?
2. Can you describe the wood box he keeps under his cot? What are some of the items he keeps locked inside of it? What is significant about the ejecta stones?
3. According to Ben's mom, which star should you look for if you are ever lost, as it will always lead you home?
4. Ben's mom, the town librarian, had many quotes taped on her refrigerator at home, but only one quote taped on her bulletin board at work, " 'We are all in the gutter, but some of us are looking at the stars.' " What do you think this means?
5. Ben had painted his bedroom black and covered the walls and ceiling with glow-in-the-dark stars arranged in the shapes of constellations. Is this something you would like to do in your room?
6. After Ben's mom passed away, he went to live with his aunt and uncle. What does he know about his father?
7. After the author introduces Ben's story in text, the first illustrated section of Wonderstruck depicts a young girl in her room in Hoboken, New Jersey, in 1927. Whose picture is she tearing out of *Moviestar* Magazine?
8. What book does Ben find in one of his mom's dresser drawers? The book Ben finds describes museums, both big and small, as collections of objects thoughtfully acquired, arranged, and displayed to convey a story. A curator decides which objects the museum will house and the best manner for the objects to be displayed. People who collect objects to be kept and/or displayed in their own homes are also curators. Are you a curator? Do you collect anything? If so, how do you decide what you'll acquire, keep, discard, and/or display?
9. Ben finds a photo of a man named Daniel inside his mother's locket. Ben and Daniel have the same eyes. Who does Ben assume he is?
10. Why is Rose so upset to see the signs at the movie theater advertising a new sound system and "talkie" movies?
11. What happens when Ben tries to call the phone number for Kincaid Books, and how does this affect his hearing?
12. Do you know anyone who is deaf? If so, how do they "listen?" For example, do they read lips or have cochlear implants?
13. What does Rose like to do with books?
14. Why does Rose run away to New York City? Does she find what she is looking for?
15. Why does Ben run away to New York City?
16. What building do both Rose and Ben end up at after arriving in New York City? Which exhibit do they both pause at?
17. Meteorites start their descent to Earth as shooting stars upon which people make wishes. What does Rose wish for? Do you think Ben wishes for the same thing?
18. How does Brian Selznick highlight Rose in his illustrations?
19. Which museum diorama are both Rose and Ben are connected to and why?
20. Who is Jamie?

21. Jamie lets Ben stay in the museum because he knows Ben has run away from home. If you were in the museum with Ben and Jamie and had access to the entire museum, what would you like to see?
22. Jamie and Ben become friends because they are both interested in the same things. Why are you and your best friend close?
23. Jamie teaches Ben a little about sign language. Do you know sign language?
24. Ben needs Jamie's help to call his aunt and uncle who he knows must be worried sick about him. Were you surprised Jamie didn't ask his dad for help?
25. What does Ben find in the file folder containing information about the Gunflint exhibit?
26. Who rescues Rose from the Museum?
27. Ben hides in one particular room in the museum. What does he discover the room to be? Which one of the pieces in his museum box fits in the decorations on the cabinet?
28. Toward the end of the story, the illustrations in the book turn from following a young girl named Rose to following an elderly woman walking into Kincaid Books. Who is the woman and what year is it? Who do we see in the illustrations for the first time?
29. Where does Rose take Ben to answer all of his questions?
30. At the end of the story Rose, Ben and Jamie are sitting on the roof of the Queens Museum of Art gazing at the night sky while they wait to be picked up by Walter. Which star is featured in the last illustration and why?
31. What do you think happens after the story ends?
32. After viewing the illustrations of Brian Selznick, what subject or storyline would you suggest he write a book about?
33. One story in the book is told in text and the other in illustrations. Though set in different decades, the two stories mirror each other. Did you like the author's storytelling technique or did you find it distracting?

Plastic vs. Plastic **Book Discussion Questions Ages 9–12**
Schooled *by Gordon Korman*

1. Who was Capricorn "Cap" Anderson? Describe his appearance and personality.
2. Cap and his grandmother, Rain, lived alone on Garland Farm. Garland Farm was considered an "alternative farm commune." Explain the lifestyle and beliefs of the people who lived on Garland Farm over the years. What are the advantages of this style of living? What are the disadvantages of this style of living?
3. Garland Farm was founded as a way for members to escape a society centered on money and material possessions. How much money or "things" should people have? Do you think the world revolves around money?
4. At the start of the story, Cap had never played a video game, watched television, or used a computer. What one piece of technology do you think you could not live without?
5. Cap and Rain were the only remaining Garland Farm residents. Did Cap have any other family members besides Rain?
6. After Rain had to be hospitalized for eight weeks with a broken hip, where was Cap temporarily relocated to live? How is it that the woman who lived in this house understood all that Cap was going through?
7. Was it an honor to be nominated and elected eighth-grade president at Claverage Middle School? What was the process and who won the election? Who was supposed to be nominated, and how did that person feel about not winning? Why did he or she not tell Cap to take his name off of the nomination form?
8. What was the nickname given to Claverage Middle School?
9. Have you ever moved to a new city or town? If so, where did you move from and to? Can you relate to Cap's experiences and fears? How would Cap have gotten along at your school?
10. Cap was homeschooled on Garland Farm, and Rain was his teacher. When he first started at Claverage Middle School, he thought it would be impossible to learn in an environment where, at the sound of an alarm, students stopped working on one subject and began studying another subject with a different teacher. How does your school work? Do you have short periods that meet every day or longer blocks of time during which students may concentrate on one subject? Are there advantages or disadvantages to either system?
11. What sorts of judgments do the kids at school make about Cap based on his appearance?
12. What did Hugh Winkleman mean when he said, "Adults are always trying to figure out what makes kids tick . . .Know what? They don't have a clue."?
13. Many characters in the story had their own reasons for treating Cap terribly or looking the other way while others did. What were the reasons for the following characters?
    a. Zach Powers
    b. Hugh Winkleman
    c. Naomi Erlanger
    d. Sophie Donnelly
    e. Mr. Kasigi, the assistant principal
    f. Mr. Rodrigo, the school bus driver

From *The Maker Cookbook: Recipes for Children's and 'Tween Library Programs* by Cindy R. Wall and Lynn M. Pawloski. Santa Barbara, CA: Libraries Unlimited. Copyright © 2014.

14. Zach and Naomi put disgusting items in Cap's locker just to be mean. What did Cap do with the dead bird they placed in there?
15. The school bus is described as the place where people act their very worst. Do you agree or disagree with this statement? How do you get to school: the school bus, car, bicycle, walking, or another way?
16. Assistant Principal Kasigi gave Cap a book of signed checks from the school's Student Activity Fund. What was the money supposed to be used for? What did Cap do with the money? What would you do with a book of signed checks from your school?
17. What unlikely duo teams up together after Cap becomes the most popular kid at Claverage Middle School? How did they set up Cap at the school's pep rally? Did they succeed in their plan?
18. When Cap did not return to school and the Halloween dance was cancelled, what were some of the rumors explaining what had happened to Cap? What did the students come together to do on the night the Halloween dance was supposed to be held?
19. Was Cap happy to return to Garland Farm?
20. What sort of transformation did Rain undergo after Cap's "memorial service?"
21. Do you think Cap will change after he leaves Garland Farm once again to live in society and attend Claverage Middle School?
22. Cap broke the law at least three times during the course of the story. Can you explain the circumstances of any of Cap's legal infractions? Of course, laws are put into effect to protect people. But if a person breaks the law while helping another person, do you think he or she should be treated more leniently? Why or why not?
23. To many of the characters in the story, Cap appeared to have fallen out of the sky or was seen as a visitor from another time period or planet. Though Cap represented the 1960s, if you could travel to any other time period, what would it be? Or, is there a particular historical event you would like to witness and/or a person you would wish to meet?
24. Cap was 13 years old when he was arrested for driving without a driver's license. Do you know at what age a person may obtain a driver's license in your state? At what age do you think a person should be allowed to drive a vehicle and why?

Fairy Tale Theater **Book Discussion Ages 5–7**
Pinky and Rex and the School Play *by James Howe*

1. This book is about two friends appearing in a play together. Have you ever been in a play?
2. What happens to Pinky when he gets nervous? Why is he nervous at the start of the book?
3. What does Pinky want to be when he grows up?
4. Does Rex want to try out for the play? Why not?
5. What part does Rex get? Why is the name of the play changed? Do you think Pinky is happy about his part?
6. Pinky says that he is never going to speak to Rex again. Why? Do you think Pinky is right?
7. In the first few rehearsals, Rex was having difficulty doing something. What was it? Did Pinky feel badly for her? Why or why not?
8. Why did Pinky decide to go to every rehearsal?
9. Pinky felt like the day of the play would be the worst day of his life. Why did Pinky feel this way? Who made him feel better? How did she do it?
10. Before the play started, what did Mr. Lacey tell the children NOT to do?
11. Did Pinky like his costume when he first saw it? Why did he change his mind?
12. What is the theater expression that actors use to wish each other good luck?
13. What two things did Mr. Lacey remind the children of just before they went on stage?
14. During the play, some of the children forgot what to do. How did Pinky help?
15. Did Mr. Lacey think Pinky performed well in the play? Why?
16. Do you think Rex will act again? Why or why not?
17. Do you think Pinky will act again? What does Mr. Lacey think Pinky might want to do?

Fondant Game Book Discussion Questions Ages 9–12
The Candymakers *by Wendy Mass*

1. The four main characters in *The Candymakers* enter a candy-making contest. Would you consider entering a candy-making contest? Describe and name the candy you would make if you did enter.

2. When we first meet Logan, he says that he doesn't have any experience with other kids. What does he mean by this? Did you know something was different about Logan right away?

3. Logan doesn't go out much, but sticks to a very steady routine. Does he find the steady routine of his life boring? Do you think you would, even if you lived and worked at a candy factory?

4. The Candymaker and his wife don't believe in traditional schooling. Logan learned kindness, baking, storytelling, generosity, reading, writing, and biology. He also learned to be hard working and to tell right from wrong. Do you think his parents have prepared him for life? Would you prefer learning on the job as Logan does?

5. Fear creeps in and whispers in Logan's ear that he "doesn't have what it takes to be a candymaker." Why do you think that happens? Have you ever doubted yourself the way Logan does?

6. Who is Magpie? Do you think people or animals make better best friends?

7. Philip has a notebook that he carries with him all the time. What does he write down in his notebook? Why do you think he hides it from the others?

8. Why does Logan think someone like Philip would never want to make candy? Is he correct? What is Phillip's real reason for entering the contest?

9. Why is Miles obsessed with the afterlife? Once Miles finds out that "the girl" is actually Daisy and she is not dead, what is his reaction? Do you think you would have reacted the same way?

10. What is Daisy hoping to achieve by entering the candy contest? Do you think she should be involved in her family's business?

11. At the Life Is Sweet candy factory, Miles can't get enough of one meal. What is it? What are some of the ingredients in chocolate pizza? If you could make your own chocolate pizza, what toppings would you add to create your own personalized recipe?

12. Why was Daisy seen talking to herself while reading her book upside down? If you could have a spy gadget like Daisy's book, reshapable wax, multipurpose pen, or tiny transceiver, what do you think would be the most helpful for you to have and why?

13. Logan's mom slips a poem into Logan's pocket every day. One of the poems she places in his pocket says, "Be kind, for everyone you meet is fighting a battle you know nothing about." What do you think this means?

14. Logan doesn't want his dad's help making his new candy because he thinks it wouldn't be fair to the other contestants. Daisy and Miles think that's "very big" of him. Philip says it is stupid not to use any advantage you have because that is how you win. Who do you agree with?

15. Miles makes up his own language. What is it? Can you talk backward like Miles? What can you say?

From *The Maker Cookbook: Recipes for Children's and 'Tween Library Programs* by Cindy R. Wall and Lynn M. Pawloski. Santa Barbara, CA: Libraries Unlimited. Copyright © 2014.

16. The Life Is Sweet candy factory has many different kinds of rooms: the Taffy Room, the Cocoa Room, the Neon Yellow Lightning Chews Room, the Tropical Room, the Bee Room, the Marshmallow Room, the Gummy Dinosaurs Room, the Some More S'mores Room, and even a library. If you were designing a candy factory, what types of rooms would you create?

17. Butterflies are repeatedly mentioned in the story. Logan is waiting to see a butterfly to emerge from its cocoon. Miles thought that living in the Life Is Sweet candy factory had kept Logan well protected like a butterfly in a cocoon. Why do you think that is?

18. Miles thinks Logan "doesn't seem to notice his scars." Daisy says that "after a few minutes, you don't really notice the scars." Do you think these statements are true or false?

19. In a gummy monster fight, who do you think would win: Gummzilla or Gummysaurus Rex?

20. What kind of candy did each of the four contestants end up creating to enter into the contest?

21. Daisy was "taught not to question the motives of the client. After all, every story had two sides. Who was she to decide right from wrong?" Do you agree with this business philosophy? Is it necessary to run a successful spy business? Do you think Daisy agrees with this philosophy?

22. Philip has a cheat notebook handed down to him from his older brother Andrew. If you could use a cheat notebook with a guarantee that no one would ever find out about it, would you use it?

23. Once Phillip found out his father's intention to take over the Life Is Sweet candy factory, what plan did he come up with to stop his father? After the way Phillip acted and all the things he'd done, would you have believed in him and taken part in his plan?

24. Do you believe that Philip's father will keep his word and drop his plans to take over the factory after Philip wins?

25. Throughout the course of the story, it is revealed that each of the four main characters has met one of the others in the past, although in every case, only one of the two remembers the meeting clearly. How did Philip know Logan? How did Daisy know Philip? How did Miles know Daisy?

26. Had you guessed what the Life Is Sweet candy factory's secret ingredient was? When the secret ingredient was revealed were you surprised or disappointed, or did you think it was exactly right?

27. At the end of the story, Logan, Miles, Philip, and Daisy all want to make some changes in their lives. What do they want to change? Do you think they should?

Appendix B: Letters and Documentation for Parents and Caregivers

Rehearsal/Class Schedule for the *Fairy Tale Theater* Program

The Children's Department is very excited to announce the rehearsal schedule for *Fairy Tale Theater*, our theater group for children ages _____. Young performers will meet together to learn acting skills through games and rehearse for a dramatic performance of a fairy tale. Rehearsals/classes take place on:

Date: _____   Time from: _____ to _____

Date: _____   Time from: _____ to _____

Date: _____   Time from: _____ to _____

Date: _____   Time from: _____ to _____

Date: _____   Time from: _____ to _____

Date: _____   Time from: _____ to _____

The DRESS REHEARSAL will take place on: Date_____ from:
Time _____ to _____.

The PERFORMANCE will take place on: Date_____ from:
Time _____ to _____. Actors should report to the stage area at
_____ sharp. The play begins at _____.

Because of the limited rehearsal time, all of the children are needed at each rehearsal. To maximize rehearsal time, it is important that <u>children arrive and depart on time.</u>

....

My child_____, has my permission to participate in the play. I have reviewed the rehearsal/class schedule above and certify that my child will be able to arrive early or on time for each scheduled rehearsal. I acknowledge that any unacceptable/disruptive rehearsal conduct will result in my child's removal from the play.

Signed: _____   Date: _____

Email address: _____   Phone: _____

Costume Conference Letter for the *Fairy Tale Theater* Program

Dear Parents and Caregivers:

Our play is such an exciting experience! Thank you in advance for helping your child learn their lines and driving them to all the rehearsals. Looking ahead, we need to plan your child's costume. Please stop at the Children's Services Desk to schedule a 15- to 20-minute conference for <u>you and your child</u> concerning his or her costume. Due to the limited amount of rehearsal time, we must schedule these meetings outside of our regular rehears-

als. Conferences will take place sometime between the week(s) of _____ and

_____. Please sign up now for a conference date and time.

Thanks! The Children's Department Staff

Costume Approval List (to be completed by the staff member)

Name-Character	Library Has	Child Will Provide	Notes
Lisa-Bo Peep	bonnet, shepherd's hook	floral dress	need stuffed sheep

How to Rehearse with Your Child for the *Fairy Tale Theater* Program

Here are a few guidelines to help make the rehearsal time with your child as productive as possible:

- Rehearse at a time when your child is not tired, hungry, or distracted.
- Remember to practice as much as you can, but have fun. Rehearsal shouldn't be something the child dreads.
- When you first rehearse, begin by telling the fairy tale together. After your child has an excellent grasp of the order of the events in the story, you can start helping him or her with his or her lines.
- If possible, make rehearsal a family event and give everyone one or two (or more) parts. The child actor should only say <u>his or her character's</u> lines.
- It is important for the entire play to be rehearsed, not just your child's actual lines. As this is a play for younger children, they may have more actions than lines, so they must know when to perform them.
- Mark off or designate a stage area (size is really not important) and use substitute props so that the children get a feel for acting within a limited area and using props while speaking their lines.
- Be sure to verbally remind your child when they enter the stage and with whom (if anyone). "You come on stage right after the farmer says . . . " or "You and the duck come on stage together."

Maker Marketplace Craft Fair Parent/Caregiver Information Handout

Dear Parents and Caregivers,

Thank you for registering your child for the *Maker Marketplace* Craft Fair which takes place on _____. We hope that you and your child enjoy your craft fair experience. In order to keep your child safe during the creation of any additional crafts and prepare him or her to act as a vendor at the craft fair, we have created a checklist for both you and your child. Once all the items on the list are checked off, you and your child are prepared for a successful day!
The Children's Department Staff

Parent/Caregiver

- ☐ Save the date of the *Maker Marketplace* Craft Fair to share with your child.
- ☐ Help your child plan any additional crafts they wish to make for sale at the craft fair, closely supervising any that require the use of a heat source.
- ☐ Answer any questions that may arise during the creation of your child's additional crafts, but be mindful that the craft fair accepts only items made by its child vendors.
- ☐ Assist your child in pricing each item, taking into account the library's price limits, if any.
- ☐ Provide a selection of small bills and coins to allow your child to make change for customers.
- ☐ Use social media to let everyone know about the craft fair and the items your child will be selling.

Child Vendor

- ☐ Discuss with your parents or caregivers what additional items you wish to make for sale at the craft fair and what supplies, if any, you need to acquire.
- ☐ Create the additional items for sale.
- ☐ Price the items for sale. Remember to take into account the library's price limits, if any.
- ☐ Discuss with your parent or caregiver who will be in charge of accepting money from customers and making change.
- ☐ Create a sign for your table to advertise what you will be selling and decide on the arrangement of your products.
- ☐ Tell all your friends and relatives about the craft fair. Be sure to let them know when and where it will take place.
- ☐ Carefully wrap all items in tissue paper, bubble wrap, newspaper, or whatever you have on hand for transportation to the craft fair. Save the protective wrapping to rewrap the items for your customers to transport their purchases home.

T-shirt *Transfer*-mations Handout

Dear Parents and Caregivers,

At the library today, your child has created a wearable work of art. BEFORE your child can wear the T-shirt, it MUST be placed in the dryer on the lowest setting for approximately 20 minutes to set the color. If your child has used fabric markers in addition to crayons, you must also _____
_____. Then, your child's T-shirt is ready to wear. The first time you wash this T-shirt, launder it by itself in case any waxy crayon residue remains. In subsequent washings, turn the T-shirt inside out before laundering. Below you will find directions for recreating this project at home.

T-shirt *Transfer*-mations is a parent/child project that lends itself to so many uses. By following the directions below, you can create this project at a birthday party and let the children take home the T-shirts in lieu of a goody bag. Any club, scout troop, or sports team would enjoy making a wearable symbol of membership. The next family reunion can be enhanced with affordable T-shirts for everyone. This project may even bring some sunshine to a rainy vacation day. Most tourist vacation destinations provide an ironing board and iron, while crayons and sandpaper can be easily acquired.

T-shirt *Transfer*-mations Directions:

For this project, you will need one white T-shirt, one piece of fine sandpaper, a piece of cardboard slightly larger than the piece of sandpaper, an iron, an ironing board, paper towels, and a selection of crayons.

1. Place the piece of sandpaper on a table, textured side up.
2. Color a design with the crayons on the textured side of the sandpaper. Press down hard when coloring, to leave more crayon on the sandpaper. For more vibrant results, go over your design multiple times, creating as thick a coating of crayon as possible. The image transferred to the T-shirt will be reversed. If you wish to use lettering as a design element, keep in mind that any lettering will have to be written backward in order to be read.
3. Once you are finished coloring your design, use a paintbrush to brush off any excess crayon wax from the areas of the sandpaper that are not part of the design. This prevents any stray wax from being transferred onto the T-shirt.
4. Preheat the iron on the cotton setting.
5. Place the T-shirt on the ironing board with the front of the T-shirt lying flat, face up on the ironing board and the back of the T-shirt beneath the ironing board so that the back of the T-shirt does not accidentally receive any of the crayon transfer. If you wish to place the design on the back of the T-shirt, reverse the T-shirt's placement accordingly.
6. Place one piece of cardboard between the ironing board and the underside of the front of the T-shirt. The cardboard should be centered under the T-shirt where the design will be transferred.
7. Center the sandpaper design crayon side down on top of the T-shirt and cardboard.
8. Place a paper towel over the sandpaper.

9. Iron on the paper towel for approximately 30 seconds.
10. Without moving the T-shirt, carefully lift up one corner of the sandpaper to make sure that your design has transferred. If not, iron in 10-second increments, checking between each, until your design transfer is complete.
11. Remove the paper towel and sandpaper and place two paper towels on top of the design now on the T-shirt and iron to remove any excess wax. Place the T-shirt in the dryer on the lowest setting for 20 minutes to set the color.
12. Enjoy!

Appendix C: Handouts for Program Participants

Maker Open House Survey

Thank you for taking the time to complete this survey. Your input is very important to us. In order to provide the most accurate information, please fill out one survey for each child in your care. Fill in the blank or place a check mark by each applicable answer.

How old is your child?_____

Which *Maker Open House* station(s) did you and your child enjoy the most?

- ☐ Art Station
- ☐ Craft Station
- ☐ iPad Station
- ☐ Computer Station
- ☐ 3D Printer Station

Which type of library Maker programs would you and your child like to attend in the future?

- ☐ Art
- ☐ Craft
- ☐ iPad
- ☐ Computer
- ☐ 3D printer
- ☐ Other (please specify) _____

Which time of day would you prefer future library Maker programs to be held:

- ☐ Weekday mornings
- ☐ Weekday afternoons
- ☐ Weekday evenings
- ☐ Weekend mornings
- ☐ Weekend afternoons
- ☐ Weekend evenings

Which day of the week is most convenient for your child to attend library Maker programming:

- ☐ Monday
- ☐ Tuesday
- ☐ Wednesday
- ☐ Thursday
- ☐ Friday
- ☐ Saturday
- ☐ Sunday

Which type of library Maker programming would you like to see more of:

☐ Family programs
☐ Programs designed for children to attend on their own
☐ Both

Which is your preferred method for learning about children's Maker programming?

☐ Signs posted at the library
☐ The library's print newsletter
☐ The library's website and/or blog
☐ Facebook
☐ Twitter
☐ Newspaper article
☐ Other (please specify) _____

Please feel free to write any other comments in the space below. Thank you for taking the time to complete this survey. The results of this survey will be used to help guide us in developing future library Maker programming.

Old School vs. High-Tech Quiz for the *Plastic vs. Plastic* Program

Name _____

Old School vs. High-Tech Quiz

Choose one statement that best answers each of the questions below. Select either statement a or statement b and circle your preference.

1. Which type of plastic in the *Plastic vs. Plastic* program do you think you will like the best?
   a. I think I will like the milk plastic object I made myself. I like to be hands on in all aspects of a product I create.
   b. I think I will like the plastic object created by the 3D printer. I think the 3D printer can make a more precise plastic object than I can.
2. In what form do you prefer to read books?
   a. I prefer to read books printed on paper. I like the smell and feel of a book in my hands.
   b. I prefer to read eBooks or book apps. I can take as many books as I want with me wherever I go and the books have additional features.
3. How do you prefer to watch movies?
   a. I prefer to watch movies on DVD. I like to watch the extras on the discs.
   b. I prefer to watch movies streamed through my computer or television. There are a lot more movies to choose from.
4. How do you purchase your music?
   a. I buy my music on CD. I like to collect the discs.
   b. I download my music. It is easier and takes up less space to keep everything on my computer, tablet, or phone.
5. How do you prefer your frozen pizza to be cooked?
   a. I prefer my frozen pizza to be cooked in the oven. It comes out crisp and evenly warmed throughout.
   b. I prefer my frozen pizza to be cooked in a microwave. I don't have time to wait for the oven.
6. How would you rather create a poster for a school event?
   a. I would rather create a poster with poster board, paints, markers, and/or colored pencils. I like my design to be just the way I want it. The only way I can get that is to make it by hand.
   b. I would rather create a poster on the computer. I can cut and paste pre-created designs and add special effects.
7. If someone were to give you a gift, would you rather receive a foot-powered scooter or an electric scooter?
   a. I would rather receive a foot-powered scooter. Too many things can go wrong with the electric scooter. If it breaks, I am out of luck.
   b. I would rather receive an electric scooter. It gets me places faster without breaking a sweat.
8. How do you prefer to play games?

a. I prefer to play board or card games. I like the feel of the pieces and/or cards in my hands and I like to move them myself.
b. I prefer to play video games or game apps. I like to immerse myself in the realistic graphics of the game.

9. Would you rather attend school in person or online?
a. I would rather attend school in person. I want to hang out with my friends.
b. I would rather attend school online. I can meet new and different people from all over the world.

10. Would you rather have a human or a robot as a babysitter?
a. I would rather have a human babysitter. You can negotiate with them and make them feel sorry for you.
b. I would rather have a robot babysitter. It can be temporarily turned off and then I can do whatever I please. I just have to hope my parents do not check the robot's computer log.

Old School vs. High-Tech Quiz Score Your Results

For every statement "a" that you chose, give yourself 1 point.

For every statement "b" that you chose, give yourself 5 points.

Add up the total number of points for all your responses to the questions to determine your final Old School vs. High-Tech Quiz score.

If your score is between 10 and 22, you are Old School. You know how to enjoy life's simple pleasures. When the batteries wear down or the electricity goes out, everyone looks to you for fun ideas to pass the time.

If your score is between 23 and 37, you are a balanced combination of Old School and High Tech. You are not stuck with one method or another, but are willing to choose the right tool to finish the job the way you want it done.

If your score is between 38 and 50, you are High Tech. You are on the cutting edge and you know what the next, new, hot gadget everyone wants will be.

From *The Maker Cookbook: Recipes for Children's and 'Tween Library Programs* by Cindy R. Wall and Lynn M. Pawloski. Santa Barbara, CA: Libraries Unlimited. Copyright © 2014.

Stop Motion Films **Storytelling Sheet**

Step 1—Brainstorm ideas—Refine your ideas into a one-sentence concept that describes the story you wish to tell in your stop motion film.

Step 2—Think about the plot—The plot is a description of what is happening, what is at stake for the characters, and the order of the events that will take place in your film.

Step 3—Determine the setting—Decide where and when the action in your stop motion film will take place.

Step 4—Choose the characters—Every character, even the lesser characters, has a story to tell. Each character's story should have a beginning, a middle, and an end.

Step 5—Use dialogue or conversation between characters wisely—Most dialogue requires close-ups, in addition to camera movement back and forth between the characters in a conversation. If the camera is constantly moving back and forth between the characters to capture their conversation, there is a limited amount of time left for the characters to actually do anything.

Step 6—Draw the storyboard—To prepare for filming, your concept and any action and scene changes need to be translated into a visual language. The storyboard forces you to think through your ideas carefully and create a visual picture of the action similar to a comic book. Your drawings don't have to be an accurate, artistic representation; they just need to communicate your ideas.

Step 7—Create a camera shot list—The brain needs time to process the action taking place on the screen. In order to provide ample time, include at least four identical shots of each scene. This also creates a smoother, more pleasant viewing experience. Remember, one second of film uses 24 photos, so you will need to take a lot of pictures.

Step 8—Begin shooting your stop motion film.

From *The Maker Cookbook: Recipes for Children's and 'Tween Library Programs* by Cindy R. Wall and Lynn M. Pawloski. Santa Barbara, CA: Libraries Unlimited. Copyright © 2014.

Storyboard Worksheet for the *Stop Motion Films* and *Silent Film* Programs

Design Box Instructions for the *Chalktography* Program

The following directions will help you measure and create a design box _____ high by _____ wide in the cordoned off–paved work area. Your design will be created inside of this box.

1. Release the tape from the tape measure equal to the height measurement written above. Lock the tape measure.
2. Place your locked tape measure vertically on the paved surface and draw one line to mark the beginning of the tape measure and another line to mark the end of the tape.
3. Draw a line along the tape measure, connecting the bottom mark to the top mark.
4. Unlock the tape measure to free the tape. Release the tape from the tape measure equal to the width measurement written above. Lock the tape measure.
5. Place the locked tape measure horizontally onto the bottom height measurement mark you created in the previous step.
6. Mark a line at the end of the measured tape.
7. Draw a line along the tape measure, connecting the two bottom marks to create a horizontal line. Unlock the tape measure to free the tape.
8. Release the tape from the tape measure to the height measurement once again. Lock the tape measure.
9. Place the locked tape measure vertically on the far end of the bottom line and draw a line to mark the end of the tape.
10. Draw a line along the tape measure, connecting the measurement mark you created in the previous step to the far end of the bottom horizontal line.
11. Connect the two remaining edges to make the horizontal line which completes the box.
12. Measure the box to be sure it has the correct dimensions.

Now the design box is completed. The following directions will assist you in achieving the best chalktography result.

1. Position the ladder or step stool in a temporary testing position in front of the box design on the paved work area.
2. Take the digital camera, iPad, or smartphone up the ladder or step stool pausing at each step to find the optimum viewing position for your photographic device. The optimum viewing position occurs when you can see the measured box created on the paved work area, but not the chalk lines of the box itself. You may need to adjust your position and/or the position of the ladder or the step stool in order to find the best angle or height for your photographs. If you are using a digital camera or smartphone with a zoom, try out your zoom settings.
3. Discuss and choose a design theme and decide how to fit the design within the box. Be sure to leave ample room for the child who will inhabit your photograph.
4. Using the sidewalk chalk, draw the outlines only of your design. When it is complete, the design box should look like a giant coloring sheet on the pavement.

5. After the younger children arrive, assist them in coloring in the design elements of the box, but do not do the work for them. They need a chance to be proud of their contributions as well.

6. Help the younger children pose to suit your design. Give them precise verbal instructions and demonstrate these instructions using your own arms, legs, etc. to show them what you would like them to do. Remember, many younger children have trouble telling their right from their left, so you may have to repeat or rephrase your directions.

7. Take the digital camera, iPad or smartphone up the ladder or step stool and make any adjustments necessary to obtain the optimum viewing angle.

8. Take three or four photos of each child in the design in order to avoid the inevitable closed eyes, moved arm, etc.

9. View the photos in your viewfinder or on your screen to make sure you have at least one great shot.

Food Detectives Score Sheet

Candy Bar Station

The candy bars I tasted from my plate were:

_____ _____ _____ _____

The candy bars shown in the slideshow were as follows:

Slide 1 _____ Slide 2 _____ Slide 3 _____

Slide 4 _____ Slide 5 _____ Slide 6 _____

Slide 7 _____ Slide 8 _____ Slide 9 _____

Slide 10 _____ Slide 11 _____ Slide 12 _____

Number of correct answers: _____

Secret Smoothie Station

The Secret Smoothie I tasted was made of:

_____ milk, _____ yogurt, and _____ (type of fruit).

Number of correct answers: _____

Conventionally Grown vs. Organically Grown Salad Station

Insert a description of the color or the pattern of the bowl in the sentence blanks:

The conventionally grown salad I tasted was in the _____ bowl.

The organically grown salad I tasted was in the _____ bowl.

Number of correct answers: _____

Chicken Nugget vs. Vegetarian Chicken Nugget Substitute Station

Insert a description of the color or the pattern of the napkin in the sentence blanks:

The chicken nugget I tasted was given to me on the _____ napkin.

The vegetarian nugget I tasted was given to me on the _____ napkin.

Number of correct answers: _____

_____

Final Score _____

Secret Smoothie Recipe for the *Food Detectives* Program

Food Detectives Secret Smoothie Recipe
½ cup of frozen fruit (use only one kind of fruit)
¼ cup of vanilla cow's milk yogurt, almond milk yogurt, or soy yogurt
¼ of a ripe banana, broken into pieces
¼ cup of cow's milk, almond milk, or soy milk

One member of the group will turn his or her back while the remaining three blend up a Secret Smoothie. The remaining three members of the group should choose the type of fruit, yogurt, and milk to use to create the Secret Smoothie. Write down the chosen ingredients on a piece of scrap paper.

In the container of the blender, add the chosen frozen fruit, vanilla yogurt, banana pieces, and milk. Place the cover securely onto the blender and blend until smooth. Fill one of the bathroom-sized disposable cups to the top for the group member who is to guess the ingredients. If desired, the other three group members may split the remaining Secret Smoothie among three additional bathroom-sized disposable cups.

Once the taster has written down his or her guesses of the ingredients on his or her *Food Detectives* Score Sheet, he or she should show the remaining members the conclusions reached. The creators should then reveal the Secret Smoothie ingredients written on the scrap paper and compare. The number of correct ingredients should be recorded on the taster's *Food Detectives* Score Sheet.

Appendix D: Auxiliary Program Materials

Recipe Planning Checklist

_____ Program Name

_____ Date _____ Time

Shopping List

_____

_____

_____

_____

_____

_____

_____

_____

Preheat Checklist

☐ Purchase and/or gather the ingredients

☐ Inspiration (slideshow, images, etc.)

☐ Create a sample project

☐ Program room reservation

☐ Registration sheet, handouts, and/or directions

Publicity

☐ Flyer/sign

☐ Print newsletter

☐ Library blog and website

☐ Social media site(s)

☐ eBlast

☐ Newspaper(s)

☐ Staff newsletter

☐ School and PTO newsletters

Program Day Necessities

_____

_____

_____

_____

_____

Post-program notes: _____

_____

Book Discussion/Fusion Box Recipe Planning Checklist

_____ Program Name

_____ Date _____ Time

Book Preparation	App/iPad Preparation	Publicity
☐ Select the title	☐ Select the app	☐ Flyer/sign
☐ Interlibrary Loan or purchase	☐ Purchase the app	☐ Print newsletter
Shopping List	☐ Download and install the app	☐ Library blog and website
	☐ Charge the devices	☐ Social media site(s)
_____	☐ App directions _____	☐ eBlast
_____	_____	☐ Newspaper(s)
_____	_____	
_____	_____	
_____		

Preheat Checklist

☐ Purchase and/or gather the ingredients

☐ Inspiration (slideshow, images, etc.)

☐ Create a sample project

☐ Book discussion questions

☐ Program room reservation

☐ Registration sheets, handouts, and/or directions

☐ School and PTO newsletters

Program Day Necessities

_____

_____

_____

_____

_____

_____

_____

Post-program notes: _____

_____

APPendix

The following is a list of apps used in the recipes contained in this book. This is merely a small representation of the fun and educational apps available for download. With a simple online search, you can find an app suitable for almost any program.

Animal Tracks Quiz

Art Maker

Bamba Toys

ColART

Doodlecast

Fairytale 123 Maze

Grandma's Kitchen

Grandpa's Workshop

Happy Campfire

Hopscotch

iZen Garden

Leo's Pad

Magic Maze

Monster Physics

Morfo 3D Face Booth

Morton Subotnick's Pitch Painter

Mouse Maze

Paint for Cats

Pettson's Inventions (1 and 2)

Play Lab

Playart

Puppet Pals 2

Snackerdoodle

Stop Motion Studio

There's No Place Like Space!

Toca Builders

Wombi Helicopter

Alternate, *Alternate Reality* Ideas, Projects, and Discussion Questions

If you would like to present the *Alternate Reality* program with a different concept or create a series of *Alternate Reality* programs, the following are some suggestions for equally interesting suppositions on which to base your program(s).

Supposition:

What if the Native American Indians conquered the European explorers?

Project: Carve an animal or Native American figure from a bar of soap using plastic knives, emery boards, and bamboo skewers to capture the essence of Native American Indian soapstone carving.

Discussion Questions: Given the Native American reverence for nature, do you think we would still be facing the ecological issues of today or do you think the damage and depletion of the Earth's resources is inevitable?

Before the European explorers arrived, the formal education of Native American Indian children included life skills and tribal history. How do you think your school day would be different if your school followed a historical Native American Indian education model?

Supposition:

What if the dinosaurs were not extinct?

Project: Make a stop motion animation film featuring dinosaurs interacting in a contemporary setting. (For program details, hints, and tips see the *Stop Motion Films* program on page 85.)

Discussion Questions: Do you think the dinosaurs of today would be held in a zoo, kept as pets, or roaming free?
Would the dinosaurs have evolved into different creatures by now?

Supposition:

What if the colonists lost to Britain during the American Revolution?

Project: Using a plain bandana or bag and fabric markers, design a new colonial flag, incorporating the Union Jack and elements from the 13 colonies.

Discussion Questions: If America was still under British rule, how do you think you would feel about the British Royal family?

How do you think you would feel if the lands, people, and economy of what is now the United States were still governed by the British?

Supposition:

What if the nuclear fallout from the Chernobyl disaster had caused a significant negative impact throughout the world?

Project: Draw or use a shoebox to create a diorama of the ideal fallout shelter.

Discussion Questions: There are communities surrounding Chernobyl in which residents have refused to leave the contaminated zone because their family has lived in that specific area for hundreds of years. Would you be able to leave your ancestral birthplace if disaster were to strike?

Would you be in favor of nuclear retaliatory strikes?

Supposition:

What if the polar icecaps melted?

Project: Have each program participant plant a hydroponic plant.

Discussion Questions: How much damage do you think the melting of the polar icecaps would actually cause?

What types of new inventions would appear as a consequence of the melting of the polar icecaps, for example, amphibious cars?

Supposition:

What if Martin Luther King Jr. had not been assassinated?

Project: Compose and/or write a tribute poem or song to Martin Luther King Jr. or follow the directions for the *Animation Exploration* program on page 67 and use the Martin Luther King Jr. actor/puppet.

Discussion Questions: If Martin Luther King Jr. were still alive, do you think race relations would be different in the United States today?

In his later years, do you think Martin Luther King Jr. would have focused more on politics or religion?

Supposition:

What would women's lives be like in America today if the Suffrage Movement had not been successful?

Project: Have each participant choose a historically important woman and draw a tribute to her on either cloth to be sewn together as a quilt, paper to be placed in a poster or collage, or on sandpaper to be transferred onto a T-shirt. (For instructions on how to create a sandpaper transfer, see T-shirt *Transfer*-mations on page 122.)

Discussion Questions: If women were joining together today to promote equality, do you think they should or would choose to focus on the right to vote or would they be united by another mission?

Do you think the men of today would be more likely to support equality than their male counterparts at the turn of the 20th century?

Supposition:

What if Benjamin Franklin were transported to our present day?

Project: Since Benjamin Franklin drew the first cartoon in an American newspaper, ask attendees to create their own cartoon or follow the directions for the *Animation Exploration* program on page 67 and use the Benjamin Franklin actor/puppet.

Discussion Questions: There have been many scientific advances since Benjamin Franklin's death. What new inventions do you think he would create using today's current science?

   If Benjamin Franklin were here today, what topic do you think he would be inspired by to create a cartoon to submit to a newspaper, magazine, or online news website?

Raspberry Pi Workstation Essentials for the
Scratch That Technology Itch Program

Currently, those interested in purchasing a **Raspberry Pi** computer may choose from Model A for $25 or Model B for $35. The two differences between the two models are that Model A has no network capability and only one port. Model B has a network connection and two available ports.

After choosing Model A or Model B, a display of some kind must be purchased. The best available option is a **TV monitor with HDMI** capabilities and an HDMI cable (the sound comes through the HDMI cord directly to the TV).

OR

Another option is to use a **computer monitor with a DVI socket and an adaptor**. With this option, you will need **speakers or a set of headphones** to hear the sound. The speakers must have a 3.5 mm audio jack.

A computer monitor with only a VGA connector may not be used without the additional cost of an expensive converter box.

A **keyboard** and a **mouse** are also necessary. If workstation space is an issue for your library, consider purchasing a smaller-sized keyboard and a mouse designed for a laptop.

The Raspberry Pi computer uses an **SD card** instead of a hard drive. The easiest thing to do is to purchase an SD card that is already loaded with the Raspberry Pi operating system. However, you may choose to purchase and prepare a blank SD card. Purchasing and preparing your own SD card does have one advantage. It allows you to choose from a variety of operating systems to use. If you are writing your own SD card, the computer you use to do this must have an SD card reader or you must purchase an external SD card reader. If you do buy your own blank SD card, purchase one that is at least 4GB. With the prices of cards becoming less expensive, consider purchasing a card with a larger storage capacity. The card must also be a class 4 or higher.

Purchase a **USB hub** to provide additional ports since the Raspberry Pi computer only provides two available ports at most and you need to connect at a minimum a keyboard and a mouse. It is best to choose a USB hub that is self-powered (it gets its power from being plugged into an electrical outlet) so as not to drain the power from the Raspberry Pi computer.

If you wish to connect the Raspberry Pi computer to the Internet, the simplest choice is to purchase an **Ethernet cable** and plug it in. Your Raspberry Pi workstation will then need to remain tethered to the Ethernet cable in order to maintain connectivity.

Cutting the Ethernet cord is a bit more complicated as neither model of the Raspberry Pi computer has Wi-Fi support. If you select Model A, you may purchase a **USB wireless adapter** to provide connectivity. If you select Model B, you may purchase a USB wireless adapter or a **Wi-Fi bridge** that is USB powered and plugged into an Ethernet socket. Be sure to research online those models that are tested and have been proven to work with the Raspberry Pi computer. There are models that are not recognized by the Raspberry Pi computer and therefore will not operate.

From *The Maker Cookbook: Recipes for Children's and 'Tween Library Programs* by Cindy R. Wall and Lynn M. Pawloski. Santa Barbara, CA: Libraries Unlimited. Copyright © 2014.

Adaptive Animal Behavior Sheet for the *Necessity Is the Mother Nature of Invention Convention* Program

The examination of natural processes and the attempt to adapt and reproduce them to solve human problems is called biomimicry. The following list contains suggested prompts for participants to use in the *Necessity Is the Mother Nature of Invention Convention* program.

The sensitive whiskers of a cat can distinguish the changes in air currents around objects. This allows the cat to successfully navigate as it moves from place to place in the dark.

Certain types of lobsters, crabs, shrimp, and snails have eyes that sit on the tip of a stem-like structure called an eyestalk. The eyestalks protrude from the body and can move in different directions, allowing these animals a wider field of vision without having to turn their heads.

Zebras assemble in large groups called herds. Within the herd, zebras move and choose to stand very close to each another. A predator looking at the herd in an attempt to isolate one zebra to attack becomes confused as the different patterns of each zebra combine, making it difficult to distinguish one individual animal from another.

Ice worms can be found living and moving through the glaciers of the Pacific Northwest and Alaska. No one knows for certain how ice worms can move through the glacial ice, but one theory is that they exude a chemical from their bodies which melts the ice as they move along.

There are five different species of flamingos, all of which are pink in color. The shades and hues of pink vary among the different types of flamingos as a result of their diet. The algae and shrimp the flamingos feed upon contain natural pigments that turn a shade of red when digested.

Although it may not be polite to talk about in front of company, every animal poops. Animals excrete from their bodies the waste products left over from the digestion process. The dung beetle, however, seeks out these waste products for food, shelter and to lay their eggs in.

Contrary to popular belief, the humps on a camel's back do not contain water. Fat is stored in the hump of a camel, providing the animal with an energy source when food and water are in short supply.

Though technically not a "fish," starfish are marine dwelling animals that have five arms, called rays, that radiate out from a small, circular, central body. If a starfish were to damage or lose one of its rays, it has the ability to grow a replacement.

Pufferfish, or blowfish, may be slow swimmers, but they are not easy prey. Not only are they poisonous creatures, but if they perceive a threat they can blow up their bodies like a balloon and double in size. This sudden change frightens other animals that will likely then leave the pufferfish in peace.

The remora, also known as a suckerfish, is a fish with the ability to attach itself to larger ocean animals by a suction organ located on its fin. In return for a ride and leftovers from meals, the remora repays the larger host animals by acting as a vacuum as it eats parasites and algae from their skin.

Surviving through winter is a challenge for many animals. The weather can be brutal and sources of food may become scarce. Some animals, such as box turtles, bats, and bears, ride out the winter season in their homes by hibernating or taking long naps. During their sleep, their heart beats and breathing rates slow down and their body temperatures drop. These animals require smaller amounts of food, as by hibernating at least some of the time, they are expending less energy. Although some animals sleep continuously, others wake occasionally to find food and/or care for their young.

Glass frogs live in the rain forests of Central and South America. Though mostly greenish in color, the skin on their abdomens is transparent. Internal organs, including the heart, lungs and liver, can be seen through their skin.

The common swift is a bird that prefers to live primarily in the air rather than on land. It may fly for months at a time and land only to care for its offspring.

The sharp, chisel-shaped front teeth of a beaver allow the animal to gnaw down trees to build dams. The teeth of a beaver endure a lot of wear and tear; but because they are always growing, the teeth maintain a consistent height.

Fireflies make their own light. This is called bioluminescence. The light they produce is very economical, as none of the energy they use to create the light is wasted.

Voting Ballots for the *Necessity Is the Mother Nature of Invention Convention* Program

---

Necessity Is the Mother Nature of Invention Convention Voting Ballot

I cast my vote for the project titled _____

_____.

Necessity Is the Mother Nature of Invention Convention Voting Ballot

I cast my vote for the project titled _____

_____.

Necessity Is the Mother Nature of Invention Convention Voting Ballot

I cast my vote for the project titled _____

_____.

Audition Ratings Form for the *Fairy Tale Theater* Program

Name	Memorization	Emotion	Characterization	Comfort	Focus	Projection	Behavior	Improvisation	Total

Sample Theater Dialogue Index Card for the
Fairy Tale Theater Program

Little Red Riding Hood	#1
Grandma, what big teeth you have!	

Index

About the Authors

Cindy R. Wall, MLS, has been head of Children's Services at the Southington (CT) Library and Museum for 10 years. She authored a chapter in *Tablet Computers in School Libraries and Classrooms*, an American Library Association publication, and she reviews books and apps for *School Library Journal*. Wall won the Connecticut Library Association Publicity Award and a Library Services and Technology Act (LSTA) grant to expand her iPad programming.

Lynn M. Pawloski, MLS, is a children's librarian at the Southington Library and Museum. She holds a master's degree in library science from Southern Connecticut State University and has worked in both school and public libraries. She enjoys developing new library programs in which children use their imaginations and are allowed to MAKE a mess!.